Teaching Practice for Early Childhood

D0148988

This fully updated new edition of *Teaching Practice* will help student and recently graduated early childhood teachers to make the most of their teaching in a variety of early years' settings.

Chapters cover vital topics such as ways of knowing and relating to children, the early childhood curriculum, and working collaboratively with colleagues and parents.

In addition, this new edition takes into account the current demands for quality, accountability and continuity in the early years curriculum and includes fresh material on:

- The importance of social and emotional development.
- The role of observation in assessing children's learning and growth, and the use of documentation as a form of accountability and teacher research.
- The value of socially responsive learning environments.

This authentic, trustworthy and engaging text is written in a style that talks directly to its readers. By presenting the experiences of student teachers, as well as those of beginning and experienced teachers, the author brings into focus real situations, dilemmas, issues and rewards which student teachers are likely to face.

Rosemary Perry has extensive experience in early childhood education, as a teacher, lecturer, researcher and consultant.

Teaching Practice for Early Childhood

A guide for students

Second edition

Rosemary Perry

RoutledgeFalmer
Taylor & Francis Group

LONDON AND NEW YORK

First edition published 1997
by RoutledgeFalmer
11 New Fetter Lane, London EC4P 4EE

This edition published 2004
by RoutledgeFalmer
2 Park Square, Milton Park, Abingdon, Oxon OX14 4RN

Simultaneously published in the USA and Canada
by RoutledgeFalmer
270 Madison Avenue, New York, NY 10016

RoutledgeFalmer is an imprint of the Taylor & Francis Group

© 1997, 2004 Rosemary Perry

Typeset in Garamond by
HWA Text and Data Management, Tunbridge Wells
Printed and bound in Great Britain by
Biddles Ltd, Kings Lynn

British Library Cataloguing in Publication Data
A catalogue record for this book is available from the British
Library

Library of Congress Cataloging in Publication Data
Perry, Rosemary
  Teaching practice for early childhood : a guide for students /
    Rosemary Perry. – 2nd ed.
      p.   cm.
  Includes bibliographical references and index.
  1. Early childhood education.   2. Early childhood teachers –
    Training of.   I. Title.
  LB1139.23.P474 20004
  372.21–dc22   200402729

ISBN 0-415-33108-0 (hbk)
ISBN 0-415-33109-9 (pbk)

To my parents, who gave me a wonderful childhood

Contents

Illustrations

Foreword

To be an early childhood teacher, you require practical wisdom. You are, very often, the first teacher with whom parents share the care and education of their child. Your sensitivity to their concerns can shape how the child adjusts to the world beyond the family. You must be empathetic and a skilled communicator, creating a shared agenda for the child based on acknowledging parental aspirations and responsive to the concerns of the inexperienced mother or father.

You must have a knowing eye that can 'see' possibilities in the most ordinary actions of the two-year-old, in the expressions of a three- or four-year-old and in the seemingly foolish experiments of a five-, six- or seven-year-old trying to understand the world. To make good teaching decisions you need to understand the minds and personalities of each child and develop a keen eye for possible teachable moments that make each child's contact with valued cultural traditions, including reading, writing and arithmatic, exciting growth-producing events.

To be able to make such wise practical decisions you require more, much more than knowledge about the practical implications of theories about children, families and subject-matter. You need to know more than how to apply a range of instructional techniques.

Herein lies a major dilemma. The usual tools of teacher educators – lectures, tutorials, texts and practice teaching sessions – seldom bring students face to face with the realities of having to make the best possible decisions within a certain time frame and within competing and often conflicting expectations. Opportunities to critically examine the types of incidents, events and situations that practising teachers typically face, are essential. Without them students will be ill-prepared for the realities of their work.

This is a dilemma that the author of this text knows well from her many years of practical experience as a teacher, teacher educator, researcher and supervisor of beginning teachers. Her search for ways around the dilemma has resulted in her current use of narrative inquiry and narrative text. Her experience has told her that teachers learn a great deal about the realities of being a good teacher by listening carefully to how other practitioners talk about their concerns. Exposure to the experiences and the language of teachers with similar beliefs and values makes it possible to insert something of themselves into what the reader and listener imagines the situation to be. Through this reflective process it is possible to confront the need to deal with multiple demands.

Enjoy the opportunity presented by this book to delve into teaching from the reflective practitioner perspective. Keep returning to the sections that speak most strongly to you and engage in quiet celebration when you get that feeling that you could cope with similar situations once you are the real teacher at work with children and their families.

In this text Rosemary Perry draws on her work undertaken collaboratively with students, beginning and experienced early childhood teachers to create resources that bring students into contact with real teaching situations.

Gail Halliwell
Early Childhood Consultant and former Senior Lecturer
January 2004

Preface

Purpose and content: My purpose in writing this second edition of *Teaching Practice for Early Childhood* is the same as for the first edition. That is, it aims to assist you, as a student teacher, to make the most of the learning opportunities teaching practice in early childhood settings provides. A number of changes have been made to the book's organization however, and new material added. In identifying the topics to be discussed in this edition I was influenced by a number of factors all of which are closely intertwined. These factors include: the growing societal demands for quality, accountability and continuity in early childhood education; the changes occurring in early childhood curriculum; the increasing recognition of the importance of social and emotional development; and the emphasis being placed on teachers becoming 'researchers' of their own teaching. Also, the changes occurring in teacher education with increasing numbers of external students undertaking independent or on-line study, and the expanding range and variety of pre-service courses and practicum placements being experienced by pre-service teachers, were taken into account.

What's new? In order to address these current topics some chapters from the previous edition have been updated while others have been substantially changed and new chapters added. For instance, the chapter focusing on ways of knowing and relating to children has been expanded to give consideration to the role of observation in assessing children's learning and the growing use of documentation as one form of accountability and teacher development (Chapter 2). The chapter on early childhood curriculum (Chapter 3) has also been substantially changed to highlight the current emphases on quality and accountability, given the introduction of quality assurance systems and early childhood curriculum frameworks. The influence of the Reggio Emilia approach on early childhood curriculum is also considered. In this edition curriculum work is presented as a problem-solving process requiring decisions and action after consideration of complex information and planning.

Two totally new chapters have also been added. Given the complexity of relationships and the conflict and violence that are evident in our world today, the chapter 'Creating socially secure environments for learning and teaching' (Chapter 5) has been included to highlight the importance of socially responsive and supportive learning environments. The final chapter 'Stories from beginning teachers: What is the reality?' (Chapter 8) is entirely new and has been added to give a glimpse of what awaits you as a beginning teacher. Six teachers who have just completed their first year of teaching in a range of early childhood settings share their very different experiences of life as a first year teacher. They have done this in the hope that by reading their stories you might be assisted in better preparing yourself for the realities of teaching.

Another change relates to the 'Suggested activities' at the end of each chapter. These have been written as activities for individual student teachers in recognition of the increased numbers of external students undertaking teacher education courses. The activities can, however, be easily adapted for tutorial use through group discussion and debate.

Approach to presentation: The approach to presentation remains the same as in the first edition because feedback from readers indicates that they like the *Guide* because it talks directly to its reader, anticipates experiences and engages the reader in the learning process. Presenting the experiences of other student teachers, as well as those of beginning and experienced teachers brings into focus real situations, dilemmas, issues and rewards which you are also likely to face. As you read these accounts you are encouraged to consider situations and behaviours, to foster your own exploration of associated theories and perspectives, and to propose appropriate strategies as well as possible consequences of actions. In short, the aim is to enable you to begin to think as a teacher.

Philosophy: As I worked on this second edition I had the opportunity to re-examine my philosophical views about teaching and teacher education that underpinned the first edition. I found they remained very much the same. These views may be summarized as follows:

- *Learning to teach is a very personal process.* Because, as a student teacher, you bring your own unique past experiences, current understandings, expectations, learning style and personality to the teaching practice setting, your experiences and learning will differ from those of others. Teaching practice will increase your awareness of your own strengths and weaknesses in meeting personal challenges. In the process of learning to teach you will begin to make explicit the beliefs and values that are guiding your actions and decision making, and, as you reflect on your experiences and seek to derive personal meaning from them, you will find your own answers to teaching dilemmas. No one else can do this for you.

- *Learning to teach involves recognizing the complexity of decision making.* Teachers have many different reasons for acting and responding in the way they do in particular situations. These reasons may relate to beliefs and assumptions about learning and teaching, understandings of children or situations based on specialized knowledge, obligations to meet syllabus requirements and professional responsibilities, as well as the recognition of personal skills and abilities that they can offer. In other words, as a teacher, you will have to make decisions about your actions in the light of your analysis of events, your specialized knowledge, your responsibilities and your consideration of possible consequences of alternative strategies. It is important that, as a student teacher, you come to recognize and accept the complexities inherent in teacher decision-making and that there is no one 'correct' method that can be applied. In order to deal successfully with this complex decision making you need to reflect on your knowledge and research your actions in ways that lead you to a deeper understanding of learning and teaching.
- *Learning to teach is a continuing and constructive process.* Just as children need opportunities to contribute to their learning, take the initiative, set goals, deal with problems and gain confidence from their achievements, so, too, do you as a student teacher. You have to become an active participant in your learning to be a teacher. Teacher education courses provide you with theoretical knowledge about learning and teaching, about curriculum frameworks and syllabus documents, and offer information as to 'how to' handle particular behaviour and situations. It is only during teaching practice, however, as you set yourself goals, take the initiative and deal with problems that arise, that this knowledge is used and a new dimension of practical knowledge constructed. Provided you critically examine and research your teaching experiences you will continue to construct 'new' knowledge throughout your years as a student teacher and then as a teacher.

This book could not have been written if students and teachers had not been willing to share their experiences – their successes and their moments of despair. Their stories are authentic although names have been changed for reasons of confidentiality. To all those who contributed I say a big thank you.

A brief background: All the student and beginning teacher contributors are from the School of Early Childhood within the Queensland University of Technology. This School offers a number of teacher education courses including a four-year Bachelor of Education degree specializing in early childhood education. These courses require students to undertake teaching practice in different early childhood settings, which include:

a childcare setting:	providing for babies to five-year-olds, for periods of up to 12 hours per day and where attendance may be on a regular or an occasional basis;
a preschool setting:	providing for three- to five-year-olds in two-and-a-half or five-hour sessions and where attendance is on a regular, although voluntary basis on consecutive or alternate days;
a lower primary school setting:	providing for five- to six-year-olds (Year 1), six- to seven-year-olds (Year 2), and seven- to eight-year-olds (Year 3) who compulsorily attend for six hours on a daily basis.

Although there is some variation in these types of settings and the use of terms to describe them, the terms 'childcare', 'preschool', and 'Years 1, 2 and 3 of primary school' have been used consistently throughout this book.

Acknowledgements

There are many people to thank. To those who commented on the early drafts – Sue Armstrong, Margaret Henry, Deborah Gahan, and Gail Halliwell – I would like to say how much I appreciated their constructive criticism and supportive comments. I would also like to express my thanks to my friends and experienced teachers, Sue Thomas, Gay Burgess, Fay Haas and Liz Irwin, who keep me in touch with the realities of teaching young children and have provided some of the revealing anecdotes and comments for this book. The practical support of the staff of the Lady Gowrie Child Centre, Brisbane was very much appreciated as were the photographs provided by Kelvin Grove State College preschool campus, the Lady Gowrie Child Centre, Northgate State preschool and primary school, Jane Roneberg, Sue Thomas and Rhonda Warner.

Above all I wish to express my gratitude to the student teachers and the beginning teachers who have so willingly shared their stories and experiences of teaching practice and taught me so much about the process of becoming a teacher. Thank you Bronwyn Aird, Samantha Lee Anderson, Kay Beattie, Kym Blank, Ben Campbell, Larissa Clothier, Allan Davison, Melissa Deakin, Kerrylyn Doocey, Fiona Dunn, Lana Edmonds, Karen Ellis, Karen Ellison, Louise Ellrott, Susie France, Danielle Frey, Susan Glass, Korina Gole, Jodie Holding, Kirsten Ivett, Lena Jensen, Lynette Kai, Esther Keilar, Luke Kelly, Cindy Keong, Fiona Langton, Rachel Martin, Tania Masci, Kylie Patterson, Sherrin Proctor, Rachell Rendall, Debbie Russo, Tammy Shaw, Tina Stannard, Louise Streets, Melinda Taylor, Maria Thurlow, Suzanne Tomkins, Monica Tresehman, Joanne Warren, Nicole Wickham and Tania Wilcox.

Chapter 1

Teaching practice in early childhood settings

In this chapter we are thinking about:

- what teaching practice is;
- professional attributes of early childhood teachers;
- opportunities for learning in teaching practice;
- preparing for teaching practice.

One day, as four-year-old Sam sat beside his teacher, he said, 'You must have to do a lot of learning to be a preschool teacher.' His teacher said, 'Mmm ... yes, you do.'

'You must have to watch a lot of kids' television programmes,' said Sam.

'Yes', said the teacher, 'that's one of the things ...'

'What else did you have to learn?' asked Sam.

'Well,' said his teacher, and paused, as Sam seemed about to add more of his own thoughts.

'You'd have to learn about making ... and gluing ... playing ... doing puzzles ... counting ... writing and reading books ... building games ... painting ... talking ... using good ideas ... and you'd do a lot of knitting them all together,' contributed Sam.

'Yes', replied Sam's teacher, 'teachers learn about those things, and we have to learn a lot about children ... and think about what they know and do... and think about what we do.'

At this point, Sue, the teacher who was recounting this conversation, said it was interrupted.

From Sam's perspective it was important that teachers learn to do all the things that children enjoy. From his teacher's perspective these learnings were important too, together with gaining knowledge about children and developing an ability to reflect and act on this knowledge. Coupled together, Sam's and his teacher's ideas about what an early childhood teacher needs to learn provide a succinct overview of the contents of this book. In using this *Guide* to assist you in making the most of your teaching practice experiences you will be challenged:

- to build relationships with young children (by enabling children to do what they enjoy doing in ways that promote respect for diversity, equity and fairness);
- to extend your understanding of curriculum (by thinking about how children learn, what they need to know and how you will assess what they know);
- to provide supportive learning–teaching environments (by recognizing the physical, social and emotional factors that contribute to learning and by becoming familiar with effective behaviour guidance strategies);
- to collaborate with other important adults in a child's life (by refining communication skills and establishing working relationships);
- to nurture your professional growth through research and inquiry (by thinking about what you do, how you do it, and why).

In developing your knowledge and abilities in relation to each of these aspects you will also be challenged to do 'a lot of knitting them all together', to use Sam's phrase. It is important that you take up this 'knitting' challenge because by doing this you will build a more complete understanding of what it means to be a teacher of young children.

WHAT TEACHING PRACTICE IS

Teaching practice is an integral component of most pre-service teacher education courses (Cohen *et al.* 1996; McBurney-Fry, 2002; Posner, 2000). It refers to the period of time in which you, as a student teacher, gain first-hand experience in working with a particular group of children in an early childhood setting. Teaching practice can be undertaken in a number of forms, such as a day per week over a semester, or in two- to six-week blocks. A number of terms such as 'the practicum', 'field experiences', 'professional experience' or 'internships' are used to refer to this period. In many institutions 'internship' is the term used to refer to the final teaching practice. This final teaching practice is generally longer than previous periods and is aimed at inducting the student teacher more fully into the professional work of teachers. As an intern you will be expected to fulfil the responsibilities of an associate teacher. In this book, the terms 'teaching practice' and 'the practicum' will be used. The one exception will be when quoting student teachers' comments in which they make reference to their teaching practice and use the student teacher vernacular 'prac'.

As you undertake teaching practice you probably will be referred to as a *student teacher* or a *pre-service teacher*. These terms will be used interchangeably throughout this book. During your teaching practice you are generally guided by the teacher responsible for the particular group or class to which you have been assigned. In this book, this person will be referred to as your *supervising teacher*, although elsewhere this person may be known as the 'centre-based' or 'school-based' teacher, the 'host' teacher or the 'cooperating' teacher. In some placements you may be paired with another pre-service teacher to work with a particular class. Paired placements can have a number of benefits if you approach the experience positively. For instance, you can share observations, plan and evaluate together, work with smaller groups of children by sharing teaching responsibilities and observe how a peer handles particular behaviours and situations.

When undertaking your teaching practice you may also have access to a representative from your university or institute. This representative, who is likely to be responsible for advising you and for liaising with the supervising teacher, will be referred to as your *liaison teacher*.

PROFESSIONAL ATTRIBUTES OF EARLY CHILDHOOD TEACHERS

Perhaps because teaching practice is regarded as such an important means of becoming a teacher, student teachers have mixed feelings of anticipation and apprehension as they commence their teaching practice. Tessa, for instance, after her first visit to her placement wrote in her journal:

> After today I can say I am excited, happy and full of anticipation. Yet I am also full of fears and worries. My excitement and all the other positive feelings come from the fact that I really relate to the type of programme at the centre. It is one that helps children learn through expressing their own ideas and making their own choices about activities. This is great, but I am a little worried as I have never experienced a programme where the children have had quite so much choice and input. For the first couple of days, I hope I can spend a lot of time observing.

Do you have the same mixed feelings about teaching practice that Tessa experienced? There's the excitement of being a part of a *real* early childhood setting, of getting to know children and their families, of planning and organizing the day and of extending a child's understanding. At the same time there are the niggling doubts about your ability to cope with unfamiliar situations, manage the whole group, or establish a working relationship with your supervising teacher.

Although all of your teaching practice experiences will contribute in some way to your understanding of teaching, it is important that you learn how to *use* your experiences in order to learn from them. Your pre-service course may require you to focus on specific aspects of teaching during teaching practice. If you are looking for your own focus, however, the numerous Professional Standard Statements that have been developed in recent years by various boards, education departments and teacher organizations to define the professional standards expected of teachers may assist you. For instance, the National Board for Professional Teaching Standards in the United States expects accomplished early childhood teachers to meet rigorous standards in nine areas (cited in Hyson, 2003: 156). These areas are: understanding young children; equity, fairness and diversity; assessment; promoting child development and learning; knowledge of integrated curriculum; multiple teaching strategies for meaningful learning; family and community partnerships; reflective practice.

Katz (1995a) has suggested that becoming an early childhood professional involves:

- developing specialized knowledge;
- using that knowledge to assess and make decisions;
- acquiring high standards of practice.

It is important that you think about how to use your teaching practice experiences to develop your knowledge and abilities in relation to each of these aspects.

Developing specialized knowledge

Although you can gain much specialized knowledge by attending lectures and undertaking readings and assignments, when you enter the teaching practice setting this knowledge can be given added meaning. As one student, Rosanna, said: 'When I came into contact with real children and parents, and real teachers and classrooms, I discovered that I became less sure about some things and learned a whole lot of new things about something I thought I knew well.' Comments made by students in discussions following a teaching practicum indicate that this is a common experience. For instance, Donna described how her knowledge of two-year-olds had been affirmed during her teaching experience in a childcare centre:

At Uni we were told that two-year-olds are beginning to pretend and I've noticed that this group just loves home corner … so yesterday I went in to them and they were making cups of tea … and I said to Jay, 'Do you think Mike would like a cup of tea? P'raps you could ask him,' and he did … and you should have seen the look on Mike's face. He was so pleased.

As Donna drew on her knowledge of two-year-olds to guide her actions and observed their effects, she was also discovering new knowledge about two-year-olds, having never worked with that age group before. She said:

They need a lot more reassurance about everything compared with three-year-olds … like three-year-olds are more able to play with each other while two-year-olds are more inclined to have parallel play. The other day I did a sociogram of two little girls, Rachel and Heather … and it was really interesting to see how Rachel moved from one thing to another without once interacting with anyone … and Heather kept coming and talking to me. She wouldn't talk to other children. She'd only talk to me. So they really seem to prefer to talk to adults than children their own age.

By the second week of his teaching practice with a group of four- to five-year-olds, Tim had become particularly aware of the respectful relationship between the teacher and the children. He felt this contributed to a very positive environment for learning. Tim said: 'I can see how Miss S. treats children as individuals. She really values their contribution. She doesn't come across as being superior. She never raises her voice and yet the children always respond.'

I asked Tim whether he had noticed anything in particular that Miss S. did in order to create this positive atmosphere. Tim paused, remembering the teacher at work:

Well, she really listens to what they say … and she often makes comments such as, 'That's a good idea' or 'That's good thinking.' And if she asks them to do something, she explains why it needs to be done … like at tidy up, they all sit down and think about the jobs that have to be done, and she makes it clear what she expects them to do. They talk about what their jobs are so it's very clear, and the tidying up gets done.

Plate 1.1 While beginning to play with others, two-year-olds seek the attention of adults. (Photo courtesy of Lady Gowrie Child Centre, Brisbane.)

Tim was aware of the children's positive attitude to learning and that the teacher was contributing to this, but he needed the question to spark further thinking about some of the specific strategies the teacher was using. Asking yourself questions about what is happening and why things are happening in certain ways is a vital part of developing your specialized knowledge during teaching practice.

Felicity, a fourth-year student, was beginning to look at her specialized knowledge and ask herself questions about it in the light of her own values. During my visit we had been discussing her goals for the children and what she felt was important for them to learn. Here are some excerpts from that conversation.

> Felicity said, 'I think it's how children get on with others ... and what they learn about themselves that's important. Sure they've got to learn subject matter and skills ... but well, I believe children have to know themselves and know how to be with other people before they can learn anything else ... because if they can't accept themselves they're not going to learn.'
>
> I asked her if that meant that the kinds of goals she would focus on would be related to children's social abilities.
>
> Felicity said, 'Yes ... though I would also aim to develop abilities in other areas too. I think other things are important as well, but to learn other things you've got to know about yourself. If a child is always going to be fighting and always on the outside that child's not going to learn anything. Do you understand what I'm saying?'
>
> I replied that I did. Then Felicity asked, 'Well, is what I'm saying right or wrong?'
>
> My immediate response was, 'There's no right or wrong answer. It's a decision you have to make in the light of your current specialized knowledge.'

Making assessments and decisions

Felicity's question – 'Is what I'm saying (or doing) right or wrong?' – highlights the dilemma that lies at the heart of every decision or judgement an early childhood teacher has to make. If dilemmas and decisions are recognized as part of teaching then teaching becomes 'a process of doing research' that stems from teachers' own questions about everyday practice (Stremmel, 2002: 62). By thinking of yourself as a teacher *and* a researcher you set yourself the goals of gaining insights into teaching and learning, becoming more reflective and bringing about positive changes in your centre and in the lives of children (Cochran-Smith and Lytle, 1993, 1999). Achieving such goals is quite a task even for the most experienced teacher. Fortunately, pre-service courses offer you time and assistance in developing the skills that contribute to your ability to make sound professional judgements. You are not expected to make these decisions in your first teaching practice. Rather, as you gain experience in different practice teaching situations you can develop the knowledge and skills that will help you make professional decisions.

From the beginning of your course, it is important to start to clarify the nature of the knowledge and skills you will need. Traditionally, pre-service courses for early childhood teachers have emphasized knowledge relating to child development and approaches to teaching. Knowledge of syllabuses, key learning areas and performance standards has been seen to be more relevant for those teaching in primary school settings. In recent years, however, mandated preschool curriculum guidelines and position statements on early childhood teacher preparation are highlighting the need for early childhood teachers to be familiar with the key elements of academic disciplines and subject matter (Wheatley, 2003).

In order to make assessments and decisions in teaching, you will need to consider the 'child', the 'content' and the 'method'. Thinking in terms of these multiple strands is rather confusing at first. At one level you learn that teaching involves:

- planning what you want children to learn;
- deciding how you will teach it and how you will determine if they have learnt it;
- teaching them;
- assessing their learning;
- using the information gained in your future planning.

At another level, however, you know that if your teaching is to be meaningful and relevant, you cannot do this in a vacuum. You must get to know the children and take their motivations, activity, ideas and interests into account. Becoming familiar with the actions in a process that is commonly referred to as the *teaching cycle* is a useful starting point for helping you think in this multi-layered way.

The teaching cycle

In order to make teaching decisions you will need to be able to:

- *Describe events*: This necessitates observing the actions of all those involved – the child, other children and adults – and recounting the situations that arise and the interactions that occur. You should also try to identify some of the factors that appear to contribute to the situation.
- *Reflect on and analyse situations*: This means thinking about the situation in ways which focus on *what* happened, *how* it happened and considering possible reasons for *why* it happened. In order to do this you may need to look in-depth at the interactions and responses of both children and adults. If you are the adult involved it is important to be as objective as possible about what you did and why you did it, while at the same time recognizing the feelings you may have about the situation.
- *Consider alternative strategies*: Having analysed the situation you are in a better position to think about the ways in which the situation was managed and how it could have been handled differently. For instance, your analysis may have indicated that the squabbles that are happening with the three-year-olds are likely to be due to there being only two trucks and four children who want them. In the light of your knowledge of three-year-old development you may decide to provide more trucks for the group. Similarly, your analysis of the unruly noise emanating from your Year 1 class may have indicated that the children are unclear about ways to use the two new learning centres you have set up. Clearly, some rules are needed but there are different ways you could handle this situation. Do you present 'your' rules to the class or do you call a class meeting and involve the Year 1 children in making rules that have particular meaning for them?
- *Decide on and carry through a course of action*: The knowledge that you have thoughtfully analysed situations and considered alternative strategies gives you confidence to put your plans into action. These plans may involve providing particular materials or equipment, focusing a discussion, or being near a child in a particular situation to provide support. Generally, well-thought-through plans succeed. Occasionally, however, even after much consideration, you may find that your chosen course of action is not working or not having the desired effect. Always be prepared to modify or change your approach in these circumstances. For this reason it is useful to have planned an alternative course of action.
- *Evaluate the effectiveness of decisions and actions*: By the time you get to do this you will feel that you have come full circle because, in order to evaluate, you are back to observing and describing the situation. After

all your effort, it is likely that you will be able to note improvements in the situation or in the children's behaviour or knowledge. You may see improvements in the children's use of the materials, or in the quality of the interactions between children or between the children and adults. These evaluations, while in one sense being an end point, also provide you with a new starting point for further planning.

Mastering the processes in the *teaching cycle* provides you with the various skills needed to make professional decisions. Lucy, a first-year pre-service teacher, used a number of these skills as she focused on her interactions with Lilly. The way in which she did this is illustrated in this extract from her teaching folder. Lucy wrote:

Description of the situation: Since my first day at the preschool, five-year-old Lilly has been my shadow, following me everywhere and attempting to monopolize my attention. I have explained to her that I have to spend time with all the children and that while I like to play with her I can't be with her all the time. This morning I was out in the playground looking at a shady patch in the garden when Lilly joined me. Lilly said, 'This is like a beautiful rainforest garden. I wish I could hear the sound of trickling water.' I agreed with Lilly that the shade and green plants did make it seem like a rainforest and we discussed her experiences of rainforests. She talked about 'the tall trees', 'walking along tracks', 'hearing water trickle over rocks' and 'little waterfalls'.

Reflecting on and analysing the situation: As we talked, I realized Lilly had quite some knowledge of rainforests that I could perhaps extend. I also knew that Lilly liked a challenge and could probably work out a way to make the sound of trickling water. I also thought that this might be a project she could undertake with other children and without me.

Carrying through a course of action: Before I was really aware that I had decided on a course of action, I said, 'How do you think you could make some trickling water?' I used lots of open-ended questions. Lilly decided she would need a pond for the water to run into, as well as some rocks for the water to run over. We began to think of things she could use to build the pond – some plastic sheeting; spades; watering cans; and some logs and rocks. I helped Lilly collect these materials and encouraged Stephanie to join in as she showed interest in what we were doing. As we couldn't find any large rocks we used two bricks instead.

When the girls began digging the hole for the pond I moved away and observed from a distance so that the girls could direct the play. Annie joined them and they worked well together without conflict. When they felt the pond was big enough I helped them line it with the plastic before they placed the bricks on top of the log to form the waterfall. They then began to fill the pond by pouring water from their watering cans on to the bricks and watched it run into the pond.

I decided to use the teachable moment and talk to the children about forests, plants and ponds. I asked them, 'What creatures live in ponds?' Annie said that frogs and tadpoles did, and added, 'If we leave the pond here, they might come to live here.' We decided that we would leave the pond there overnight. The children continued to play in the pond, floating leaves and bark in the water. They particularly enjoyed pouring the water over their feet. I found myself reminding them to be careful not to stand on the plants that were nearby. Lilly suggested they could make paths to the pond by putting rope down so the plants wouldn't be trodden on. This proved to be successful.

Evaluating the effectiveness of decisions: The next morning I decided not to mention the pond so as to see if the children were genuinely interested. Lilly and Stephanie went to the pond immediately they entered the playground. After a few minutes, Lilly came and grabbed my hand and asked me to come to their pond, which I did. After noting there were no tadpoles yet they began to play in the pond and added more water. Lilly did not seem to need me so I moved away and observed from a distance.

I feel that this experience was worthwhile and meaningful for all concerned. The activity related to the children's past experiences – they knew about trickling water and rainforests. Working on the pond gave the children a range of sensory experiences – smelling and feeling the water and moist earth and listening to the sound of the running water. I tried to get them to talk about these sensations to increase their awareness of them but they found this difficult. Lilly, Annie and Stephanie maintained a high level of attention and they explored a range of concepts such as sinking and floating; full and empty; plants, growth and forests.

Self-evaluation: I am happy with the way I guided this activity. I realize that I may not always be able to give so much attention to one small group when I am responsible for interacting with the whole group. My initial questions for getting the children to be more aware of their senses need to be improved. When I talked to my supervising teacher about this she suggested that, instead of asking, 'How does it make you feel?' I could have shared some of my thoughts – 'This trickling sound reminds me of bath time when the tap is turned on just a little.' She said she has found that such examples often help children to express their own thoughts. She also suggested posing some 'wondering' type questions – 'I wonder why the soil here feels so moist and cool?' I will read a book tomorrow about rainforests with a view to developing their concepts further.

From this extract it is apparent that Lucy, in writing about the event after it had happened, used the skills that are a part of the teaching cycle as a useful framework for clarifying her thinking about the experience. Her account shows that she became aware of the learning opportunities inherent in Lilly's comment, analysed the situation and decided on a course of action almost simultaneously. She then described 'the action' and 'interactions' in some detail before seeking to evaluate the effectiveness of the experience from both the children's perspective and her own. Written in this way her account suggests that the skills outlined in the teaching cycle are used in an ordered, sequential fashion. Although this may sometimes happen, it is far more usual that two or more of these skills are being used simultaneously. One experienced teacher told me that she frequently found that in her teaching she was simultaneously using all the skills in the teaching cycle. They were 'jumbled together'.

When Melanie told me of her interactions with Owen during her teaching practice in a Year 1 classroom I was reminded of just how 'jumbled' the use of these skills can be. Melanie said:

> One of the best things that has happened to me this prac is that the children have really responded to me ... well ... except for Owen. He just won't stand up and participate in morning talk. He seems a very bright child, and on the odd occasion when he does say something or join in, he has a great contribution to make. I've been trying to reinforce his behaviour when he does participate ... giving him lots of praise. But then at other times he gets a look on his face ... an 'I'm not going to do this' look. I know he can do it, but at these times he just won't, and I don't know why.
>
> The other day we were playing 'Doggie Doggie where's my bone' and I asked who hadn't had a turn ... and he put his hand up and I chose him. I don't know why I did that because the whole day we'd been having these tussles. Anyway, after I chose him he wouldn't go and get the bone ... so I went over to him, took his hand and walked him over to the bone ... and he picked it up ... and I thought, 'OK

we're fine now' ... but when he got back to his place he wouldn't sit. So I stopped the game and I said it was a pity that we couldn't go on playing because we would have to wait for Owen to sit down. But Owen kept standing there and the other children were becoming restless and, I don't feel good about what I did, but I felt it was the only thing left to do ... I said, 'OK, if you don't want to join in the game then there's no point being here' ... and I took him to the corner. I felt really awful but I made him sit there while the other children worked on their ideas for the circus ... and then I went and talked to him, and I said, 'It was because you weren't participating I put you here ... I thought you didn't want to be involved in the class.' He started crying and I felt terrible. I asked him if he could tell me what the problem was but he wouldn't talk, although I knew he was listening to me. So I kept on talking ... saying how I had been sad because I knew he could join in and do all these things ... and I said a lot of positive things about him ... and I said that I couldn't understand why he wouldn't join in. ... And something must have clicked ... because yesterday he did join in!

The principal came in when I was taking a group ... and I picked Owen ... and then I thought, 'Oh no, what have I done?' But he responded ... and a few other times during the day he joined in. You could see he thought hard ... but then did it. And he responded to the music teacher this morning ... and he's never done that before ... and this morning at the end of the group when I said I was going to write on the blackboard he came up to me and gave me this piece of chalk. He looked so pleased as he gave it to me ... and he said, 'You won't have to look for a piece now.' I don't know where he got the chalk.

From listening to Melanie's description of her experiences with Owen, it was apparent that her observations had contributed to her understanding of the situation. As Melanie interacted with Owen, she was constantly reflecting on and analysing the situation as well as thinking about the strategies she could use that would encourage his participation. In the game of 'Doggie Doggie', Melanie was faced with one of those moments when immediate action is required. With Owen standing and obviously flouting the rules of the game, and with the other children becoming restless, Melanie had to decide on a course of action. She did not have the luxury of time to consider alternatives. She decided to act, and followed through on her decision to remove Owen from the group. But that wasn't the end of the situation. Later Melanie went and talked with Owen. She shared her reasons for her actions with Owen and told him she valued him as a person and wanted to understand the reasons for his behaviour.

Melanie's evaluation was able to include some very positive outcomes for Owen and herself.

> I really would have liked to find out why Owen was behaving in the way he was ... because I didn't like what I did ... although I had tried all the positive things first. But it worked ... and I'm able to give him lots more positives now. Like yesterday when I was with him I said, 'I feel so happy to see you joining in like you have been.' He said, 'I'm just so tired I want to go home.' It really is an effort for him ... and he came to me this morning and talked to me. At the end of this prac I'm really feeling I can teach ... that I can problem solve. I think my experience with Owen has helped me to do that.

Melanie's account of her experience is a good illustration of using all the skills highlighted in the teaching cycle, many of them simultaneously, and of the complexities of assessing situations and making decisions.

Acquiring high standards of practice

As a pre-service teacher undertaking teaching practice, you may feel that the need to adopt professional standards of practice or a code of ethics is something for the distant future when you gain a position and officially enter the early childhood profession. You do have responsibilities in this regard, however. Because you are undertaking teaching practice in settings where there are young children who are powerless and dependent on adults for their physical and psychological well-being, standards of professional practice become particularly important (Katz, 1995b). Although you may not have full responsibility for the children, there will be many occasions when you make decisions or act in ways that can have considerable impact on their lives.

Early Childhood Australia, like many other national early childhood associations worldwide, has developed a code of ethics that focuses on 'optimal conduct' to be aimed for by *all* personnel whether qualified or unqualified, who work with young children (Stonehouse, 1998: 17). You also may have been given guidelines for ethical practice as part of your pre-service course. It is important that your own behaviour is in keeping with expectations regarding ethical behaviour when undertaking teaching practice. Some of the aspects highlighted by such guidelines, together with other issues associated with ethical behaviour, indicate that acquiring high standards of practice involve:

- acting in ways that best serve the interests and well-being of children;
- ensuring that confidentiality about children and their families is maintained;
- adapting and responding to the unique services and features of the setting;
- recognizing, accepting and valuing diversity among children, families and members of staff;
- acting in accordance with the legal and industrial aspects relating to the teaching practice setting.

Serving children's interests

As a pre-service teacher in the process of developing your professional expertise, it is not always easy to know which is the best way to act. It has been argued that the difference between professional and non-professional behaviour is that non-professional behaviour is 'determined by personal predilection, common sense or folk wisdom' while professional behaviour is influenced by specialized knowledge and accepted principles of practice (Katz, 1984: 9).

There will be times when you find yourself taking a commonsense approach or acting in ways in which your parents or a respected teacher treated you. This is not something to feel guilty about, but it is something you need to consider in the light of the specialized knowledge you are acquiring. It may well be that after reflection you will want to add new strategies to your teaching repertoire because you can see that they are consistent with your new knowledge or with accepted principles of practice. There may well be other strategies you decide to discard.

Maintaining confidentiality

Sometimes a supervising teacher will share confidential information with you so that a child may be better understood, or a family situation may be discussed at a staff meeting to enable staff to support the family. It is essential that you respect the confidential nature of this information and do not discuss it with peers, friends or parents. Even comments made to another staff member, if overheard by a parent or child, can be misinterpreted or repeated causing much heartache to those involved. When writing or discussing observations and child studies or when participating in seminars relating to teaching practice, you should take care not to use real names so that particular children, parents or staff members are not identified.

Plate 1.2 High standards of practice require you to recognize, accept and value diversity among children, families and members of staff. (Photo courtesy of Northgate State Preschool.)

Adapting to the uniqueness of the setting

Different early childhood settings may demand very different responses from student teachers. For example, if you are undertaking teaching practice in a childcare centre you may be required to attend at the time of a particular shift. If you are in a classroom where parents are regular participants in classroom activities, you will need to be prepared to welcome and work with additional adults in the room. If you are undertaking teaching practice in a centre that shares its facilities with another organization, you may be asked to assist in packing away materials and equipment. It is important that you recognize and accept the unique features of your teaching practice setting and show that you can adapt to the demands made.

Valuing diversity

In early childhood settings you will encounter children, families and staff members with many different cultures, languages, religions, ways of living and family structures. Given that our society values the importance of showing respect to all, it is important to develop understanding of and sensitivity to this range of differences in order to interact and respond appropriately. This is quite a challenge as even committed, experienced teachers can feel overwhelmed by this task (Copple, 2003). During your teaching practice you will find it helpful to explore ways in which you can demonstrate and communicate respect in your own interactions with children and adults, as well as developing strategies to assist children to develop positive attitudes towards others with different backgrounds, social customs and abilities.

Becoming familiar with legal and industrial aspects

Because laws, regulations and industrial awards vary between states and local authorities it is important that you become familiar with the particular legal and industrial requirements relating to the school or centre where you are undertaking teaching practice. Some issues you should inquire about relate to licensing, funding, child space and building regulations, liability and duty of care, protective care and the reporting of abuse, occupational health and safety regulations, as well as the industrial conditions and awards that apply to the staff at your school or centre.

OPPORTUNITIES FOR LEARNING IN TEACHING PRACTICE

In this chapter we have been considering teaching practice in terms of the opportunities it offers you to extend your specialized knowledge, to use that knowledge to assess situations and make decisions, and to show that you are beginning to acquire high standards of practice. As you commence your teaching practice and begin to get to know the children and adults, become familiar with the routines and work out what is expected of you, it may be that you feel more overwhelmed than excited by these learning opportunities. Don't be alarmed if you feel this way. Many pre-service teachers have similar feelings initially. Take heart from the fact that by the end of the teaching practice most agree that they have learned a lot from the experience. Here are just a few of their positive comments.

JAY I've learned so much. I've never had a group quite like this ... and I've had to use a lot of management strategies ... and develop them. I've never had to do that before.

TESSA I've had to learn to plan from my observations. Mrs H. doesn't believe in putting out activities just because there's a space. In this Centre everything that's put out is there for a reason. So I've learned how to go about doing that.

DONNA I hadn't realized that working with toddlers was just so full on. You can't switch off for a second.

MELANIE I've learned that I can teach Year 1 children. I've really enjoyed planning a unit of work. I've loved putting my ideas to the children and seeing them work on them ... and having children respond to me as if I was their teacher ... and I've proved to myself that I can problem solve ... and handle difficult situations.

On rare occasions, some students have difficulties in their teaching practice and feel far from positive about their experience. I well remember a practicum I had in a preschool in the first year of my course that left me feeling frustrated and bewildered. At the time I couldn't put into words what it was that concerned me but, with the benefit of hindsight, I'm sure my frustrations stemmed from my supervising teacher's desire for order and tight control. I was expected to keep the children occupied doing activities set by the teacher. I could see that the activities held little enjoyment or meaning for the children and allowed them no opportunity to diverge or imagine.

I remember one day being told to sit at the sewing activity and teach the children to sew according to the teacher's set procedure. While two children were managing to remember to thread the bodkin *down* and then *up* from *underneath*, the third child, Sarah, was becoming hopelessly confused and upset. Rather than persisting with the set task, I encouraged her to make stitches as best she could and soon she had a much-stitched, scrunched-up ball of fabric and a beaming face. 'It's a new ball for Joey, our kitten,' she said as she put it in her locker.

That afternoon my supervising teacher informed me of the error of my ways with Sarah. I was told of the importance of teaching a correct procedure and of getting children to persist at a task so they could achieve. I felt a failure and yet I felt that Sarah had achieved. She had made something of which she was proud. I felt, too, that my encouragement had contributed to her achievement. Was I really such a failure? There were many similar experiences during that teaching practice. I wanted to encourage the children to play, to diverge from the set activity that seemed to be in direct opposition to what my supervising teacher wanted. Which approach was most appropriate? Was I right or wrong to think this way?

I have often thought about that teaching practice. As I became more aware of my emphasis on meaningful activity and play in my own teaching, I realized that I, and my supervising teacher, had experienced a very clear mismatch of values and teaching approaches. Even though at that stage my teaching approach was embryonic, I was coming to recognize that encouraging children to act on their own ideas and valuing what children perceived to be of value were important aspects of my teaching. At the time I considered that particular teaching practice had been a disaster. In retrospect, I realize that it helped me make some important discoveries about my own teaching. It also helped me define things I would *not* do as a teacher, although it was some years before I could explain why I believed they were not good strategies. So you see, even negative teaching practice experiences can result in positive learning!

The student teachers' comments and my own experience indicate that the learning derived from teaching practice will be different for every participant. Given that every group of children, every supervising teacher and every pre-service teacher is different, this should come as no surprise. As you come to reflect on your own experiences in becoming a teacher you will realize that learning to teach is a very personal process. As you undertake readings, assignments and lectures, observe experienced teachers, listen to the teaching practice experiences of others as well as reflect on your own, your understanding of teaching will continue to deepen. These events will also be 'mixed together or integrated with the changing perspective' provided by your growing awareness of your own values to form your own 'practical theory' (Handal and Lauvås, 1987: 9). There is no one way to teach. Every teacher is continually developing a personal approach to teaching. In becoming a teacher you have to be prepared for some personal challenges.

PREPARING FOR TEACHING PRACTICE

Once your practice teaching placement has been confirmed there are a number of actions you can take that will help you feel 'prepared'. Here are some suggestions that may assist you.

- Telephone the centre or school and arrange a mutually convenient time to meet your supervising teacher.
- See if it is convenient to make a number of classroom visits to familiarize yourself with the children and the setting before your period of teaching practice officially begins. (In some courses this may be a set requirement.)
- Gather as much information as you can during these visits. Record the names and birth dates of children in the class. Become familiar with the children, the staff, the facilities and resources available within the setting, the nature of the programme and the administration of the school or centre. (It is also helpful to know the names of administrative staff.)

- Accept that your supervising teacher may not be able to spend a lot of time with you during these initial visits because priority must be given to the children and parents. Be prepared to use your initiative during these visits, but remember, too, that you are still a visitor.
- Ask questions of staff members when they have time available. They will not think your questions silly but will be pleased that you are keen to find out.
- Make contact with your liaison teacher. Discuss any concerns and share your hopes for the teaching practice.
- Be sure that you fully understand the expectations of your institution regarding your role as a pre-service teacher during teaching practice. If you are uncertain, discuss these expectations with your liaison teacher before teaching practice commences.
- As you become familiar with your particular setting consider the ways in which you will be able to meet the requirements set for your teaching practice.
- Discuss these requirements with your supervising teacher and be prepared to negotiate ways of achieving these (for example, ask if there are preferred ways to record your observations as well as to plan and evaluate).
- Be prepared to seek and accept advice. Let your supervising teacher know that you are keen to learn and would appreciate any feedback.
- Think about ways in which you can share your thoughts, ideas and 'wonderings' with your supervising teacher.
- Avoid jumping to conclusions about whether the teaching you are observing is 'good' or 'bad' after only one or two visits. Be prepared to keep an open mind until you have observed and experienced the situation for a considerable length of time.
- Think about the level of your commitment to the teaching practice. Remember that you will have to allow time for written reflection and preparation, apart from the time you are with the children. Work out how you are going to handle other personal or job commitments during the teaching practice.

Being prepared for the unexpected

As you prepare to undertake teaching practice be prepared for one more thing – the unexpected. There are many circumstances, and combinations of factors, that can influence the nature of the experience. These reflections highlight a number of unexpected factors encountered by some pre-service teachers.

SUSAN I have a two-year-old son, so I thought doing a prac with the toddler group would be easy because I felt I knew that age group ... but I've found it difficult interacting with several toddlers at the one time. I also found myself dealing with my own emotions about putting my child in childcare when any of the toddlers became upset.

JENNY I'm supporting myself through Uni and have this job in after-school care. It's very hard to juggle prac and my job. It makes for some very long days ... and nights.

ROSS I've found it very difficult coming into this primary prac. I've been in preschool and childcare pracs before this and I've found it difficult to adjust this time. There seems to be a different form of organization here. You have to stick to the timetable and the children have to go to the library and music at set times. I also have to be more aware of the syllabus documents when I'm doing my planning.

These comments highlight factors that resulted in some unexpected challenges for pre-service teachers during their teaching practice. Although you are the one who has to meet the challenges, remember that you have others who can assist you. Talk over a situation with your supervising teacher or your liaison teacher. Share a difficulty with a fellow student or friend. Consider their perspectives together with your own as you think through ways of meeting the various and unexpected challenges that will inevitably arise during teaching practice.

SUMMARY

Teaching practice enables you to gain first-hand experience of working with young children in early childhood settings and provides countless opportunities for developing professional understanding and teaching skills. The extent to which you learn from these opportunities is largely up to you, and will depend upon your willingness to:

- think about your practical experiences in the light of your theoretical knowledge;
- practise and refine those skills that are a part of the teaching cycle;
- develop an understanding of achieving high standards in teaching and ethical practice.

Your supervising teacher and liaison teacher are there to support you in your learning, but you will need to share your aims, concerns and feelings with them if they are to assist you. There are a number of steps you can take to prepare for your teaching practice. These include familiarization visits, clarifying the requirements expected of you during the practicum, and organizing other aspects of your life so that you can give priority to teaching practice.

There will be many occasions during your teaching practice when you will ask, 'Is what I'm doing or thinking right or wrong?' While your supervising teacher may help you find some solutions, it is vital that you seek your own answers and make decisions that have meaning for you. Be prepared to accept that there may be no clear-cut answers or absolutely correct ways of handling particular situations. Rather, there may be a number of alternatives that need to be considered in making a decision. You will be required to be a teacher and a researcher as you seek solutions to teaching dilemmas. You will need to ask questions and do your own thinking in the light of your growing specialized knowledge and understanding of effective practices for young children. These are the challenges and rewards that teaching practice offers.

SUGGESTED ACTIVITIES

Although these activities have been written for students studying independently they could be easily adapted for tutorial use through group work, discussion and debate.

• Jot down your thoughts and feelings about making your initial visit to the centre or school where you will undertake your teaching practice. Consider the people you are likely to meet and the impression you hope to make. Imagine or role-play the visit, making sure the perspective of each participant is presented (for example, the supervising teacher, pre-service teacher, aide, children, director or principal). What are some strategies, attitudes and questions that you as a pre-service teacher can adopt in order to make this initial visit a positive experience for all? What actions are best avoided?

• After your initial visit, reflect on the information you have gathered. Ask yourself 'what else do I need to know about the setting that will help my teaching?' You might want to know more about the daily schedule, how transitions are organised, what the 'rules' for the group are, or how you can best guide a particular child's behaviour. Now you are more familiar with the setting, devise possible ways of obtaining this additional information.

- Think more about the processes that make up the teaching cycle. Re-read Melanie's story of her experiences with Owen in this chapter. How would you have handled Owen? Use the processes suggested in the teaching cycle to make some decisions about a course of action. Outline *your* strategies and develop criteria you could use to evaluate their effectiveness.

- Consider the standards of practice expected of student teachers that are outlined in this chapter. List some practical ways in which you can demonstrate that you are acquiring high standards of practice in your particular setting.

- Read and consider the professional code of ethics that is adopted by teachers in your area. Explain why it is important for the early childhood profession to have a code of ethics.

Chapter 2

Ways of knowing and understanding children

In this chapter we will think about:

- teachers and children: building relationships;
- the nature of observation;
- what can be observed when getting to know children;
- using observations in curriculum decision-making;
- some questions about observations;
- the role of observation in assessing children's learning.

TEACHERS AND CHILDREN: BUILDING RELATIONSHIPS

Coming to know children and building relationships with them are two of the most exciting yet demanding challenges you will face as a teacher. If you are to assist children to engage in meaningful learning experiences and to approach their learning with confidence it is vital that you and the children know each other well and build mutually trusting relationships. In order to develop this knowledge and construct these relationships both you and the children will need to find out how the other thinks and feels, what each can do, and how each is likely to behave in particular situations. Building an effective relationship requires contributions from both parties. It is to be expected, however, that as the teacher you will have more detailed knowledge of children than children will have of you, and that you will show more empathy and unconditional positive regard than the children.

It also takes time to achieve these goals. Trusting relationships are generally built as children and teachers talk and join together in play and other activities, as well as observe each other in everyday situations. If the duration of your teaching practice is only a few weeks, the challenges of building trusting relationships are even greater. You will be surprised, however, at the amount of knowledge you can gain in a short period of time, and at the strength of the relationships that can develop if you really set out to 'come to know' children. In developing relationships you should be prepared to accept that you may not always be 100 per cent successful. Leanne's account of her experience during a teaching practicum provides a reminder that success in establishing relationships is not always assured despite your best efforts. Leanne wrote:

> Forming relationships with children is something I have always taken for granted. It is easy to do, isn't it? Well, before my last prac I thought it was. Until then, this had been the case for me. At my last prac, there was a child who displayed quite a lot of negative behaviour. I believe in being positive, so I aimed to focus on positive aspects. Unfortunately, I did not ever have conversations with him, although I tried. He answered my questions and then would ask me to leave him alone. I do not think he disliked me, nor do I feel I spent my time harassing him. It seemed more that I was a stranger, an intruder, someone who was interrupting him. I simply wanted to get to know Larry as much as I wanted to get to know all of the children. Larry stood out in the group. He was not afraid of defying anyone, or of being different. I was concerned that I was not getting to know him.
>
> One day I did a transition activity with the children to get them to wash their hands before morning tea. Larry refused to move. My mind raced with strategies I could use to persuade him to join the others. I knew telling him to do it was not going to work. I sat at his level and said his name, loudly enough to gain his attention, yet in a way that I thought would avoid a confrontation. Before I had finished he turned his back to me and shouted, 'SHUT UP'. The teacher came over and told him it was time to get ready for morning tea and he joined the other children. I had not even uttered a sentence.
>
> It hit me right then. I had no relationship with Larry. I had tried but I had only been at the centre two weeks. This was my first real taste of not getting to know a child as well as I would have liked. The teacher told me she still struggles with Larry and she has been with him all year. I got to know almost all of the children at my prac, yet when I left I still didn't know Larry. They say, 'Out of sight, out of mind'. Well Larry may be out of my sight but he certainly is not out of my mind. Larry taught me that forming relationships is a challenging task, more challenging than I had ever imagined!

As you set about getting to know children and building relationships with them, you may find it useful to recall Leanne's experience. Although you will be able to build positive relationships with most children, don't be too hard on yourself if you find relationships have not flourished to the extent you had hoped. Remember, developing trusting relationships takes time and effort from both parties.

Some suggestions for getting to know children

Here are some ideas and experiences of other pre-service teachers which may help you think about how you can use your time most effectively in getting to know the children in your teaching practice setting.

Become familiar with names and faces

If you can visit the centre a number of times prior to commencing your teaching practice, write down the first names of children from the class roll and begin to link some names with faces as you observe the children in their play or class activities. Coming to know children, however, means far more than getting to know their names and faces, or even observing them from a distance.

Talk with the children

Observing from a distance provides a different form of knowing someone from that experienced when you are able to talk with a person directly. For instance, getting to talk with someone at a party whom you had only observed across the room, provides you with opportunities to check out your initial impressions. Being able to interact with young children as they play provides you with similar opportunities. It also offers the child a chance to get to know you. In your visits prior to the teaching practice, ask your supervising teacher if you can talk with the children and join in class activities.

Think about how children might see you

Are you this tall person who towers over them, or are you someone who squats or sits down with them as you talk? Are you another child's mother or father who is visiting? (How many times have I been asked, 'Are you Jay's mum ... or grandma?'!) Do you explain who you are and why you are there? If you ask a child their name do you tell them yours too? That seems only fair. Do the children see you as someone who is watching them or as someone who is interested in what they are doing and will join in their game?

Plate 2.1   In getting to know children it is important to show them you are interested in what they are doing. (Photo courtesy of Sue Thomas.)

Join in activities with the children

Jeannie discovered that it wasn't as easy to join in the children's games as she thought it would be. She described her experiences this way:

> Well ... there was this group of children ... and they weren't in any particular area so I approached them ... but they just looked at me when I tried to talk to them ... so throughout the day I made a deliberate effort to go and talk to them ... individually. They were mostly role-playing, so I'd go up and ask if I could join in with them ... and later during the day ... they seemed much more comfortable and they began approaching me. If they're uncomfortable with you ... they just won't talk to you.
>
> My supervising teacher told me that a good way to join in the children's role play is to take on an 'as if' role ... so ... if they are playing hospitals I could act 'as if' I'm a nurse ... or a mother with a sick baby. I saw the teacher doing that the other day. She dabbed some red paint on the doll's arm ... and went into the hospital ... and she said, 'Doctor, could you look at my baby. She's hurt her arm.' The doctors and nurses responded like it was real ... I was amazed. ... They bandaged the doll ... and one wrote out a prescription and told the teacher she had to take it to the bank! I don't feel very confident about doing that sort of thing ... but I'll give it a go.

As Jeannie found, you have to make a deliberate effort to join with children in play. Taking on a role in keeping with the game, or contributing some additional materials that the children can use, are useful ways to enter the play. Such actions also give the children 'cues' that you are a player too.

Share something of yourself

Many student teachers have found it useful to introduce themselves to the children by telling the children something about themselves. Anne showed the children a photo of herself at their age. The class was particularly interested in family photos at the time. Marie found herself telling a group of children who were discussing how hot they felt that she had been so hot the previous afternoon she had gone to a friend's house and plopped in her swimming pool. To her surprise she had seen a water dragon on the side of the pool watching her. The children were immediately fascinated by the water dragon and wanted to know what it looked like, so Marie promised to bring a book that had a picture of the water dragon. As soon as Marie arrived the next day, Jason asked her if she had brought the book. Marie felt that this mutual interest helped her establish rapport.

Keep a journal

Although not a requirement, Bella kept a journal of her thoughts and experiences during the days she visited the centre prior to her teaching practice because she felt it helped the familiarization process. Although her journal covers many aspects of the centre's functioning, such as the organization of the day and what the teacher and aide did, only extracts which focus on getting to know the children are included here.

Monday, 25 July
I found the children's 'show and tell' to be mostly 'tell', which was great. Sarah spoke about riding on a ghost *train*. This triggered a memory in Joe about visiting the place where his mum had formerly lived and was now a ghost *town*.

Monday, 1 August
The day's programme began with a group discussion. Emma had a self-made folder of drawings to show. Dean had a postcard of Puffin' Billy. Dominic brought a book about space and showed the page with a picture of a dish for receiving satellite images. This led to talk about the reception of sound waves by our ears. The group discussion

concluded with the children talking about their ideas for indoor time. Emma made a house. When I visited, she was cutting up brown paper to make chocolates to put in a chocolate box.

Dean made his Puffin' Billy from blocks and cushions. He also made some stop and go traffic signs. Gary, after discussing Puffin' Billy with Dean, decided to make Thomas the Tank Engine and used the large hollow block into which he fitted two chairs. Patrick set up a bowling alley with Edward. They kept a score sheet. Dominic constructed a message-receiving space station from blocks and an umbrella. Melissa, Belinda, Katherine and Jalyce were ballerinas and stuck numbers on the chairs in their theatre.

One aspect I find fascinating is the amount of discussion which takes place. The detailed plans for what and where, with whom and with what equipment the children will work must surely help prevent conflict. Negotiations concerning positions of buildings and equipment take place publicly, so that other children are able to help the parties involved come to an agreement. This also must build a sense of community as they find out how they can pursue their interests without infringing the rights of others.

A comment on problem solving. ... When an argument brewed with Dean's group re the action to take at the amber light ... slow down or wait ... the teacher advised the children to watch what their parents did when they were driving. She did not give her opinion as to the right and only option.

Monday, 8 August
The children appear to need to dress up before they begin their play, although the outfits do not necessarily reflect their roles. While the children are beginning to accept my presence and request my help with physical needs, I feel I have not become a 'playmate' as yet. For example, when I requested an appointment at the hairdressers, Emma said she was busy with her family. Later at group time she must have remembered this incident, and said, 'You can come tomorrow.' As my imagination can carry me away I must be careful to follow their lead and not take over or direct their play.

While I cannot generalize from only three mornings with the group, I am interested that the children with ideas for games seem to be Sarah, Emma, Andrew, Patrick, Gary and Joshua ... or, at least, these are the vocal ones. It will be a challenge to see whether this bears out research that we discussed in class that there are dramatists, explorers (builders) and spectators. I look at Melissa and Belinda and wonder what is going on inside their heads. They seem too quiet. (Gary thinks Melissa is wonderful!)

Monday, 15 August
Gary occupied a great deal of the teacher's time today as she sat explaining the consequences of his behaviour to him and giving him the social phrases which will help him make friends. Many of the children must struggle to see another's point of view. Their own desires close their vision. The support they are being given while they learn these skills is really warm in this centre. An example of this scaffolding was when Gary announced, 'Melissa, I'm gonna sit near you.' Melissa refused and Gary reacted angrily. The teacher explained to Gary that if he were to get a mat for Melissa and put it near his mat he could say, 'Melissa, you can sit beside me, here.'

In her journal Bella was making some interesting 'getting to know you' type observations. It is worthwhile examining these in more detail as they provide some insights into the nature of observation as well as suggesting ways in which initial observations can be focused effectively.

THE NATURE OF OBSERVATION

Have you thought about what it is you are doing when you are observing children? Some experienced teachers, when discussing this question, described it in these terms (Perry, 1989: 2):

ANNE When I'm observing I'm trying to build a picture of a child.
JANE For me, observation is more than building a picture of a child. It's more than looking at what a child is doing. I have to act on the observation in some way ... try to understand what I'm seeing ... make some sense of it.
SARA When I'm observing I think I gather snippets of all types of behaviour that help me come to know the 'Tim-ness of Tim!' I want to know all those things that make Tim, Tim ... that demonstrate his uniqueness. Things like the way Tim does things, the way he approaches other children or adults, the complexity of his dealings.

If we look more closely at Bella's observations made in her journal, we can see a number of the features of observation highlighted by these experienced teachers. For example, Bella was actively involved in her observations, gathering snippets of information about individual children in order to build a more complete picture of them and making connections between this new information and her previous readings and knowledge. Although each of us has to work out our own ways of observing and building relationships, it is useful to consider and try out some of the methods and processes that others have found helpful. Here are some of the processes that were a part of Bella's initial observations.

Processes that are a part of initial observations

Identifying characteristics of individual children

Bella did this by noting what particular children were interested in doing; what they liked to talk about; how they went about doing things; what their particular needs seemed to be; and how they got on with other children and adults.

Noting general characteristics of children

For Bella these general characteristics included: the children's interest in making connections – how one child's talk of ghost trains led to talk of ghost towns; the children's apparent need to dress up before they commenced their play; and the children's difficulty in seeing another's point of view. She also observed that some children are very vocal and able to express their ideas while others are very quiet and reveal little of their thoughts.

Describing how the group functions

The amount of discussion and negotiation concerning what, where, with whom and how ideas and games would develop surprised Bella, and led her to ponder on the value of discussion in preventing conflict and promoting the sense of community. Similarly, the warm support, scaffolding and modelling of phrases by the teacher for Gary was considered likely to foster more social behaviour.

Assessing how the children respond to you

Bella found that she had to earn the children's acceptance in their play and that this took time. Being prepared to accept Emma's initial negative response to exclude her from the hairdressers was important, as was being aware that she must not take over the children's play by imposing her own ideas when Emma eventually invited her into her game.

Considering new information in the light of specialized knowledge

Although it is not easy to consider your observations in the light of your specialized knowledge, it is important that you try to do this. In some courses pre-service teachers are asked to focus on particular aspects of child development and learning during teaching practice. This was the case for Bella. She had chosen to focus on two teaching issues: helping children to resolve conflict, and helping children to become confident problem solvers. By reading articles on these topics prior to teaching practice she was aware of some of the issues involved and so was able to focus some of her observations from the outset. The readings also provided her with some specialized knowledge against which she could consider her own observations and experiences.

Having a purpose for your observations

In getting to know children, Bella's aim was to discover 'their strengths and needs' so she could plan in ways that challenged and enhanced their learning. Although discovering children's strengths and interests are useful starting points for your planning, you will need to go on to find out far more about each child if your teaching and the children's learning is to be meaningful and purposeful. In fact, getting to know children is a never-ending process. On the last day of your teaching practice you should be discovering something new about the children.

WHAT CAN BE OBSERVED WHEN GETTING TO KNOW CHILDREN?

Because there are countless numbers of things that could be observed in getting to know children it is often difficult to make decisions about what you will observe. Here are some aspects that experienced teachers indicate they aim to observe in getting to know children:

- areas of development (e.g. physical, cognitive, social, emotional, moral);
- the children's knowledge;

- the particular skills and strategies used in learning and interacting;
- the children's dispositions;
- the children's feelings;
- the dynamics of a group of children.

These aspects may provide a framework for your observations too.

Areas of development

Knowledge of child development provides you with an understanding of the changes in children's thinking and behaviour as they grow from birth to adulthood, and with an awareness of the general characteristics likely to be shown by children in their various stages of development. Although children are whole beings and you want to come to know them in a holistic way, sometimes it is necessary to think about particular areas of development to get a more in-depth understanding of an individual child.

If you know what is involved in social and emotional development, for example, then you will be able to observe these areas of a child's development in a meaningful way. Because Moira was aware that strong attachments to parents are an important base for a young child's ability gradually to establish bonds with adults and peers outside the family (Honig, 2002; Kostelnik *et al.*, 2002), she was able to recognize the significance of three-year-old Rae's behaviour. Frequently, during the first week of Moira's teaching practice Rae asked 'Is my Mummy coming now?' Early in the second week, however, Rae asked about her mum less frequently and, when Rae ran to hug Moira before she departed with her Mum, this observation was seen as a significant step in Rae's developing ability to establish relationships with other adults. Having some knowledge of this area of child development, Moira was able to bring some specialized information into her thinking about Rae and ask some relevant questions:

> Is Rae's behaviour typical for her age? What situations are likely to be difficult for Rae? Is it important to be close by when Mum is departing and to work on developing my relationship with Rae? Would a more predictable daily routine help Rae establish when her Mum will come?

From Moira's example you can see that knowledge of areas of development provides information that helps you formulate numerous questions and think about how you can respond to children in ways that assist their learning. Numerous texts on child development such as Berk (2001), Nixon and Gould (1999), Santrock (2001) and Woodhead *et al.* (1998), provide detailed discussions of the various developmental areas. You are strongly urged to become familiar with such texts, if you have not already done so, in order to extend your specialized knowledge of child development. These texts can provide you with some pointers concerning what to observe in specific areas of development. Your knowledge of development may also help you to understand what you have observed better. This was Anne's experience. She wrote:

> I couldn't understand why Caitlin, a five-year-old in a Year 1 class, was having such difficulty doing the task I had set. Groups of children had been asked to look through magazines and cut out pictures of items for their particular shop. We were making big posters displaying what was sold by various traders such as the butcher, baker, hardware merchant, jeweller and fruiterer. Caitlin was in the butcher's shop group, but, instead of cutting out items for the butcher's shop, she cut out pictures of things that she liked and wanted. At the end of the time she had pictures of dolls, diamond rings, a bicycle, nail polish and ice-creams. Although she could tell me that butchers sold meat and recognized pictures of chops and sausages, she seemed unable to cut out pictures of meat that obviously didn't interest her. As I observed Caitlin's behaviour, I realized that this might be an example of pre-operational thinking in which Caitlin's egocentrism was preventing her from breaking out of that particular mind set. This knowledge of development helped me accept Caitlin's behaviour and lessened my frustration. I realized she wasn't being naughty. She just could not see why she needed to cut out pictures of meat when there were so many interesting pictures of things she wanted to have.

The children's knowledge

Although children's knowledge is frequently talked about, there are various views as to the nature of that knowledge. Some writers (Edwards and Knight, 1994: 39) argue that knowledge not only means facts 'but also skills and procedures, as well as a system of interrelated concepts'. Others, such as Katz (1996: 138), suggest that young children's knowledge can be thought of more broadly in terms of 'understandings, constructions, concepts, information, facts, stories, songs, legends and the like'. Debate revolves around the actual content of these understandings and concepts, what needs to be taught and how it needs to taught, in order to achieve the knowledge and skills a community considers necessary for adults in their society to have (Siraj-Blatchford and Yeok-lin Wong, 1999).

For those of you undertaking teaching practice in settings where children have reached compulsory school age, observing children's knowledge may not seem to be such an issue, because with the introduction of national curricula in many countries, the *what* of children's learning is generally specified in syllabus documents. You may see observing children's knowledge in these settings as just a matter of observing whether or not children know the content that is prescribed. Leaving aside the thorny question of how best to assess this knowledge, there are many other questions and issues, however, relating to children's knowledge that you need to consider. Does the focus on prescribed content provide a sufficient base for the under-standing of children's knowledge? Is prescribed knowledge the only knowledge that is important to young children? Are there different types or domains of knowledge? (For example, is knowing how to climb a ladder a different type of knowledge from knowing how to count to ten?) Is the way in which children construct their knowledge important? And what about the knowledge of children who are below the compulsory school age? What is the nature of their knowledge?

Perhaps this observation shared with me by a teaching colleague, Sue, will help you think further about some of these questions and the nature of young children's knowledge.

Sue, the teacher, was walking past a group of five-year-old girls chatting together. She heard Alicia comment, as she flipped her long blond hair back over her shoulder, 'If you don't have long hair when you go to school, the boys won't love you.'

Sue paused and interposed, 'Oh I don't think that's right. ... I've got short hair and I know lots of people love me ... and Bridget, you've got short hair ... do you have people who love you?'

Bridget said thoughtfully, 'Yes, Alicia! People love me. ...'

Sue continued, 'Yes ... and it's not what you look like or whether you've got long hair or not. People love you if you're kind and think nice things inside. ... But they don't like you if you're unkind and do unkind things.'

The teacher left the group at this stage, but later in the session Alicia came up to her and said, 'Miss T. ... I'm unkind, but my Daddy says he loves me.'

Sue responded with a question, 'Oh, are you really unkind? What things do you do that are unkind?'

Alicia replied, 'I kick people ... and sometimes I lie on the floor and scream if I can't get what I want.'

Sue replied, 'Well ... Mummies and Daddies like yours are really special people and they love you no matter what you do.'

'Mmm,' said Alicia, thinking hard.

'But, you know', said the teacher, 'not everyone is like your Mummy and Daddy. Most people, if they see someone doing unkind things feel sad and upset ... and they think "I don't want to be friends with someone like that!" ... and often people who do unkind things end up feeling very sad and lonely.'

'Mmmm,' said Alicia again as she walked away.

What can be learned about young children's knowledge from this observation? Alicia spontaneously shared her knowledge with her friends. She seemed confident about the understandings she'd constructed, and, without the teacher's intervention, she and her friends could well have gone on holding this view. The teacher, however, challenged Alicia's statement by presenting some evidence that contradicted it, and invited Bridget to present some opposing evidence too. Having set up this dissonance, the teacher went on to provide some further information for Alicia to think about. In essence, this was that it is not what you look like that counts but rather what you do. Sue's observation of Alicia's knowledge could well have ended here but it didn't. The fact that Alicia came back to the teacher in the way she did, shows how children keep on trying to make connections between what they know and new information they are given. In this instance, just as the teacher had done, Alicia had some contradictory information to present – 'I'm unkind, but my Daddy says he loves me.' It is interesting to note how the teacher responded in this situation. She accepted Alicia's evidence but then added more information for Alicia to take into account as she went on constructing her own understandings.

For me, this example illustrates the nature of young children's knowledge. It reveals some of Alicia's understandings and concepts, as well as something of the way in which she goes about constructing these by testing ideas and considering new information. It also highlights an aspect of the teacher's role in extending – or in this case, challenging – children's knowledge. Although the knowledge that the teacher sought to build – 'that being kind is what counts' – was not specifically prescribed content, it was in keeping with the teacher's goals for the children to value and respect everyone. The teacher's initial observation, which very much involved *hearing* what Alicia was saying, was the catalyst for the learning episode. The teacher acted on her observation by providing additional information and evidence that played such an important role in helping Alicia construct new knowledge.

While it is important to observe and monitor children's knowledge in relation to prescribed content or learning outcomes, it is equally important to observe the children's understandings, concepts and connections which may be revealed in their discussions and interactions, as well as in their activities and play. Knowledge acquired in this way, as young children go about making sense of their world, is strong because it is embedded in 'motivating circumstances' and is full of 'social and cultural meaning' (Carr, 2000: 7). Such observations also offer teachers important cues for extending and challenging children's knowledge.

Skills and strategies used in learning and interacting

Skills are usually thought of as actions that indicate some mastery. Because they are actions, they are generally easily observed. Learning strategies too are actions but when they are associated with learning they are seen to be actions used with a particular purpose in mind (Nisbet and Shucksmith, 1986). Sometimes learning strategies are more difficult to observe and have to be inferred from behaviour.

It is important that you observe skills related to all aspects of learning and interacting. These include verbal and communication skills, social skills, thinking, reasoning and problem-solving skills, as well as skills associated with creating, constructing and expressing ideas. Skills inherent in the development of literacy and numeracy should also be observed. Many pre-service teachers have indicated that when they first start making observations, they find they focus mainly on physical skills, because these seem 'more obvious'. While observing the 'more obvious' may be a good starting point, remember that your observations should help you come to know more about a child. If you have several observations showing that a child has established hand dominance, then there is little point collecting further observations that give you similar information. Aim to observe other skills that will provide you with different or additional information.

Also, when you are observing skills, try to connect that knowledge with other information you have about the child. As one of her observations, Jan had written: 'In their physical education class Troy was able to throw the ball with his right hand and catch the ball with both hands.' When I asked what the significance of this observation was Jan said: 'I'm not sure. We're supposed to get all these observations during prac ... so when I have a spare moment ... like when the phys ed teacher was taking the class ... I just wrote anything I could.'

Although this is not a good rationale for making observations, it is, nevertheless one that is used when pre-service teachers feel pressured to fulfil the practice teaching requirements. As you become more skilled in observation, however, and experience how observations can assist you in your work with children, your purpose for making observations will change. In Jan's case, as we talked about Troy, she realized that she had noticed that he was having difficulty with his writing but had not observed him closely enough to note possible reasons for these problems. She decided that she needed to observe more closely the ways in which he went about his writing tasks in the classroom. She also realized the importance of making connections between the snippets of information she had about Troy if she was to assist him in his learning.

It is often after observing a child's actions or experiencing the effects of a child's behaviour that you become aware of particular strategies that are being employed. Have you had a child engage you in conversation or present a persuasive argument to keep you with them, especially when they sense you are about to leave? My four-year-old niece, with whom I was 'surfing', persuasively argued that I shouldn't leave the water, 'because the waves haven't finished yet. There are plenty more waves to come!' Natalie, undertaking teaching practice with a Year 2 class, became aware of James's strategy when she was taking a maths lesson. She wrote in her journal:

> I noticed that James seemed to rely on Sam and Nicholas to help him with his maths sheet and to explain the directions to him. He was sitting with them initially, and when I asked him to move to his own desk he was reluctant and took several minutes to do so. Then he kept turning around and asking Sam and Nicholas what to do.

Natalie reflected on her observation this way:

> While I think it is important that children support one another, I think children should know that they cannot expect their peers to do or explain everything for them. This seemed to be the strategy James was using. Encourage James to do things for himself and build his self-esteem. Explain that he can ask group members for help but that he needs to have a go himself first.

Observing and being aware of the strategies children are using are essential if your own strategies are to be effective in assisting their learning and development.

Children's dispositions

'Disposition' is a term that comes from developmental psychology and is increasingly being used in the early childhood literature to focus on a different type of learning from that involved in learning knowledge and skills. Dispositions can be thought of as

> habits of mind, tendencies to respond to situations in certain ways. Curiosity is a disposition. It's not a skill, and it's not a piece of knowledge. It's a tendency to respond to your experience in a certain way.
>
> (Katz, 1988: 33)

Behaviours such as cooperativeness or quarrelsomeness can be regarded as dispositions, as can a desire to make friends or to learn. You can generally observe children's dispositions in the way they go about doing things.

The notion of learning dispositions has been developed further in the context of the New Zealand socio-culturally oriented national early childhood curriculum. As a result of this development Carr (2000: 21) discusses learning dispositions in terms of 'participation repertoires' and suggests five domains of learning dispositions that should be fostered. They are:

- taking an interest in aspects of the early childhood setting that might be the same or different from home; coping with transition and changing situations;
- being involved at an increasingly complex level;
- persistence with difficulty or uncertainty; an interest in 'learning' and a capacity to risk error or failure;
- communicating with others, expressing a point of view, an idea or an emotion;
- taking increasing responsibility in a range of ways.

  (Carr 2000: 17)

Another anecdote from my teaching colleague, Sue, illustrates some of these domains in this example of four-year-old Jack's learning disposition.

> It was in the first week of term and Jack was being helped to become familiar with the arrival routine. The aide was standing near the basket where children were placing their lunch boxes. The teacher observed that Jack seemed concerned about placing his lunch box in with all the rest, and heard him say to the aide, 'How will I know it's mine?' The aide replied that they would be able to find his lunch because his Mum had written Jack's name on it. Somewhat reassured Jack went off to play, but later in the morning the teacher was aware that Jack seemed a little troubled. On talking with him she discovered that Jack was still

thinking about how he would find his lunch. 'I sure hope my Mum wrote my name on the crusts, 'cos I eat the soft part,' Jack said.

By observing Jack the teacher noted aspects of his learning disposition. For instance, she noted his initial interest relating to what he needed to do with his lunch box at preschool that was different from home, as well as his persisting concern about how he would find his lunch. The teacher supported his learning disposition by enabling Jack to express his concerns and ideas about how he would recognize his lunch and encouraged him to take some responsibility for finding his lunch box for himself. In the process she gained a fascinating insight into his point of view about the way his Mum would write his name on his lunch. She was also reminded that young children's views of the world may be very different from those of adults.

Children's feelings

The importance of engendering positive feelings in children about their competence, their sense of belonging and their ability to learn and solve problems cannot be over-emphasized. Failure to observe a situation closely and respond sensitively to it can often result in children experiencing less than positive feelings. Vicki describes a situation she experienced on her last teaching practice that made her aware of the need to handle situations sensitively. She wrote:

> Anna, a four-year-old, wet herself at morning tea while sitting at the table. Miss D. took her outside to the lockers to get changed while the aide cleaned up. Miss D. told Anna to take off her shirt and skirt as they were wet and to put on the other dress that was in her locker. Miss D. then went back inside. Later, I discovered that Anna had taken off her shirt and put the dress on over the wet skirt. Following up on Miss D.'s instructions I told her to go and take her skirt off. She went to her locker to do this but didn't re-emerge so I went to see what was happening. There was Anna standing beside her locker crying because she couldn't undo the button on her skirt.
>
> Once I realized Anna couldn't undo her button I felt so guilty. Why hadn't I asked her why she had left her skirt on? Why had I acted in an irritated way? Why wasn't I thinking? Basically I think I was just following the tone of the other staff, irritated that Anna had wet herself at such an inconvenient time and place. This is no excuse. No wonder Anna didn't feel she could approach anyone when she found she couldn't

get her button undone. In fact, she did the only logical thing she felt she could do – put on her dress over her skirt.

I realized I had not been sensitive to Anna's feelings. I had not observed and thought about the situation closely. Why would she keep on a wet skirt when she could have a clean, dry dress? I thought about how intimidating teachers as authority figures could be. I want the atmosphere in my classroom to be encouraging so children are not afraid to ask for help, or give suggestions. I learned a lot from this incident ... that I need to put myself in children's shoes more often and think about how they are feeling and why they are behaving in certain ways.

Vicki's experience reminds us of the importance of looking at situations not just from an adult's perspective but from a child's point of view, particularly a child who may be feeling embarrassed, shy and vulnerable. Although we may not be able to observe some feelings directly, we can become sensitive to behaviour that reflects feelings.

The dynamics of a group of children

Although there is much emphasis given to observing individual children in early childhood education, it is important to remember that these individuals are also members of a group. Jane, an experienced teacher, describes her thoughts about individuals and groups this way:

My centre is not a place where 25 children roam about independently. We are a social setting where personalities, ideas, characteristics and emotions merge to form the dynamics of the group ... and sometimes the dynamite! This is the setting in which each individual operates, so it is important for me to observe the group so that I can place my growing knowledge of the individual in context.

It is also important for me to come to know the group as it develops certain characteristics over the year so that I can make predictions about reactions to teaching strategies. If I can be aware of what stimulates, satisfies or calms I am more likely to aid the learning in the play. If I can be aware of what is likely to occur when different individuals and personalities merge, I can be more productive as a teacher. As the year progresses, the whole class or some friendship groups can develop patterns of behaviour. It may be that these group characteristics are productive and positive or they may be negative ones that I need to redirect in order to promote growth.

(Perry, 1989: 9)

Jane's reflections highlight the importance of coming to know the group dynamics as well as considering observations of individual children in a group context. As you come to know which children are likely to dominate, lead or be passive participants in group situations, you are able to plan your teaching strategies more effectively.

In thinking about observing individual children's development, knowledge, skills and dispositions as well as their group behaviours, you have probably thought of many other aspects you could observe that would help you come to know children. Observing the nature of children's play, or the ways in which they interact with materials, or engage in mathematical thinking, for example, also can provide valuable information.

As you develop your observation skills and come to know your children you will find it easier to make decisions about what to observe. Jane, when describing her understanding of observation indicated how knowing a child helped her focus her observations. She said:

> For me observation is an active process in which I am internalizing a new awareness of a child that in turn changes *my* perceptions or behaviours. It is a conscious thought process that interacts with what I knew in the past, what I am doing in the present and influences how I will act in the future. For instance, I might observe that Tom is crying. Because I know that Tom does not usually cry, my observation seems to focus on why Tom is crying. My initial observation that Tom is crying is only a starting point and therefore not productive in itself. For me, the observation becomes productive when I search for why and make decisions about what I will do.
>
> (Perry, 1989: 4)

Jane's experience suggests that when you 'know' children you become more attuned to 'different' behaviours, comments or reactions which create a new awareness that prompts you to observe a particular aspect more closely. For Jane, observation became useful when it increased her understanding of the child and assisted her to make curriculum decisions.

USING OBSERVATIONS IN CURRICULUM DECISION-MAKING

As your experience in teaching increases, the usefulness of observations will become more apparent. Because you know something about children's interests, particular areas of development, or their dispositions and feelings you are in a far better position to make appropriate curriculum decisions and develop teaching strategies. For instance, observations can be used in curriculum decision-making to:

- provide supportive and responsive learning environments;
- understand specific behaviour.

Using observations – to provide supportive learning environments

If you are to teach effectively, it is vital that you use the knowledge you have gained about children from your observations when you plan learning experiences for them. Although this use may seem obvious, you may discover, as Suzette did, that it is easy to overlook the knowledge you have. Suzette, a pre-service teacher, shared with me one chaotic experience she had with a two- to three-year-old group because she did not use the knowledge gained from her observations when planning. She said:

> Because Christmas was coming up, we were talking about what presents the children could make for their parents. I'd seen this idea for hand prints made from plaster of Paris in a book … so we decided we'd do

Plate 2.2 A casual observation might suggest a child painting a box – a detailed observation revealed that a boat was being made. The challenge of observation is to gather detailed information without being intrusive. (Photo courtesy of Lady Gowrie Child Centre, Brisbane.)

that. I didn't test it out beforehand ... which I should have ... and we couldn't get the plaster the right consistency and I spent ages trying. This meant the children were becoming upset and restless ... and then we couldn't have them crowding around, which they all wanted to do. When they did get a turn, they really couldn't manage it by themselves and I had to put their hand in the plaster ... and some didn't like that and cried. ... And then I'd forgotten they wouldn't be able to wash their hands by themselves and I didn't have a bucket of water nearby for them to wash their hands ... and everything got splattered with plaster. It was just chaos!

In reflecting on it later, Suzette realized that she had been so enthused with the hand print idea that she hadn't stopped to consider whether two-year-olds had the physical skills to handle the activity. Nor had she thought about the extent to which they would be able to participate or whether the activity would hold any meaning for them. She said:

If only I'd thought about it. I've observed how messy two-year-olds are with the paints. They just don't have the fine motor skills that this activity needed ... and I've observed that they can't wait for any length of time, and yet I kept them waiting. I know that while we're encouraging them to be more independent they still need help washing their hands ... and I should have thought how I was going to manage that part of it. I just went ahead because the hand prints sounded like a fun thing to do. I just didn't think about whether the children could handle it.

Suzette's experience shows how essential it is to use the knowledge derived from observations if you are to provide supportive learning environments. This knowledge not only helps you to decide whether or not the experience you are planning is appropriate, but it can also help you to think through ways of organizing the environment so that children can participate fully in the activity, and be as independent as possible while being safe.

Using observation – to understand behaviour

If a child is demonstrating difficult behaviour, focused observations may help identify factors that trigger particular behaviours, as well as conditions that help the child control or improve the behaviour. Leona, a final year pre-service teacher, observed a change in Andrea's behaviour. She wrote:

By the end of my first week Andrea refused to play in the hospital. She cried and refused to even walk near the area when she went to the bathroom. She also began hiding her face and sticking her fingers in her ears at story time when hospital stories were read. The crying for Mum increased at times when she didn't like the activities offered, was expected to follow a routine, or took offence at other children's actions.

Leona noted a number of factors that could have been the cause of Andrea's behaviour. For instance, the aide Andrea was particularly fond of left the centre; she began complaining of stomach pains; and the home corner where Andrea loved to play became a hospital as the result of some other children's particular interests. Leona reflected:

> Originally I thought Andrea's behaviour might have been due to the changes in the room, including having a prac student take on the teacher's role, and followed my supervising teacher's suggestions to be firm and insist she behave appropriately. This seemed to make the problem worse. As our concerns increased, the teacher and I spoke with Mum, who was also worried, and took her to the doctor. Andrea did receive medical treatment and at the same time I changed my strategies to simply accepting her feelings and concerns. I kept reassuring her that she could settle down and feel better, and that she did not have to play in the hospital. I also tried to plan activities that I thought would interest her. Whether it was using different strategies, an improvement in her general health, or simply becoming accustomed to hospital play, I don't know, but on the last day of prac Andrea was again playing in the hospital. She was 'fixing Jo's head by injecting it with medicine' and happily joining in the other activities.

Although Leona felt there were probably multiple causes for Andrea's behaviour which stemmed from coping with a number of changes and feeling unwell, it was Leona's thoughtful observations and reflections which led to her successful teaching strategies.

SOME QUESTIONS ABOUT OBSERVATIONS

As you gain experience in observing, it is natural that you will have some concerns and questions. Be prepared to express these and seek advice. It is only in this way that you will develop your skills as well as clarify your beliefs concerning the value of observation. Here are some questions about observation that pre-service teachers have asked during their teaching practice.

What methods of observation should I use?

> Are we expected to do running records and anecdotal records and all the other observation methods we've been told about? I find it very difficult to walk around with a notebook. I found the first couple of days I could, but now I want to get in with the children, rather than stand there with a pad and pencil and write things.

This was Tracey's question when I visited her. In a previous teaching practice Tracey had been required to gather certain types of observations such as anecdotes, running records and event samples in order to develop her skill in using these particular methods. In her current teaching practice there was no such requirement, and Tracey was faced with having to decide on methods of observation as well as how to observe while she was teaching. In talking further about her concerns Tracey realized that her decision about the type of observation method to use had to be made after asking some questions:

- What type of information is wanted?
- How will the information be used?
- Why is the information needed?

She decided that if she wanted to build her knowledge of individual children then she would use anecdotal records, which are short, narrative summaries of directly observed, significant incidents. On the other hand, if she wanted to find out about children's writing skills and social skills then she would use a check-list in combination with anecdotal observations. She decided to use check-lists because she knew good check-lists contain clearly defined items that would help her quickly assess whether a child had specific skills or characteristics. She felt, too, that these check-lists could help build her knowledge about the skills necessary for writing or building social relationships, which in turn, would assist her to develop more focused and responsive teaching strategies. After thinking it through, Tracey realized that the type of information required and the reasons for its collection must guide her selection of the observational method.

If you are not familiar with the variety of methods which can be used to observe and study children, there are many texts available to inform you (for example, Beaty, 2002; Bentzen, 2000; Curtis and Carter, 2000; McAfee and Leong, 2002).

Is it OK to observe some children more than others?

In discussing her teaching, Paula commented that she seemed to focus her attention on the noisier children and spent her time with them so they did not disturb the rest of the group. Paula went on to say that giving so much attention to the noisy ones worried her. 'When I go to write up my observations I sit there and I see the name, David ... and I think ... I didn't even notice him today ... and I think ... it's ones like him I should be giving my attention to ... not the ones who demand it.'

Paula was voicing a dilemma experienced by all teachers, not just pre-service teachers. How does a teacher share her time and attention appropriately with all children? Paula said that her supervising teacher had told her that if a child or group of children had a problem or particular need, then you had to spend time with them, but that she felt 'things evened themselves out over the year'. Although somewhat reassured by her teacher's comments, Paula still felt uncomfortable and anxious about not knowing her 'quiet' children, so we talked through some practical strategies to try. These included ideas for getting the aide to work with the attention-seeking children so that Paula was free to interact with and observe the quieter children.

I also told Paula about how Tessa, who was experiencing a similar difficulty, was attempting to ensure that she didn't become so involved with a particular group that she was unable to move around and see every child in the time available. To increase her knowledge and awareness of every child Tessa set herself the task of filling in a daily observation record in which she noted something she had observed about each child. An extract from Tessa's record is shown in Table 2.1.

Table 2.1 Extract from Tessa's observation record

Child	Observation
Alicia	Music with Mrs H. Wanted to sing me a song she learned at ballet with Hannah. Really enjoys music and movement.
Sara	Made blotting paper – wanted to keep Rosie there – 'Are you going to do another one?' Really enjoyed the experience. Talked well with other children at the table.
Michael	At collage table by himself. Made a mask with Adam. Did dance for the class.
Christopher	Mother on roster. Very enthusiastic about papermaking. Helped Thomas and Richard do theirs. Explained the steps.
Philip R.	Not interested with paper activity – wandered off after a few minutes. Just seemed to flutter around – watched while other children did activities, then wandered off. Played on swings with Christopher.

After reading Tessa's brief observations, those of you who are familiar with a variety of observation methods may be saying that they are not proper anecdotal records. Tessa herself said that to me when she explained her notes. She said:

> I know more detailed anecdotes give me more information about a child (and I write those up separately) ... but I find the brief daily notes useful because they make me think about what each child has actually been doing and what they are interested in. They give me ideas for the next day.... That's where my planning really comes from. There seem to be so many things we could do ... the children have so many ideas ... but I guess that is because, on this prac, I seem to be observing all the time. I found it really hard observing this way at first, because in trying to see what everyone was doing I felt I wasn't really committing myself to anyone's play ... but I think I've developed the knack of joining in with the children ... and being aware of everyone else.

Tessa's method of observation is certainly a very practical one, particularly if your purpose is to know something of each child's interests, abilities and needs. Tessa's final comment indicates that she has reached a stage where her observations have become a part of her interactions. This is the nature of observation for most experienced teachers.

How do I know if my observations are accurate?

During my visit with John, he said, 'Sometimes I get really bothered when I'm writing my observations. I keep asking myself, "Am I right about this child? Are my observations accurate?" My biases, beliefs and feelings must have an influence on my observations.'

This is a common concern shared by pre-service and experienced teachers. Some try to allay their concerns by testing out their observations or by checking their view against another person's observations. Others like to observe when there is verbal interaction between the children or when they talk with a child, as this may reveal children's thinking, understandings and explanations and also provides teachers with opportunities to test some of their own interpretations.

In the kinds of observations that take into account socio-cultural factors and interactions, measures of validity and reliability can be replaced by judgements of 'plausibility' and 'trustability' (Walsh *et al.*, 1993: 472 cited in Carr, 2000: 182–3). Carr highlights four ways in which this type of accountability can be achieved. These are:

- *Keeping the data transparent* – by ensuring there is sufficient information available to allow other staff and families to understand the interpretation given or to present an alternative interpretation.
- *Ensuring that a range of interpreters have their say* – by having a number of staff collect observations or 'learning stories' on any one child, discussing their interpretations and deciding together what to do next.
- *Refining the constructs as they appear locally* – by developing a common understanding of a particular behaviour being observed. For instance by checking out what colleagues see 'persisting with difficulty or uncertainty' to be, in behavioural terms, and comparing their views.
- *Being clear about the connection between the learner and the environment* – by taking into account the nature of the relationship between the child and the 'environment'. As an example Carr cites childcare staff discussing Joseph's transition to the over twos program. Because Joseph was seen as 'a learner-in-relationship', staff wanted to understand the relationship that had worked in his present setting so as to plan for the development of relationships in the next setting.

(Adapted from Carr, 2000: 183–4)

Although, as Almy and Genishi (1979: 37) maintain, our 'emotional responses colour what we see and hear and we cannot eliminate their effect', we can take steps similar to those proposed by Carr (2000) to ensure the judgements on which our teaching decisions are based are as trustworthy as possible.

THE ROLE OF OBSERVATION IN ASSESSING CHILDREN'S LEARNING

With the recent introduction of national curricula and the specification of learning outcomes, a greater emphasis is being placed on children's achievements relating to outcomes. These changes have led to much debate concerning how these outcomes should be measured, particularly with young children (Kagan, 2000; Hyson, 2002; Carr, 2000). Advocates of early childhood education have argued strongly that any form of standardized testing is inappropriate for children in the early years of schooling, given the uneven nature of young children's learning and development and lack of reliable instruments (McAfee and Leong, 2002; Meisels, 2000; Shepard *et al.*, 1998). This stand has placed pressure on early childhood teachers to demonstrate alternative ways of assessing young children that are appropriate to their stage of development, while providing the information that is required in terms of accountability.

As a consequence, the value and role of observation in assessment is coming under scrutiny as the nature of assessment in early childhood education continues to be defined. Copley (2000: 23) argues that assessment can be seen as 'the process of observing; gathering evidence about a child's knowledge, behaviours and dispositions; documenting the work that children do and how they do it; and making inferences from that evidence for a variety of purposes.' Such a definition recognizes the important role observation can play in assessment although a further clarification of this role is necessary.

The recently released position statement – *Early Childhood Curriculum, Assessment and Program Evaluation* by the National Association for the Education of Young Children (2003) sets out a number of indicators of effective assessment. These include using assessment instruments for the purpose for which they were designed, ensuring that what is assessed is developmentally and educationally significant and that the information gathered is used to improve learning. The position statement also incorporates previous guidelines (Bredekamp and Rosegrant, 1992, 1995) that indicate that assessment should be appropriate for the age and characteristics of children taking into account culture and home language, be made regularly, in a range of natural classroom situations over time, and support children's self-esteem. The use of a range of methods, including systematic observations, recording of conversations and collections of children's work samples is also emphasized.

Along with the increasing recognition of the important role observation can play in the assessment of young children there is also a growing awareness of the need to respect children's rights in the observation process (Alcock, 1999). The worldwide interest in the type of documentation and observation that is used extensively in the preschools of Reggio Emilia in Italy also attests to an awareness of this responsibility. The inclusion of the children's perspectives is a key element of the Reggio Emilia documentation. For Reggio Emilia, staff documentation generally consists of written observations, transcriptions of children's words, photographs and audio and videotapes – as well as children's projects or creations that relate to their learning. It is a way of making 'visible the process of children's learning', the ways knowledge is constructed and 'the emotional and relational aspects' (Rinaldi, 1998: 120–1).

Documentation in this form (and in variations of it) is becoming more widely practised around the world because it is seen to have numerous benefits for children, their families, the community and teachers (Abbott and Nutbrown, 2001; Edwards *et al.*, 1993, 1998). With children's words, perspectives and creations being included in documentation, children are viewed not as 'dependent' objects about whom others make judgements but rather as 'citizen' subjects whose perspectives are respected and considered (Alcock, 1999: 3). This contributes to children becoming confident learners and communicators and is seen as a means of empowering learners and promoting and respecting children's rights. There are other benefits of this kind of documentation as well. As they prepare documentation, teachers' own understanding of children's development and thinking is deepened, and as children's learning is made visible and discussed with parents and colleagues, children's competence can be publicly appreciated and teaching strategies can be modified and refined (Rinaldi, 1998).

If you want to take your 'teacher as researcher' role seriously you will find it helpful to consider the Reggio Emilia approach to documentation in-depth to see if it is a useful tool for you. Such documentation can provide you with information about children's learning and progress 'that cannot be demonstrated by the formal standardized tests and checklists' (Katz, 1998: 39). This is because documentation allows you to focus on actual interactions between the children and their environments.

As you gain more teaching practice experience and discuss assessment processes with your supervising teachers you will become aware of the pressures for more formal testing of young children's learning. If, however, along with many others, you are convinced of the inappropriateness of standardized testing for young children, then you will need to understand alternative forms of assessment and how they can be used to provide comprehensive information on a child's progress. There are a number of alternative forms of assessment including portfolios and a variety of documentation processes (for example Carr, 2000; Cooper, 1998; Danielson and Abrutyn 1997; Gronland, 1998; Helm *et al.*, 1998; Wortham *et al.*, 1998).

Your supervising teacher may be willing to share with you some of the documentation of the progress of individual children gathered over the year. In some schools each child may have a portfolio, either hard copy or electronic, which could contain dated observations, anecdotes, check-lists and samples of the child's work. By examining this documentation you can become more aware of developmental patterns and the comprehensive information that can be gathered over a lengthy period. This detailed information enables teachers to assess progress and problems in a systematic way, as well as to prepare profiles or written summaries of a child's capabilities constructed from integrating information from a variety of observations and other sources.

Ask your supervising teacher how the information is gathered and consider the type of information that is documented and the extent to which children's perspectives are included. Also discuss with your supervising teacher how the information is used. For some teachers this information may provide the basis for discussing a child's progress with parents or colleagues who may be working with the child. Some teachers may also use it to generate hypotheses, to extend learning opportunities and to promote their own professional growth. Because the nature of the information obtained impacts on its usefulness, you will need to carefully consider the form and nature of information gathered in assessment processes.

SUMMARY

Coming to know and understand children is one of the most challenging yet rewarding experiences you can have. In this chapter a number of suggestions have been made, based on the experiences of pre-service and experienced teachers, which will help you get to know children and build relationships with them. Remember though that developing a relationship is a two-way process, and you must be prepared to 'give' to that relationship and accept that you will not always achieve the desired relationship with every child, particularly if your teaching practice period is short.

Talking with and observing children are key elements in developing relationships. As you gain experience you are urged to ask yourself:

• what can I observe about children?
• how can I observe most effectively?
• how can I *use* my observations of children in my teaching?

The discussions based around each of these questions in this chapter only begin to scratch the surface, and it is anticipated that in finding some of your own answers, many more questions will be sparked. For instance, in thinking further about how to use the knowledge derived from your observations and documentation you will be faced with questions concerning the role of observation in assessing young children, particularly in terms of learning outcomes. If you are like most other pre-service teachers you will also have queries as to your methods and uses of observation and how you can ensure that children's rights are respected in the process. Share your concerns and 'wonderings' with your supervising teacher, undertake your own investigation of alternative forms of assessment and seek advice. Remember that the more you come to know children, the better your relationship with them will be and the more successful you will be in your teaching practice.

SUGGESTED ACTIVITIES

- Recall some of your own experiences in establishing a relationship with a child. Focus on one particular relationship and try to identify the factors that contributed to its development. List some skills that you have which help you build relationships with children. What other skills could you develop that may be helpful?
- Having read the views and concerns of both experienced and pre-service teachers relating to observation, think about your own experiences. Jot down any issues or questions that have arisen for you. Remember that it is important to be honest with yourself, to ask questions and to seek advice and support in finding some answers.
- Gather practical ideas relating to observation, documentation and assessment (for example: how to recall significant incidents and write up detailed observations after the event; effective documentation systems you have used, seen or read about; strategies for observing and interacting simultaneously).
- Write down your observations of a situation in which you have interacted with a child. Then put yourself in the child's place and write an observation of that situation from the child's perspective. Try to see 'the world', which may include you, the teacher, other children and the situation, through the child's eyes. How does the child's perspective differ from yours? In what ways could a consideration of the child's perspective assist your teaching?
- Arrange a time to talk with your supervising teacher or another experienced teacher about the school's expectations regarding accountability and assessment. Prepare some questions in advance. Try to clarify what the expectations for assessment are and how they are achieved in practice. Ask if you can view some portfolios and/or other documentation and assessment procedures.
- What strategies will you use to ensure that children's rights are respected in your observation, documentation and assessment processes?
- What are your views relating to 'formalized testing' for young children? What reasons would you give when explaining your position to colleagues and parents?

Chapter 3

Early childhood curriculum

In this chapter early childhood curriculum will be explored by considering:

- the nature of curriculum;
- examples of curriculum work;
- how curriculum is embedded in a set of beliefs;
- developing knowledge and beliefs about children, learning and teaching;
- influential factors;
- ways to achieve curriculum goals;
- a framework for decision making.

THE NATURE OF CURRICULUM

I've lost count of the number of student teachers, who, when reviewing their teacher education course, recall that the word that most filled them with confusion was 'curriculum'.

Suzie, who was in the final year of her course, graphically described her encounters with curriculum in her teaching story which she titled *A Brutally Honest Account!*

> I vividly remember the first year of my teacher education course. This one certain word seemed to evoke fear among us all. Yes, we're talking … CURRICULUM. I recall writing my first assignment on curriculum from a multi-cultural perspective, but not understanding at all what I had written. Over the three years my thinking about curriculum has developed, but it took until this year to confront the fearful creature called curriculum and attack it with a vengeance.
>
> My primary school practicum in the first year was my initial encounter with the beast. I struggled with acknowledging the content areas and searched the syllabus documents for some meaning.

Curriculum at this time meant: Language at 9 a.m.; Maths from 9.30 to 10.30 a.m.; Morning Tea; Science 11 a.m.; followed by Social Studies at 12 noon, and after lunch (on a Friday of course), Art. It seemed so easy. All the curriculum areas were in single blocks, left out by themselves like wheelie bins in a dark street. But where were the children in all this? Did they need to be considered or was teaching about getting ideas from the 'ready to teach from' source books? This was my initial fight – the beast was too structured for me to tackle, and I needed to tame it. ... But how? Curriculum (the beast) didn't even exist in preschool settings, did it?

I was to encounter this beast again and again in the next two years. These encounters were always gut-wrenching adventures but in my third-year primary practicum we found some common ground. Hello – why were the children singing in Maths? At last, the beast and I had made friends! I found this experience uplifting. Suddenly some creative thought was being used. I was able to prepare, as my supervising teacher did, experiences that were of interest to the children and addressed their needs. Incidental learning experiences were used to extend children's learning and the children were excited about their learning. Music took a part in Science, and Drama took a part in Social Studies. The curriculum seemed to flow throughout the total programme for the combined Year 1/2 class. I couldn't actually categorize one subject area as being by itself. It all seemed to make more sense to me. The fog had cleared. I had begun to look at curriculum as everything that happens in the classroom,

Suzie's vivid account of her curriculum encounters highlights some of the complexities associated with the notion of curriculum. Some of these complexities arise because the word 'curriculum' is used to mean different things.

In Suzie's initial encounter, she was seeing curriculum in terms of the subject matter or *product* of the children's learning and the set timetable. In her third-year encounter, she recognized that the curriculum was also focused on the children, with the children's interests and needs being addressed and extended by the teacher. The *process* of learning had an important place in this curriculum together with the *product*. The subject matter was integrated (not separated like wheelie bins) and interwoven with the children's interests so that learning was meaningful and relevant. Suzie and her supervising teacher were able to match their *intentions* for the children with the children's own *intentions* and interests. In this sense, intentions were a part of the curriculum. At the end of her course Suzie was coming to see curriculum as everything that is experienced in the classroom situation. In other words she was coming to see curriculum in terms of the *reality* of the classroom. Each of these terms – product, process, intention and reality – can be legitimately used when discussing the curriculum (Smith and Lovat, 2003).

Suzie's growing understanding of curriculum fits with the view that curriculum work involves teachers in making decisions and taking actions and that these processes need to be guided by critical reflection if they are to be effective. As Smith and Lovat (2003) suggest, the curriculum process is

> a series of **decisions and judgments** ... based upon the planner's **beliefs, assumptions, perceptions, and biases** and upon the ways in which *teachers*, and others, **make meaning of the teaching reality** in which they are located. The curriculum process then is seen as a **problem solving process**, in which **the teacher processes a complex variety of stimuli and information and uses this to make decisions and solve problems**: the teacher's key roles in this are those of **information processor, manager, decision maker and problem solver**.
>
> (Smith and Lovat, 2003: 2)

Because of the complexity of the stimuli and information that has to be dealt with in this curriculum process you will hear experienced teachers and your peers talking about curriculum in many different ways. Rather than feeling frustrated that there is no simple definition of curriculum, we have to remind ourselves that curriculum is a dynamic concept, like 'love' or 'happiness', and means different things to different people.

EXAMPLES OF CURRICULUM WORK

It is important that you start thinking about curriculum work from the very beginning of your course as it is such a vital part of becoming a teacher. Listening to your supervising teachers talk about what they do and why, can give you some useful information. I was reminded of the complexities of curriculum work as I reflected on conversations I had recorded with a number of early childhood teachers who had just completed their first year of teaching in a variety of early childhood settings. As we chatted over coffee they shared with me some of their curriculum decision-making experiences. (You can read more of their teaching stories in Chapter 8.) Their accounts range across many facets of curriculum. The snippets of conversation presented here provide 'windows' through which you can glimpse aspects of the curriculum process, as well as the challenges they faced in trying to remain true to the beliefs and ideals they held regarding effective teaching.

Curriculum work relating to 'product'

Both Jessica and Janine were a little overwhelmed by the emphasis their schools placed on the *product* of the curriculum. Jessica has a Year 1 class in a primary school in the non-government sector. She commented:

> I felt huge pressure to meet the content base. We had planning days where they said, 'in this week we'll do this … these two letters … and this science unit, and this booklet … and the next week we'll do that.' I was trying to cover so much and I just couldn't ever get it all done. I was forever rushing. I didn't feel able to express that feeling of pressure because my colleagues and the Deputy who had set up most of the content requirements were just lovely and so supportive. As a first year I didn't feel I could say, 'I don't want to do this.'

Janine who also has a Year 1 class in a state primary school had a similar experience. She said:

> There's so much curriculum to cover … but I really wanted some play so I put play into my maths and language. I did so much reading at Uni and I was up on every theory … then when I got into a school and saw what I had to teach … and all the specialist lessons I had to fit in, some of my ideals went out of the window. I had a lot of trouble getting to specialist lessons on time. I can still see the music teacher standing there with her arms folded waiting for us to arrive. We'd just get engrossed in something in our classroom, then I'd look at my watch and realise we were supposed to be somewhere else. It was quite exhausting really. I thought it would be so much more relaxed and easy going.

Curriculum work relating to 'processes'

Kylie who had taken the position of director in a community kindergarten in a rural town focused her comments on some of the *processes* and interactions that were occurring in the learning–teaching situation as a consequence of some of her curriculum actions. She said:

> I've developed particular teaching strategies this year. Like at Uni we were presented with all these different ideas and I'd think 'I'd love to do that'. And I was particularly interested in using puppets so I thought if I'm going to use puppets then I've got to use them right from the beginning of term or I'll never use them. So I made this puppet Burke. He actually went home with the kids. And the parents and children

wrote up what he did and took three photos on Burke's disposable camera. It was the best thing. Both the parents and kids latched on to it and it brought everyone together. It really helped the kids to take part of their preschool home and to bring something of their home back to preschool. The parents are asking if we'll do it again next year. We probably will, but it won't be Burke. He went off with Santa. I want to try a different puppet.

I've changed some of my strategies during the year, too. I started out being the sort of teacher who said, 'Right everybody sit with your legs crossed and hands in your laps and listen' and now I've changed to more individual reinforcement like 'Oh Sofie you are sitting up beautifully with your hands in your lap.' And they all look and do the same. I know we talked about that strategy at Uni but I'd forgotten about it until one day at rest time. We usually said, 'OK everybody, heads down, lying still.' I really used to hate it because it seemed like I was giving orders all the time. Then Maxine my aide, came into the room this day and she said 'Wow! Look at Pip. She's lying so beautifully.' And I thought 'Oh I'd like to get that kind of approval.' And from that point on I put myself in the kids' shoes more and thought 'How would I like to be asked to do things?' The kids really took to that approach so that's what I do now. And I use the puppets to give that positive reinforcement too.

Curriculum work relating to 'intentions'

Amy who is a preschool teacher in an independent school became aware that, at times, what she intended to happen, didn't. She gave this example of a time when her *intentions* regarding what should happen were in sharp contrast to what actually did happen. She commented:

> Because we focus very much on transition to school we do some more formalized lessons in literacy and numeracy towards the end of the year. One day I was doing a lesson and I got the feeling that the children just weren't focused and engaged … and one girl said to me 'This is really boring Miss L. Do we have to do it?' And I said 'No! Let's go outside and do something else!' I guess with things like that I found that, while I thought something was great and would work with the children … when I listened to what the children were saying and saw what they were doing, I discovered that what I thought, wasn't always what the children thought.

Kate, a preschool teacher in the state system came to realise from her curriculum work that she needed to develop *intentions* for herself as well as for the children. As she reflected on what actually happened in response to her teaching actions she clarified what some of her strategies should be. She said:

> The thing that I had difficulty with was following something up when it occurred. One example was with Tim in the water play. One day Tim had started to build the water wheels and he was asking me why these things happened … and I thought, 'OK I must follow that up tomorrow.' But I should have explained it then, because the next day his water wheel structure wasn't nearly so complicated and half way through our discussion he decided he didn't want to do that any more because there was another child doing something more interesting. I really want to make the most of the teachable moment.

Curriculum ideals and classroom reality

Julie found that, given the expectations of her school in terms of the syllabus and teaching methods, she was not always able to approach teaching and learning with her Year 1 class in ways that were consistent with her own beliefs and values. She commented:

> At Uni you have all these great ideas … and then when you get to a school you're given the content and told, 'this is what we do.' I tried to fit in my ideals … but it was very difficult. I fitted some in but not as many as I would have liked. In the last couple of weeks of the year we had a shop … a Christmas shop. I'd wanted to have a shop all year but we just couldn't get to it … and I was determined because this was something the children really wanted. They brought in toys and they shopped and just loved it. During the year we had free play on a Friday afternoon … but it was the sort I'd seen on some pracs and felt uncomfortable with. I felt that this type of play did not match what I knew about learning through play. There was a constant dichotomy between what I felt I had to do and what I felt I'd like to be doing … and not liking what I was doing added to my stress. I started the year trying to schedule a time each week to teach cooperative skills. By about week five I just dropped it because I had so much trouble fitting in the 'required' content. It was a difficult decision because this was part of my philosophy. Now I've had more time to reflect I realize I compromised some of my core beliefs. Next year I'm not going to panic so much about the content.

These comments by beginning teachers indicate some of the challenges you may have to meet, the types of skills you need and the kinds of decisions you have to make as part of your curriculum work. The ability to critically reflect and to make decisions in the light of complex and sometimes conflicting information and expectations takes time to develop. Coming to recognize personal beliefs and values is an important early step in this process as they influence your curriculum decision-making and actions

HOW CURRICULUM IS EMBEDDED IN A SET OF BELIEFS

Have you found yourself responding positively or negatively to different curriculum experiences? Often it is difficult to express why we react or feel the way we do in different situations. Even when we can say what we like and don't like about a particular classroom or setting it is hard to go that one step further and give reasons for our likes and dislikes. This is because our responses are generally in line with our underlying beliefs and values. Although these beliefs and values can influence our thinking we often remain unaware of their effect.

It was only after Kellie reflected on her negative reaction to one of her teaching practice experiences in a Year 2 class that she was able to clarify a value she held. She wrote:

> I was told the topics to be covered, and when I was going to teach them before I even started my teaching practice. My first lesson was to cover the geographical features of Australia – rivers, bays, islands and mountains. This introductory lesson, as I saw it, was to draw on the children's prior knowledge and build from there. When I outlined my plans which included getting them to discuss aerial photographs, I was told, in no uncertain terms, that this was a waste of the children's time and mine. I was reminded of the topic to be taught and told that what children already knew was irrelevant. I bit my tongue and tried to do the job expected of me. I was to pass on the information and the children were to learn it. I found the whole experience frustrating, impossible and very demeaning. I gained something from this prac though. I now know how I will never teach.

In reflecting further on her experience Kellie wrote:

I believe that I valued the children's backgrounds, interests and attitudes far more than their teacher did. I am not saying that she was wrong ... just that I am different.

As Kellie discovered, her supervising teachers' actions seemed to follow from her views about the learner, the learning process and the nature of teaching. Kellie's reactions also stemmed from her underlying beliefs and values. It was her experience in the teaching practice situation that stimulated her to clarify further her own beliefs. It is important, that in thinking about curriculum you consider your beliefs about learning and teaching. For instance, you need to think about the questions that Kellie faced:

- Is it important for teachers to find out what children know in order to build on that knowledge?
- Should the child be an active contributor to the learning process?
- What is the teacher's role in promoting learning?
- Are first-hand experiences important in young children's learning?

Clarifying your views in relation to these types of questions will prepare you for dealing with even bigger questions such as

- What is it that young children should learn?
- What are the most effective ways for helping young children to learn?

As you read the literature relating to learning and teaching as well as child development, and talk with experienced teachers and colleagues in order to find answers to these important curriculum questions, you will also make your beliefs and values about learning and teaching more explicit.

DEVELOPING KNOWLEDGE AND BELIEFS ABOUT CHILDREN, LEARNING AND TEACHING

By the end of your teacher education course you should be able to describe the characteristics of young learners and the types of environments and interactions that will assist them in their learning. In clarifying what you know and believe, you will develop your own ideals – your own ideas of teaching.

You may be interested to read Kellie's statement of her philosophy. She wrote this at the end of her teacher education course as she was preparing her job applications:

Introductory statement: From birth, children are establishing themselves as social beings, firstly as members of their families and then as members of a larger community. Although they have had little experience they are competent learners. They are innately motivated to learn even when they are not being 'taught'. They use the language they acquire and draw upon their experiences to practise and consolidate communicative and problem-solving skills. The children's existing interests and abilities are extended and refined as they form concepts of themselves as social beings, communicators, creators and problem solvers. These concepts will determine their views of their own abilities and worth and, in the longer term, influence their attitudes towards learning, towards themselves and towards others. For these reasons, I believe that, as an early childhood teacher, I have a very special responsibility to the young children and their families with whom I work.

I see my role as an early childhood teacher being influenced by my beliefs about children and learning.
   I believe that:

- Children are unique individuals, with their own timing of social, emotional, cognitive, linguistic and physical growth and development.
- Children not only have individual personalities, learning styles and dispositions, but also unique experiences stemming from their family and cultural backgrounds which are to be valued.
- Children develop skills and strategies as they learn through an interactive process between their thoughts and experiences with materials, ideas, adults and other children, using all their senses.
- Children's play has an important role in facilitating their social, emotional, cognitive and physical development.
- Children learn when they have positive self-esteem and are in an environment where there is mutual respect and cooperation.

I believe that children's learning and development is promoted when:

- opportunities for children to make connections and build on what they know are maximized through extending children's interests and supporting curiosity and the exploration of ideas;
- learning experiences are negotiated with input from both the children and the teacher and there is a variety of individual and group experiences;

- materials and resources provided are meaningful, developmentally appropriate and contain no bias towards a specific gender, culture or religion;
- parents, families and carers are encouraged to participate in their children's learning and when strong home–school links are established and maintained;
- children feel comfortable and secure, are supported in their inter-actions with others and have a sense of ownership in their learning environment;
- there is rhythm and routine to the day, with flexibility to cater for unexpected episodes;
- all children have opportunities to use and experience language, number, problem-solving and creativity.

If you were writing a personal statement of your philosophy would you outline similar beliefs to Kellie's, or would they be different? Do you think it's important to take into account the views of the families and the community in which you will be working? Would you want to add more on the 'what' or 'content' of learning to your statement? If the task of developing your own statement of beliefs seems too difficult for you at this stage, delve into some of the early childhood textbooks and web sites, early childhood curriculum frameworks, position statements of professional associations and reports on early education. They can help you to clarify your ideas. It is vital that, as you seek to clarify your ideas about curriculum work and educational philosophies, you do your own thinking and consider what you are reading in the light of your own experiences and values. If you fail to do this you will end up with a statement of other people's beliefs which will be of little use to you. You need to develop your own vision of what you want the curriculum to be for the children you will teach.

FACTORS INFLUENCING EARLY CHILDHOOD CURRICULUM

In developing your own vision of curriculum you need to take into account the many changes in society and recent developments in education that are influencing early childhood curriculum today. A number of these influential factors are considered here, in particular those that relate to concern for the disadvantaged; the emphasis on quality and accountability; the introduction of quality assurance systems and early childhood curriculum frameworks; and the Reggio Emilia approach. As we consider these factors you will see that they are not isolated influences. They are connected with curriculum

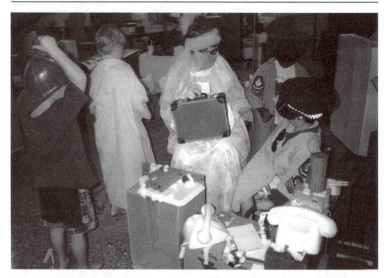

Plate 3.1 Children's play has an important role in facilitating their social, emotional, cognitive and physical development. (Photo courtesy of Sue Thomas.)

priorities resulting from changing societal, economic and political views and realities, as well as evolving psychological, socio-cultural and educational theories. You will see also that educational change is not confined to one country. Rather, curriculum change in one country influences early childhood curriculum in other countries.

Concern for the disadvantaged

From your historical studies of early childhood education you will be aware that in the 1960s, particularly in the United States of America, there was increased government funding and an emphasis on early intervention programmes that aimed to relieve the effects of poverty and social disadvantage. Programmes such as Head Start and Project Follow Through wanted a curriculum that was best able to promote cognitive and academic development and, as a consequence, curriculum models based around different theories were promoted and used to compare the effects of different approaches. These models, which included the Montessori Method, the Developmental-Interaction Approach, the Direct Instruction Model, and models derived from Piagetian theory such as the Kamii–DeVries Approach and the High/Scope Curriculum Model were structured in ways that enabled early childhood curriculum to be transported (Goffin, 1994; Goffin and

Wilson, 2001). As a result, early childhood education in many other countries, including Australia, was shaped and influenced by these models throughout the 1970s and 1980s.

Concern for quality care and education

In the 1990s, in many developed countries around the world, government interest in the care and education of young children was again renewed. This interest was prompted, not so much by concern for the disadvantaged, but by the increasing numbers of mothers/carers from all socio-economic levels who were in the workforce and were requiring care for their young children. At the same time there was concern to reform all levels of education to ensure an appropriately educated workforce for the emerging global and technological society. The reforms emphasized outcomes, and greater accountability was expected in order to show that outcomes were being achieved. These changes impacted on early childhood education in a number of ways. In Australia, there was a concern to ensure quality care for the increasing numbers of children who required long hours of care. At the same time, in the light of the general reforms occurring at all levels of education, there was a demand for greater continuity between preschool and primary education and increased accountability in terms of outcomes.

The introduction of quality assurance systems

The concern for quality long day care led to the setting up of the Quality Improvement and Accreditation System (QIAS) in Australia in 1994. This Australian Government initiative now requires that all childcare centres in Australia be accredited every two-and-a-half years in order to operate and be entitled to Childcare Benefit funding. A centre achieves accreditation from the National Childcare Accreditation Council (NCAC) after under-taking the QIAS Process that includes writing a self-study report and receiving a validation report by an external validator. These reports, together with results from parent surveys, are taken into account by a moderator who assesses whether a satisfactory rating on all 10 quality areas have been achieved before making recommendations to the Council (NCAC, 2001a). Similar quality assurance systems are now being extended to family day care and outside school hours care services.

The *QIAS Source Book* (NCAC, 2001b) can be regarded as providing a model of quality care in the sense that it defines a standard by listing principles and key concepts, together with indicators of unsatisfactory,

satisfactory and high quality practices for each quality area. The specified key areas of quality childcare are: relationships with children, respect for children, partnerships with families, staff interactions, planning and evaluation, learning and development, protective care, health, safety, and managing to support quality. You should be familiar with the *QIAS Source Book* when you undertake teaching practice in a childcare setting as it can assist you in your planning.

Introduction of early childhood curriculum frameworks

Concern for quality in the preschool education sector funded by government departments was reflected in the introduction and mandating of preschool curriculum frameworks in Australia. These documents promoted greater curriculum continuity between preschool and primary education and were the logical extension of the trend toward a common or national curriculum for compulsory schooling evident in the 1980s. Countries like England and Wales introduced a national curriculum in 1988, while the Australian government introduced national goals for schooling in 1989 with a view to establishing a common curriculum. As a consequence, most schools today work within curriculum frameworks which specify key learning areas or core and foundation subjects such as English, mathematics, science, studies of the environment and society, technology, the arts, health and physical education and languages other than English.

Just as you need to be familiar with the curriculum and syllabus documents for primary schools if your teaching practice is in a lower primary setting, so too, you need to study the early childhood framework used in your state or local area for preschool and/or preparatory education. Examples of such documents include: *Foundation Areas of Learning: Curriculum Framework for Early Childhood Settings* (1996) by the Department for Education and Children's Services of South Australia; *Preschool Curriculum Guidelines* produced in 1998 by the Queensland School Curriculum Council; and a statement for schools and communities on the education of children three to eight years of age entitled *What Is Good Early Childhood Education?* (1998) developed by the Education Department of Western Australia. Such documents are continuing to be developed, with the draft *Early Years Curriculum Guidelines* developed by the Queensland Studies Authority (2002) currently being trialled.

In general, these curriculum frameworks are regarded as guidelines for practice. Because they were developed in consultation with practitioners and academics they highlight key principles, influences and decision-making processes that are consistent with traditional early childhood practices and current theories. Components of early childhood curriculum such as the importance of understanding children, partnerships with families, flexible learning environments and play are emphasized. Foundation learning areas and their indicators of learning or outcomes are also presented, and the connections between preschool foundation learning areas and the key learning areas of the primary school curriculum shown.

The introduction of early childhood curriculum documents was also occurring in other countries besides Australia in the 1990s. For instance, in New Zealand in 1996 the Ministry of Education implemented *Te Whaariki: Early Childhood Curriculum* with the expectation that it would support quality education programmes and quality care. The metaphor of the woven mat is integral to the development of *Te Whaariki* because the curriculum is seen to be 'woven' to meet children's needs in diverse settings. The teacher/ adult plays a vital role in this 'weaving' of curriculum by interpreting, developing, refining and reflecting on practice, processes and outcomes (Garbett and Yourn, 2002: 1).

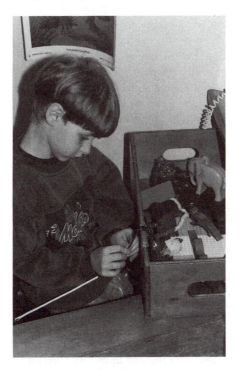

Plate 3.2   Is setting up an electric fence to keep intruders out of the wildlife park he has created, a legitimate aspect of this child's curriculum? (Photo courtesy of Northgate State Preschool.)

As you study different curriculum documents and frameworks and think how you will use them in your own teaching, ask yourself

- What does this curriculum document tell me?
- How will it assist my teaching actions and decisions?
- Will this document help me improve the quality of my teaching?

For instance as you review the *QIAS Source Book* you may find it helpful in that it provides you with criteria for quality care and indicates practices that help you achieve these criteria. Having such a model is often a very useful starting point – a 'survival kit'. As your experience grows, however, you may become aware of other aspects or criteria which, in your particular childcare setting or context may seem more important in promoting quality. You may want a curriculum framework that assists you to move beyond a 'standardized recipe for quality' (Maloney and Barblett, 2002: 14).

The Developmentally Appropriate Practice framework (Bredekamp and Copple, revised 1997), known as DAP in its abbreviated form, is also seen by some as a 'standardized recipe for quality'. This is because it highlights practices drawn from developmental theories that are appropriate to the age of the child, and responsive to a child's individual needs. DAP was initially produced in 1986 by the National Association for the Education of Young Children in the United States in response to concerns regarding the trend towards more formal and academic teaching of very young children. Although DAP has been helpful to many early childhood teachers in many countries who have used it to justify a developmental curriculum, it has also fuelled much debate amongst academic writers. Criticisms have been leveled at its over-reliance on developmental theory and the notion of universal norms (Penn, 2000), its reliance on Western cultural attitudes, and its failure to recognize the interconnectedness between the child, the family and society (Cross, 1995; Lubeck, 1998a, 1998b).

The importance of the interconnectedness of children's experiences is currently being recognized in the development of curriculum frameworks that are placing more emphasis on socio-cultural theory which originated in the work of Vygotsky (Lambert and Clyde, 2000; Woodhead, 2000). The socio-cultural perspective suggests that rather than focusing solely on the 'individual' developing through the predictable, sequential stages, it is also important to consider the contexts in which children are participating with others, as well as the effects of the guidance and support offered. From a socio-cultural perspective then, an individual child's development can be perceived as both contributing to and being constituted by the socio-cultural experiences in which the child participates (Rogoff, 1998).

Such a view causes us to look more closely at the learning and teaching processes that are embedded in the social and cultural life of the classroom or setting and consider their effects on children. For instance, if we see children as competent learners, listen to their ideas, encourage them to share their thoughts with others and recognize that their ideas are inextricably related to their experiences and contexts, then teaching and learning are likely to be collaborative processes. In classrooms where the interconnectedness of children's experiences is not recognized, teaching is often based on a deficit view of the child because a specified outcome has not been reached, or the child's experiences are different from those of the dominant culture. The child in this situation is treated far more as a passive learner rather than an active competent participant in learning.

As you examine the early childhood curriculum frameworks you will find that they provide scope for you to take into account the interconnectedness of children's experiences and, in fact, actively encourage teachers to do this. For instance, the *Queensland Preschool Curriculum Guidelines* (Queensland School Curriculum Council, 1998: 7) state:

> Creating a curriculum that is individually appropriate, socially relevant and culturally inclusive involves teachers in:
>
> > Considering the characteristics of young children as learners;
> > Recognizing, understanding and valuing the differences between contexts;
> > Reflecting on their own personal attitudes, beliefs and values and how these interact with those of families and the local and school communities;
> > Understanding practices that are fair, equitable and inclusive;
> > Identifying and challenging inequitable practices and relationships;
> > Building links between contexts;
> > Building partnerships with individuals and groups in various contexts.

Curriculum frameworks such as this provide you with a scaffold – not a recipe or formula for teaching. The curriculum scaffold, just like scaffolding on a building site, enables you to work on the 'more difficult – hard to reach' areas of the construction. As you use a curriculum scaffold you will need to consider the complexities of the task, draw on your professional knowledge and negotiate with learners in order to achieve the goals. This is the difference between *creating* an early childhood curriculum and following a curriculum 'recipe'.

The Reggio Emilia Approach

Yet another influence on early childhood curriculum is the Reggio Emilia Approach (Edwards *et al.*, 1993, 1998). The preschools operated by the municipality of Reggio Emilia in Emilia Romagna, Italy, since the end of the Second World War, have caught the attention of early childhood educators from around the world because they incorporate high-quality childcare with a clearly articulated philosophy of education. They demonstrate early childhood ideals in practice.

A high value is placed on cooperation and collaboration, with learning seen as a communal activity and the child as an active inquirer. Teachers are regarded as collaborators in learning rather than transmitters of knowledge and there is close cooperation with parents in the child's learning process. The preschools have been designed aesthetically and incorporate spacious entry ways, attractive dining rooms and well-supplied art areas. Emphasis is given to enhancing communication and visual and aesthetic awareness with an *atelierista* (a trained art teacher) being employed. The project approach to learning that incorporates art, science, numeracy and literacy, field experiences and community involvement is another key feature. A *pedagogisti* is also employed to provide pedagogical leadership, supporting teachers to develop and refine their teaching practices.

Despite the lively debate about whether or not the Reggio Emilia Approach, which is so much a part of its Italian culture, can be adapted successfully in other countries, the Approach continues to evoke interest. Teachers from different countries continue to visit the Reggio Emilia preschools and are inspired to emulate the approach, or at least some elements of it, in their own centres (Abbott and Nutbrown, 2001). In Australia this has resulted in more use of documentation (discussed in the previous chapter), renewed interest in the project approach (Helm and Beneke, 2003) and the emergent curriculum (Jones and Nimmo, 1994). The incorporation of some key elements does not, however, do justice to the Reggio Emilia approach that is 'the result of decades of hard work' and a commitment to an ongoing questioning process 'that seeks to do right by children as well as adults' (New, 1994: 36).

Perhaps a major reason why the Reggio Emilia Approach continues to be influential in terms of early childhood curriculum today is because it challenges us to re-examine our own early childhood practices in the light of those evident in Reggio Emilia preschools. New maintains that Reggio Emilia practices remind us of the ideal that children and adults can 'engage in a cooperative learning adventure with others' if teachers share that passion. New argues that, in order to have a cooperative learning adventure, we must 'think hard about our values, reconsider some of our more cherished beliefs, and reflect more sombrely on our goals and practices in early childcare and education' (1994: 36).

If you want your early childhood curriculum to be in keeping with your ideals you must undertake this type of critical reflection during your teaching practice experiences and throughout your career. Being a researcher and a learner are among the roles of the teacher in Reggio Emilia. In fact, 'professional development is actually part of the job description, an ongoing and continuous process, rather than a qualification for employment' (Phillips and Bredekamp, 1998: 447).

ACHIEVING CURRICULUM GOALS

Achieving your curriculum goals and ideals is a difficult task as some of the conversations with beginning teachers indicate. They can be achieved over time however, particularly if you recognize the importance of the planning–teaching connection in your curriculum work. Some student teachers focused on this connection as they asked questions in a tutorial leading up to their period of teaching practice.

For instance, Jo indicated her concerns about planning for the toddler group. She said, 'I'm doing my next prac in a childcare centre. I know how to plan for older preschoolers but how do I plan for the toddler group?'

David was concerned about the requirement that he plan for children early in his practicum. He commented: 'I have to plan for the children in the preschool group in my second week. Getting to know them takes time ... so how do I plan while I'm getting to know them?'

Penny was worried about her first teaching practice in a primary school. With some hesitation she said, 'I know this sounds a silly question but what do you actually teach in a Year 1 class? Do I have to focus on the content prescribed in the syllabus documents, or can I follow the children's interests like I did on my preschool prac?'

Questions such as these highlight the vital planning–teaching connection that is inherent in all curriculum work (Smith and Lovat, 2003). As we went about finding some answers to these questions it was apparent that each student had a 'picture' of what and how they wanted children to learn. They were not sure, however, how to bring that picture alive – what actions to take. This led to a discussion of teacher decision making and planning and how translating some ideals into achievable outcomes can assist.

Teacher decision making and planning for the under threes

In discussing how to plan for toddlers the pre-service teachers first shared their vision of curriculum for this age group. This suggested toddlers being responded to with warmth and hugs – being surrounded with a sense of security, yet being encouraged to explore and to touch; playing alongside others; participating in interesting sensory experiences; their physical needs being met and their parents' views taken into account. Felice, who had undertaken a practicum in a toddler group, shared her thoughts about her planning experiences. She said:

> Well … it isn't like the planning you do for preschool children. I feel like you've got to seize the moment and go with what's happening. At my preschool prac I could write a plan for the day and generally I was able to carry it through … but with toddlers you can only have a broad plan. And I think you've really got to get to know the children … and then when those moments arise you know how to respond … you know the ones you can encourage to be more independent … and the ones with the short attention spans. You think, 'Get in there, now, while Josh is doing something.' Like one day we were playing with the 'put together blocks' … some of the children have just learnt to put them together … and I was talking about the pictures on the blocks. … Anyway this day Andrew just didn't seem to want to play with anything … he just watched. All the other kids were standing around the blocks … and Andrew started to reach out for them … just pointing … so I gave him a block … and then he began to pick them up, one at a time, and gave them to me. … I made a real game of it … thanking him for each block and stacking them carefully.
>
> I guess I had aims for Andrew … to start to play with some toys and to play alongside other children, but I couldn't plan a set activity because Andrew wouldn't have been interested. I just had to respond when Andrew indicated he was interested in the blocks. I guess you have to have the right environment for that to happen … and you have to plan that environment too.

Getting to know the children through observing them closely and inter-acting with them helped Felice develop some broad aims for each child. In order to achieve them, however, she had to 'seize the moment'. This meant having a close relationship with the children so she would be sensitive to that moment and their actions and responses.

Plate 3.3 Sharing 'the moment' can help a child build connections. (Photo courtesy of Rhonda Warner.)

This discussion led Rowena to share a similar 'discovery' from her previous teaching practice in a childcare setting. She said:

> I was working the late shift ... and I was tired and the children were tired. I was getting Jock ready to go home by putting on his shoes and socks, and, to help the process I started to sing ... although I didn't feel much like singing. Jock loved it ... joining in and clapping his hands. He rarely joins a group for singing ... and I thought then ... this is more important to Jock than my planned music group time was.

Rowena's previous understandings of the importance of having activities planned and prepared were being challenged as she looked at the reality of the setting through the eyes of children and responded to their interests and needs as they arose. As we went on to discuss the content of curriculum for one- to two-year-old children, Rowena said she was coming to understand that children are learning all the time – not just from the activities that teachers plan for them, but from all their actions and interactions throughout the day. From the comments of others in the group there was a recognition that while teachers can influence children's learning, they certainly can't control it. There also seemed to be consensus that some of the most memorable learning–teaching moments can arise spontaneously as adults respond to children's interests and needs.

Teacher decision making and planning for three- to five-year-olds

All students in the tutorial agreed with David that it was difficult to plan effectively for preschool children before knowing them well. I shared with them how Tania had attempted to overcome this difficulty in her teaching practice with a group of four- to five-year-olds. In her first week at the centre Tania had observed that five of the children had a very strong friendship group and spent most of their time outdoors together. They did not welcome other children into their games and, when approached, 'ganged up' to exclude them. The 'excluded' children came up to Tania and the supervising teacher on several occasions complaining that no one would play with them. Although the other 'excluded' children were not unduly upset by their exclusion, Nicole persisted in wanting to join the group and became increasingly upset.

In thinking about the situation Tania used her knowledge of child development. She had observed that Nicole's feeling of being rejected was beginning to affect her view of herself adversely. Although she did not know the history of 'the gang', she recognized that something needed to be done to rectify the situation. In keeping with her own vision of a preschool curriculum she wanted the children to show more concern for one another and to be aware of how their actions could affect others. In the light of these considerations Tania made plans, enacted them and then made her evaluation (see Table 3.1).

Although Tania did not know each child particularly well after only one week, in making decisions about how to handle the situation she was influenced by her general views of the children as learners. Her outcomes, for example, suggest that she saw them as problem solvers, capable of expressing their thoughts and ideas at their level of understanding. She also saw thinking and content as being closely related, with the development of problem-solving skills being fostered as the children dealt with a 'real' problem.

The pre-service teachers in the tutorial were impressed with Tania's approach. 'But', they asked, 'how did Tania get the idea to introduce the discussion with a letter?' I had wondered that, too, and when I asked her she said she had seen a video where a teacher had used a similar technique to start a discussion. She had been fascinated by the way the children had responded by expressing so many ideas, and had jotted down the technique so she could try it for herself. When she was thinking about how she could discuss the problem without making Nicole feel worse, she had remembered this technique and thought it seemed a useful way of approaching the problem indirectly.

Table 3.1 Extract from Tania's planning book

Objectives	Teaching strategies	Evaluation
To encourage children to show concern for others To encourage children to express their ideas and thoughts To pose a real problem for the children to solve To help children develop problem-solving techniques in an indirect manner	Introduce discussion by showing and reading children a 'letter' I received from a girl I had taught at another preschool. Dear Miss Williams I have a problem and I was wondering if you could help me. My problem is that I have no one to play with. Sometimes when I do start playing with other children they tell me to go away. I am very sad. What do your preschoolers think I should do? Can you please write back and tell me? Love Melissa Encourage children to share ideas about what Melissa could do.	The letter aroused much interest. The children were genuinely concerned about Melissa and her problem, and suggested that Melissa should come to our preschool. Seth said she could go and tell the teacher. Other comments were: – she could tell the children that's not a very nice way to talk, and they should let her play – she could just play by herself – she could tell the children that she doesn't want to play with them if they are going to be mean – she could do the same back to them. We discussed each of these solutions to see which ones were useful to Melissa. We decided that we should write to Melissa and say that she should tell the children she would like to play with them, and if they say 'No' then she should say, 'That's not a very nice thing to say', or 'I don't like it when you talk to me like that', or' We should all be friends and play together'. Nicole just sat and listened to the whole discussion. I feel the children really did think about how to solve the problem using solutions that many of them tend to use. It will be interesting to observe whether this discussion has any effect.

In considering Tania's example, the tutorial group agreed that by drawing on her existing knowledge about children as well as her ideals, Tania had shown that effective planning and action can be undertaken as you are getting to know individual children. They also discussed how Tania's evaluations of the children's responses showed that the objectives she had set had been promoted and that the open-ended nature of the activity had enabled the children to respond at their level of ability. The documenting of children's comments was also seen to be a useful means of reflecting more deeply on the nature of the children's thinking.

Teacher decision making and planning for five- to eight-year-olds

From your studies you know that ideally, decision making and planning in a Year 1 classroom involves dealing with how to focus on prescribed content while at the same time taking into account the abilities of individual learners and building on their prior knowledge and interests.

Because we ran out of time in the tutorial we agreed to discuss Penny's question 'What do you actually teach in a Year 1 class?' the following week. A number of students who had previously undertaken teaching practice in primary settings agreed to share their planning experiences. Linda was the first volunteer and she described how she had linked prescribed content with children's interests through what is variously described as a topic, a unit or a thematic approach.

Linda said that she was expected to be totally responsible for planning in the third week of her teaching practice and that she decided to build the learning activities for the week around the topic, 'When the circus comes to town'. This was because the children had been discussing animals, and some children had mentioned that the circus was their favourite place, so she felt it linked with their current interests. She discussed the curriculum web she had developed, which showed how related concepts could be incorporated into the key learning areas.

In order to recall her feelings and experiences accurately, Linda shared some of her journal entries with the tutorial group. She had written:

> I feel like a real teacher planning an entire week's work. I think the curriculum web is OK, but my daily plans might be a bit ambitious. I do want to incorporate the children's ideas as well. I think I might have to tone down the related activities a little. Mrs D. has approved my plans which is really exciting. I am getting such a BUZZ!

Table 3.2 Linda's curriculum web, 'When the circus comes to town'

Science	English	Maths
Investigate circus animals: • what animals? • why these animals? • what do they eat?	Write a letter to a friend about the circus Poem – 'Circus circus' Talk about the jobs of circus people Think of words to do with 'circus' beginning with 'b' and 'p'	How many people are coming to the circus? Money: entry price for each child's family? Marching band: how many pairs of boots needed?
Art		
Design a poster Draw favourite animal Make clown faces Create ringmaster's hat Make money	Research circuses Read other stories about the circus Write a circus programme	Patterns for clown outfits Calculating/predicting food
Music	**SOSE (Studies of Society and the Environment)**	**Drama**
Band instruments: drums, cymbals, recorder, triangle Sing circus songs	Think about life in circus (people/animals) Relationships between people and animals Responsibilities to animals Ringmaster's role (can be a girl)	Marching hand: how to march Movement: putting up tent Pretend you're an animal Have a performance

In her daily programme Linda had planned how to involve the children in sharing and developing their knowledge of circuses as well as integrating the topic with the key learning areas.

Daily plan, Tuesday, 7 May
9.00–9.30   Assembly
9.30–10.00   Library
10.00

1   Read a story about a circus.
2   Discuss circuses ... encourage children's input ... think about the people and the animals who could be in the circus. Could we create a circus?
3   Children to write about who they would like to be in the circus (ringmaster, acrobat, lion tamer, clowns, ticket seller, animals ...) and draw picture.
4   Reflection as a group (Who did each decide to be? Why? Who were the same?)

11.30

5　Group the children according to the roles they had decided upon. ('Discover' roles for children who may not have decided.)

6　Tally how many in each group.

7　Sequencing ... discuss what needs to be done in setting up a circus
first – decide who is in it
second – decide on name
third – decide how much it will cost to see the circus.
Different prices adults/children?
fourth – decide on the acts
fifth – advertise.

8　Make money

12.30

9　Read story about one of the animals in the circus.

2.00

10　Group children – get them to discuss costumes ... something they could make for their costume.

In discussing her experiences with the tutorial group Linda again referred to her journal entries:

May 7

I introduced my plan today. It worked! The children were very enthusiastic, adding lots of their ideas. They were even chatting about the circus in the playground at lunch time. The children have made most of the choices so far. Tomorrow we are deciding on a name for the circus. (They are thinking about it overnight.) We have an acrobatic troupe, some clowns, some animals and even a juggler.

May 8

I mentioned that my circus ideas might be a little ambitious – seems so! The 'practice' session got out of hand today. Although the practice session went well yesterday it wasn't the same today. Three children were hurt (not badly) in the space of a few minutes. I dealt with this by stopping the practice session and discussing the problem with the children. We decided to make a list of rules for the circus so that everyone's safety was assured. I should have done this in the first place. Tomorrow the practice session will be held in the activity centre to avoid the problem of lack of space.

The children thought very hard about names for the circus. We ended up with 'The Scary Acrobat Circus'. It felt good knowing that I was incorporating maths into the process of naming the circus. We voted and represented votes with tally marks using the tally symbol for five. Madeline did well during maths. I asked about admission prices to the circus. I said, 'If someone paid Stuart (our money taker) $9, how many people would be going in to the circus? Madeline answered correctly that it would be one adult and two children (prices = $5 adults, $2 children). Mrs D. gave me some constructive criticism about my strategies today that I will take on board tomorrow.

May 9
The children worked on their circus posters this morning. Most children had their own ideas, so the posters are all different with some interesting border patterns. I felt each child used the space competently. They also enjoyed themselves. They told me they did! This is probably the most important aspect of all to achieve.

May 10
The circus became a production today with a real audience of parents. The children arrived with costumes and we spent time preparing the classroom and the performers! The circus itself was more a concert with circus acts. On reflection, it would have been useful for the children to have watched a circus performance on video. Although they could talk about aspects of the circus, not many of the children had concepts of the processes involved as few had actually been to a real circus. Unfortunately, this realization came too late. Still they enjoyed themselves, and learned a lot. I have learned many things too ... that I can implement a week's planning using my ideas and the children's ideas; that I can succeed in challenging children; and that I can tap into and use their interests to benefit their learning. I have also learned more about children: what they like; their humour; and how they learn.

In discussing Linda's approach the tutorial group decided that it offered her a way of focusing on the prescribed content in all the key learning areas in a context that was of interest to the children and enabled them to explore and develop new concepts. Linda also added that she had realized that the processes of learning that she had encouraged – expressing thoughts and ideas, making choices, negotiating, reaching decisions, making rules – were an important part of the content too, and matched her beliefs that children should be actively involved and enjoying their own learning.

There were several in the tutorial group who said that in their prac teaching experiences they had not seen teachers using topics or themes in their curriculum planning. Emily had, however, and wanted to share her experience of integrated learning with a Year 1 class during her teaching practice. Emily said that her supervising teacher, Marta, encouraged her to link her curriculum content with the children's interests as much as possible. Emily explained:

> My supervising teacher Marta had prepared a unit of work based on transport. The orientating phase was nearly complete and the children were all quite engaged in their activities and contracts ... then I read the children a story about a bus. It was a three-dimensional type book with movable parts. The children became totally engrossed with this book and the song 'The wheels on the bus' ... and this lasted for several days. Marta suggested that we have a brainstorming session with the class so we could gauge where their interests were heading. The children said they wanted to make a bus so we encouraged this idea. The children decided they could sing the song when the bus was finished. As the class was due to present an item at the school assembly, Marta suggested they consider dramatizing the song. The children spent nearly two days making the bus, rehearsing the song and dramatizing their roles.

Emily said that she was surprised when Marta disregarded the original work she had planned – for the time being, anyway – but that she was even more surprised when she and Marta looked closely at what the children were learning as they followed their interests. Emily said:

> I could see that they were still dealing with key areas of learning. They were using their knowledge of mathematics in measuring windows and doors and counting seats, and they had to visualize size and shape in initially designing and drawing the bus ... and there was much compromising and negotiating, with language being constantly used as they worked in groups. There was also a lot of writing and problem solving as they designed and wrote advertising posters for the sides of the bus and provided notices for the school about their assembly item. Someone said that their singing might not be loud enough for the assembly to hear so they decided to tape themselves and play that, as well as sing with it, to increase the volume.

Emily said that being a part of this experience added another dimension to her understanding of curriculum. She said, 'I saw how children spontaneously integrate their learning ... and I also saw how subjects can be integrated.' She did admit, however that she still had a niggling concern.

She said, 'I still wonder about how you know when to intervene in a child's experience to ensure that learning is occurring. With all the emphasis on learning outcomes, how can a teacher be sure children are really learning when they follow their interests like they did with the bus?'

This question sparked much discussion in the group. One suggestion was that the project itself was a form of documentation that 'made public' children's thinking and learning. Emily commented that her supervising teacher had said that because she was so familiar with the curriculum content, and because she observed the children closely, she felt she was able to make reasonable judgements about the children's learning. She said that these judgements helped her to decide whether or not she needed to intervene with a particular child. She also added that she used other forms of assessment as well.

A FRAMEWORK FOR DECISION MAKING

From these students' experiences in planning it is evident that, regardless of the age group they were working with, their curriculum work involved them in making decisions. They each had to:

- *decide to act* (e.g. Felice – to engage the toddler Andrew with materials; Tania – to try to overcome the adverse effects 'the gang' was having on Nicole's self-esteem; Linda – to design a curriculum topic for Year 1 children; and Emily to follow through on an interest);
- *decide how to act* (e.g. Felice – to give a toddler security, but encourage playfulness; Tania – to provide relevant experiences which matched the learners' needs and her outcomes for the group and Nicole; Linda and Emily – to guide classroom behaviour while teaching prescribed content in ways that encouraged active participation and choice);
- *decide whether or not actions were effective* (e.g. in all the examples the pre-service teachers observed, noted and reflected on the children's responses in order to understand their thinking and behaviour better, as well as considering the children's responses in relation to their outcomes).

This is a simple framework for curriculum decision-making which you may like to use. In making decisions you will find yourself drawing on your beliefs about children and the way they learn, and on your 'picture' of the kind of experiences you want children to have. As you reflect on whether or not your decisions and actions were effective in achieving your outcomes, you will also begin to clarify some of the many things a teacher must do as part of curriculum work and recognize the importance of the planning–teaching connection.

SUMMARY

Throughout this chapter curriculum has been presented as a concept that is dynamic in nature, has many facets and means different things to different people. Curriculum is often viewed only in terms of the product or the content to be taught. It is far more encompassing than this, however. Curriculum must also be considered in terms of the processes relating to learning and teaching, the intentions that both teachers and learners hold, the differing social and cultural experiences learners and teachers bring, and the realities that arise from classroom interactions and situations. You need to think of curriculum work as a problem-solving process in which you will make decisions after considering complex information, and planning and acting in the light of those decisions.

As you undertake teaching practice in different early childhood settings, you will become more aware of the ways in which curriculum documents and quality assurance systems are being used to promote quality care and education. You will develop strategies to support children so that they experience greater continuity between home, childcare, preschool and lower primary education and you will experience, first hand what it means for a teacher to be accountable. As you undertake teaching practice in settings that you 'like' or 'don't like' you will begin to clarify your beliefs about children, learning and teaching, and draw on your professional knowledge so that you begin to develop a vision of your 'ideal' early childhood curriculum. These ideals will, in turn, influence the nature of your curriculum planning, decision-making and teaching actions.

SUGGESTED ACTIVITIES

• Before you undertake teaching practice draw a picture or diagram of your current understanding of an early childhood curriculum. Include some representation of your view of the teacher's role as well as your view of children as learners. Date it and keep it so that you can refer to it at a later time. (Sometimes presenting your ideas graphically can help you clarify ideas that are hard to express in words.) After undertaking your next teaching practice – or at the end of your course, draw another picture or diagram. Compare the two drawings. Have your understandings changed or been clarified?

- After your next teaching practice, jot down (or share with a friend) an example of a child's successful learning experience to which you contributed. Using the decision-making framework suggested in this chapter, reflect on why you decided to act, how you planned and acted on those plans, and why you decided that your actions were effective. Suggest ways you could have made the experience even more successful.

- You are preparing for a job interview. There will be parents from the centre or school on the panel and you have been told they are particularly interested to find out about your teaching approach. How would you answer questions such as these in a job interview.

  'What do you think our children will gain from attending your preschool class?'

  'I want to be sure my Sarah will learn to read and write and be able to do maths. How will you go about teaching her to do that in the prep year?'

  'I'm not sure our two-year-old, Tom, will cope with being with other children. Do you expect them to socialize?'

- Read further about the Reggio Emilia approach. Explore aspects that are of particular interest to you or that challenge your thinking. What can you learn from the Reggio Emilia approach?

- Write a brief statement of your beliefs about how young children learn and what you see the role of the teacher to be. You may want to include this statement in your job application.

Chapter 4

Creating physical environments for learning and teaching

In this chapter and the next, ways to develop enriching environments for learning and teaching will be considered. Enriching environments are characterized by 'flexibility, accessibility and responsiveness to children' and require that teachers make decisions about the physical environment (including the use of time), as well as the social and affective environment (Queensland School Curriculum Council, 1998: 26). Although the physical and affective aspects are closely intertwined in this chapter we will focus on the physical environment by:

- considering the organization of the physical aspects of the setting;
- becoming aware of the 'messages' and effects of different forms of organization;
- recognizing the links between beliefs about learning and teaching and organizational decisions;
- reflecting on the importance of preparation.

ORGANIZING THE PHYSICAL ENVIRONMENT: WHAT IS INVOLVED?

For early childhood teachers, the organization of the physical environment is an important consideration as it both influences and reflects their teaching approach. I found it interesting that most of the beginning teachers I talked with spontaneously raised the organization of their environment as one of the problematic issues they faced, particularly at the start of the year. Here are some of their comments. Amy who was a preschool teacher at an independent school said:

> As I started talking about what my expectations were for my room with my teacher aide, I realized I wasn't really sure about what I wanted.

Our rooms are huge and I had to grapple with the realization that I was the teacher responsible for this room. That was hard and I was anxious about what other teachers and parents would think about what I did. We have people coming through our rooms every day and there is a strong expectation that our rooms are immaculately presented ... all the paintings have to be mounted and labelled. Setting up the room was difficult because there seemed to be so little furniture for such a big space. I asked the teacher in the room next door for ideas and she was very helpful ... and very willing to share.

Kate was initially told she would be the teacher of a second preschool group that was being established because of increased numbers in the area and that she would have her own room. Just before the term started, however, because numbers of children in the primary school had also increased, this plan was changed. Instead of having two separate groups in two spaces it was decided that the two teachers and two teacher aides would work together with 40 children in the existing purpose-built preschool unit designed for 25 children. Kate said:

My biggest problem was that I had no sense of 'ownership' of the children. As a beginning teacher I felt I wanted to have my own children and my own parents but from day one, I was sharing them ... and that was a major problem for me, especially as we were doing interviews ... and I just felt like the third wheel.

After about three weeks the parents started to complain because they felt the children weren't relating to one particular teacher ... there were too many parents coming in together in the morning ... and they didn't like the set up. I really agreed with them but I couldn't side with them because the principal wanted something different. I had to be very diplomatic. But after five weeks I did have my own class in my own little classroom in the primary school with some preschool furniture ... but I had to share all the resources and materials from the other preschool teacher's room, and use her room for painting and other messy activities. So nearly all of first term was spent working out how we could share without losing time ... and remaining positive.

Jenny commented that when she first saw her Year 2 room it was empty apart from four shelf units, a teacher's table and chairs, the children's desks and chairs, and a small amount of maths equipment. Jenny said:

I thought I would have a lot more equipment. Now I realize that at Uni when they say 'make resources' you really need to. ... At the end of the year I was able to look around my room and think, 'Gee I have a lot of things.' If I see anything in the school that could be useful and is about to be put in a cupboard I say 'Could I put it in my room ... and then you can get it from there?' Everyone seems quite happy with that arrangement. I got the data projector that way. I promised to lock it away every night in the cupboard in my room. People know they can have it anytime ... but the children and I use it a lot.

When you take up your first teaching position you must be prepared to handle situations such as those faced by Amy, Kate and Jenny. Because you are likely to undertake teaching practice at a time when your supervising teacher has arranged the physical environment and settled the children into the routines, it is possible to remain unaware of the many factors that need to be considered in order to create a smooth-functioning learning environment. Remember that the organization of the outdoors is just as important as the set up of the classroom for learning. There are a number of steps you can take during each teaching practice to help you be better prepared to organize the learning environment when you begin teaching. The first step is to become aware of the key aspects of the physical environment and note the different ways in which these key aspects can be organized.

Key aspects of the physical environment

In building your awareness of important physical aspects, become familiar with research and textbooks which indicate the design features, aesthetic aspects, equipment and forms of organization that contribute to effective learning environments (for example, Bronson, 1995; Carter and Curtis, 2003; Eaton and Shepherd 1998; Lunt and Williamson, 1999; Wellhousen and Wortham, 2001). In your teaching practice settings make note of the environmental features by making sketches or, with your supervising teacher's permission, take photographs of the room organization, furniture arrangements, playground designs, storage provision and aesthetic features. You will find that you will refer to these when you come to set up your own environments. Writing down the schedule of the day and noting how this relates to the particular circumstances of the setting can also provide you with a valuable base for the development of your own scheduling.

Some key aspects of the physical environment are:

- the arrangement and use of space and equipment;
- the selection and storage of materials;
- the schedule of the day.

The arrangement and use of space and equipment

From your observations and experiences you will note that there is wide variation in the use of space and the arrangement of equipment in early childhood settings. For instance, some lower primary classrooms have desks grouped into fours, a carpeted space for group discussion as well as other learning centres or interest areas containing computers, collage and art materials, blocks and manipulative materials, maths games and books. Other classrooms appear far more austere with all desks facing the board, books and number games stacked on shelves but not displayed, and children's work folders for different subjects prominently stored. In some schools you may notice separate adventure playgrounds for the younger children, while other schools have no such provision.

Similarly, preschool settings vary in appearance. In some, activities provided by the teacher are set out on tables, with areas for home play, painting, blocks, puzzles and manipulative equipment clearly defined. In other preschools there are large open spaces in which children construct buildings such as 'houses', 'boats', or 'hospitals' before playing in them. In some preschools, blocks are stored on fixed shelves and played with on the carpet, while in others, blocks are stored on non-tippable, mobile trolleys and placed around the room near to the 'building sites'. Some preschool

Plate 4.1   Finding space for a quiet writing corner can pose some challenges where the room is small. (Photo courtesy of Sue Thomas.)

teachers require that all equipment be packed away at the end of the session, while others arrange for buildings and games to be left up so that play can continue in the next session.

The selection and storage of materials

From your experiences you will also note that settings differ markedly in terms of the quality and quantity of materials available, as well as in the ways in which the materials are presented and stored. For instance, you may have observed that some childcare centres have a plentiful supply of equipment for the under threes which caters for all areas of their development. You may have seen dress-up clothes and accessories, a variety of animal and people figures and transport vehicles to use with blocks or sand, fit-in puzzles, simple matching and sorting games which encourage exploration and problem-solving and a large collection of sturdy books. Simple instruments, scarves and dancing accessories to promote music and movement may be provided together with a supply of art materials to encourage visual expression. Adjustable, low climbing structures, ride-on and wheeled toys, balls and materials for sand and water play may also be available for fine and gross motor activity. Other centres for the under threes, however, may have minimal equipment available and, as a consequence, you may have seen more friction because children of this age group are not able to cope easily with sharing and turn taking.

If you observe closely you will become aware that there are different ways in which materials are made available to children. For instance, in some settings the four- to six-year-old children have access to a wide range of materials which are stored in open shelving units or in an open storeroom adjoining the main activity area. Recyclable materials such as small plastic coils and spools, pieces of leather and cardboard, boxes, artificial flowers, wooden furniture factory off-cuts and the like may be stored in clearly labelled and colour-coded boxes. The colour coding enables children to return the red box to its rightful place on the bottom shelf where all the other red boxes are stored. Materials that teachers do not want children to access daily are kept on high shelves out of the children's reach.

You may also find that teachers vary in their expectations concerning the children's use of equipment. James had experienced these differing expectations in a practicum and shared his observations in a tutorial. Although James had worked with several teachers who required children to read the books in the book area, and to use the scissors and masking tape at the making table, his last supervising teacher had let the children use the equipment or materials where they were needed. Provided the children handled the materials responsibly and had a reason for wanting them, they could be used anywhere in the room. James told of how a child was able to take some puzzles into his 'hospital' so that the sick children would have something to do.

The schedule of the day

Have you discovered yet, that developing a schedule is more than just filling in time slots? Various factors have to be taken into consideration depending on the setting and age groups of the children concerned. For instance, teachers in primary classes have to consider the schedule of other specialist teachers and work around times for visits to the library as well as school assemblies. Having specific times for morning tea and lunch breaks also means that lessons and activities may end abruptly rather than flow on if the children are actively engaged.

Developing a daily schedule for the under threes in childcare settings can also be challenging. Three students who had undertaken teaching practice in childcare settings highlighted some of the complexities they had discovered in a tutorial. They compiled a list of factors that they felt had to be taken into account in developing a flexible yet predictable daily schedule for children. These factors included:

- being able to respond immediately to toddlers' needs;
- avoiding waiting times;
- adapting the length of activities to individual children's attention spans;
- providing some regular routines and rituals relating to meals and rest;
- allowing for unhurried one-to-one interactions between children and staff to foster language and relationships;
- the varying staff–child ratios at particular times of the day;
- timing the use of the playground if it is shared with older children;
- allowing time to talk with the children's parents at arrival and departure times.

In thinking about scheduling, pre-service teachers often raise questions about how to provide for a balance of activity in terms of time. For instance, should the same amount of time be spent indoors as outdoors? What amount of time should be spent in whole-group situations compared with the time spent in individual or small-group activity? Can more time be spent indoors on some days but then balanced by having a longer period outdoors on other days? Should children be involved in the decisions with their teacher about where they will play or the amount of time to be spent on an activity?

Clearly there are many factors inherent in the physical environment that can separately, and in combination, influence children's experiences in early childhood settings. You will no doubt discover many more factors once you start to look at the way your teaching practice settings operate and are organized. It is not enough to just note these factors, however. You also have to consider the ways in which they influence the children's experiences.

CONSIDERING THE MESSAGES AND EFFECTS OF THE PHYSICAL ORGANIZATION

In one tutorial discussion some student teachers talked about how children could be affected by the physical organization of the setting. Jane recalled that her supervising teacher had said that as she arranged her room she thought of the messages she wanted to send to children. If you view organization in this way then the physical arrangement of the setting becomes a matter of great importance, because:

- it sends messages to children about what they are expected to do;
- it has consequences for children in terms of what they can do.

Do you think that the way in which a room is arranged sends messages to children? In a room where puzzles, threading, potato prints and lacing boards are set out on tables it seems likely that children will get the message, 'There are certain tasks you are expected to undertake here.' In a room where there are cardboard boxes and blocks, dress-up clothes, space for building and an accessible storeroom, however, it seems more likely that children will get the message, 'Here is a place where you can play, make choices and act on your own ideas.' I told the tutorial group about a visit I had made to a preschool in the first week of the school year. Just inside the door the teacher had placed a small table and chairs. A bright cloth covered the table and it was set with plastic plates, cups and saucers, spoons and a teapot. A teddy bear and a doll sat on two of the chairs. A child only had to take a step into this room to get the message that here was a place to play. This teacher strongly believed that the room arrangement signalled a message.

The type of materials available and the ways they are presented also send messages to children and have consequences in terms of what children can do. If children can only use the coloured pieces of paper set out on the table to decorate their boxes, then they don't have to make too many choices or decisions. If, however, they can go to the storeroom and select any materials that they think can be affixed to their box, then they have many more choices and decisions to make. They also have opportunities to make predictions about what will or won't stick, as well as opportunities to test out their predictions.

Messages are also conveyed by the way in which time is used. Have you ever imagined what children must feel when they are told to pack away their intricate block building only minutes after they have completed it and before they have had a chance to play with it? The space the block building is occupying may be needed for a group time so, in one sense, the request to pack away may be justified, but what message is this request sending? Is it saying, 'Your building and your concentrated efforts are not valued. Just pull down your building and stack the blocks away ... you can build another building tomorrow. Today's building was of no great significance'? If your hard effort had been treated in a similar way on several occasions, would you build another building tomorrow? Children need lengthy periods of time in which to represent their ideas in some form and then to develop their play. The organization of the daily schedule needs to be such that it sends the message, 'There is plenty of time for you to develop your ideas and to play.'

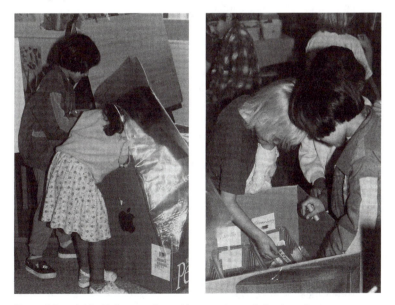

Plates 4.2 and 4.3 Only a cardboard box, a piece of plastic and some paper on sticks but this 'freezer' was in constant use as these children selected their favourite iceblocks at the iceblock shop. (Photos courtesy of Northgate State Preschool.)

Upon reflection, the members of the tutorial group agreed that, although they had noted ways of organizing the room and had thought a little about the effects of this organization on behaviour, they had not thought about physical organization in terms of the messages it sends. They also began to question why there is such a wide variation between settings, even for children of the same age, in the arrangement of space, the provision of materials and the use of time.

Examining reasons for particular organizational arrangements

Some tutorial members suggested that, while they recognized that organizational decisions influenced children's behaviour they had also noticed that, on some occasions, the reverse was true: the behaviour of children in the group could affect a teacher's organizational decisions and actions. Ann, for instance, recalled how one of her supervising teachers moved the doll's house with its delicate furnishings into her office because the play had become too boisterous and some furniture had been broken when it was situated in the main activity room. All children were still welcome to play with the doll's house, but the smaller and quieter space afforded by the office meant that only small groups of children could be involved at the one time. Ann observed that, in the office setting, the play appeared to be more focused and less inhibited as the children took on the roles of the family figures they were holding. She thought this change in play may have stemmed from a greater sense of privacy. Ann said that when she shared her observations with her supervising teacher she had agreed, and had indicated that her decisions about the positioning of equipment were often influenced by observations of the children and the way in which particular settings seemed to affect their behaviour.

Others suggested that the physical design of the building and playground, or even weather conditions, could influence the way in which the physical environment is organized. Mike described a situation he had experienced which had made him realize that weather and lack of space did affect the children's behaviour and level of activity, as well as his own. He said:

> We had two weeks of non-stop rain and both the children and I were beginning to go a little crazy ... and my patience was beginning to wear thin. One morning ... another wet one ... I was on the verandah talking to Rachel about her painting when I heard a group of children running inside. Without thinking I said, 'Don't run inside! You might slip and hurt yourselves.' That's when I realized I was beginning to say 'don't' and 'no' too often. After all, if I was five I would have wanted to run

inside ... or anywhere! It was after that ... and a discussion with my supervising teacher ... that I decided to set up a mini-obstacle course indoors to compensate for the children's lack of physical activity outdoors. I also tried to avoid negative directions and use more positive comments when I could.

By thinking critically about the children's behaviour and his own responses Mike was able to see that the confined space was impacting on the children's actions and his own. In proposing and trialling an alternative arrangement to overcome the impact, Mike was, in fact, taking an important step in preparing to organize his own classroom.

Proposing alternative arrangements in particular situations

As a pre-service teacher in your supervising teacher's setting there will be few opportunities for you to make or trial any major changes to the organization of the environment. Situations are likely to arise, however, as they did for Mike, which will provide you with the chance to test out some minor changes in arrangements. In the tutorial, Alicia recounted how she had realized that even little things, such as where she sat to read the story to the three-year-olds, could influence their behaviour. Alicia had positioned herself so that the group was looking at some open shelves. She hadn't realized that the teacher had placed some very attractive puppets on those shelves just that morning. As Alicia was about to read the story one of the children noticed the puppets and, with an excitement that was contagious, immediately picked up the mouse puppet. Needless to say, that was the end of Alicia's planned story that day. After that experience, Alicia said she checked out what the children would be looking at before she positioned herself at group time and, where possible, eliminated any distractions.

At the end of the tutorial, some pre-service teachers said they felt reasonably confident about planning and organizing the physical environment for learning and teaching. Others, however, said that while they were aware of some of the influencing factors, they often didn't realize what the effects of these factors might be. In other words, they had difficulty predicting what might happen. Because the ability to predict the 'possible trajectory of events in classrooms and the way specific actions affect situations' (Doyle, 1990: 355) is essential for effective teaching, it is important that you develop this skill. If you find predicting difficult, here are some actions you can take during your teaching practice that may help to improve your ability to predict:

- Select a particular incident (e.g. a child who refuses to come and sit with the group or a child who swears at you when you ask for the puzzles to be put away).
- Write down at least two alternative strategies you could use in that particular situation.
- Make yourself 'predict' the possible consequences of each of these strategies.
- Outline the message you think each particular strategy might convey to a child.
- Decide on your action and trial the chosen strategy at the next opportunity.
- Observe children's responses to your action, and consider whether or not their behaviour or response is consistent with the message you thought they would receive.
- If the children's response was not what you anticipated, try to work out the reasons why. If their response matched your prediction, give yourself a pat on the back ... then write down why you thought your action was successful.

Messages resulting from organizational decisions

In an effort to become more aware of the messages that can be conveyed by actions and decisions, the tutorial group members visited early childhood settings to look for the main message they felt teachers were conveying by their organization of the physical environment. In looking for the message, not only the organization of space, resources and time were 'researched', but also the apparent effects of these on the children's responses and behaviour. The teachers who agreed to these visits were aware that the pre-service teachers were looking for messages in their environment and were happy to talk with them at the conclusion of the visit. Jocelyn, after her visit to a preschool for four- to five-year-old children, said that the teacher seemed to be conveying this message: 'Here is an environment that invites and challenges you to use your initiative and resourcefulness.' She presented her reasons for arriving at her conclusion this way:

> When I first walked into the classroom before the session started I couldn't help noticing how different it looked from many of the other preschool rooms I have seen. It looked rather bare, with lots of empty spaces on the floor. The ceiling wasn't decorated with loads of bright coloured hanging 'things' but there were children's paintings displayed

on the walls. The room still contained all the resources of any other preschool – puzzles, books in a corner with lots of comfy cushions, a writing corner and an area for easel painting. The other resources were arranged differently, however. There were large, hollow blocks stacked against one wall with the project blocks on two different trolleys in other parts of the room. The storeroom door was open and it was full of a great variety of recyclable material neatly organized in boxes. The collage trolley was easily accessible from both sides and close to a work bench. I was surprised at the numbers of sticky tape dispensers, staplers, and pairs of scissors that were provided.

Of particular interest to me was how the room changed from this quiet empty space to a hive of activity after the group discussion. During the discussion the children shared their ideas for play with the teacher and the other children. The children took advantage of the space normally occupied by tables and chairs to create their own play areas. Having the different types of blocks spread around the room meant that many children, both boys and girls, had access to them and used them for many different purposes. Where the children chose to play was up to them, and problem solving occurred in many instances. For example, Jay wanted to build his house in the storeroom doorway, but how would people be able to get in and out of the storeroom? The children were challenged to think about everything, from where to play, to the types of resources they could use to make the wings of the plane, or to clean up the oil spill that was affecting the penguins. (This was a pretend game that some children had decided to play. Such a spill has been featuring in television news programs.)

I felt that it was not just the physical environment to which these children were responding. Sue, the teacher, had set up an environment where the children had stimulating, thought-provoking discussions that enabled the children to take the initiative and show resourcefulness. By organizing the room in a way that allowed the children to impose their own organization, the children also had freedom of expression and opportunities to explore materials, as well as their ideas. It seemed that the children were learning through hands-on experiences, through making decisions, solving problems and using their initiative. The most interesting aspect for me was that all the children's actions seemed purposeful and personally relevant.

When Jocelyn talked with Sue, the teacher, at the end of the session, she found that Sue had, in fact, written down the messages she was wanting to convey in her philosophy statement in *The Diary of a Preschool Teacher*

(Thomas, 1991). This philosophy is expressed in terms of the type of environment Sue wants to provide for children. Jocelyn was unaware of this diary when she visited, and was interested to compare her own impressions with what Sue had written. These are some of the statements taken from Sue's introduction to her diary:

> I want preschool to be a place where:
> - Children can work in a 'real' climate – real in the sense that their ideas and thoughts may be constructively criticized but their efforts of doing and thinking will always be valued.
> - Children's thinking and talking about their ideas is valued as much as the products and actions which can be seen.
> - Children can use materials as tools in posing and solving problems.
> - Children can develop their own style of pulling out the facts about the world rather than learning the facts about something.
> - Children can work at their own pace and level of development so that they feel a sense of satisfaction and achievement.
> - Children can develop skills in a real way and for a real purpose. The need for these will inevitably arise through play.
> - Children can have the freedom to play with materials, with each other, and with their thoughts and to re-create important events in their lives.
>
> (Thomas, 1991: 1)

What are your views concerning the match between Jocelyn's impressions and the kinds of messages and experiences Sue was hoping her environment would provide? For me, Jocelyn's description of the room arrangement seemed to illustrate clearly Sue's statements. For instance, the room's organization encouraged children to impose some of their sense of order, to use a wide range of open-ended materials in creating their buildings and games, and to be active in expressing their ideas in play. In these ways children were able to work in a 'real' environment which challenged them to use their initiative and resourcefulness.

LINKING BELIEFS ABOUT LEARNING AND TEACHING WITH ORGANIZATIONAL DECISIONS

If you think about Sue's statements, you can see that they are expressing her views about the kinds of experiences that she believes assist young children

Plate 4.4 As these children prepared to feed the animals in their wildlife park, they had the freedom to play with materials, with each other and their ideas. (Photo courtesy of Northgate State Preschool.)

to learn. She has taken these beliefs and translated them into a picture of her 'ideal' environment for young children – what she wants children to experience in her preschool. In talking about how she arrived at this point in her thinking, Sue said that it had taken many years of working with young children and many years of thinking about the nature of that work. Sue's experience may provide you with some pointers for developing your thinking about your 'ideal' environment.

As a *beginning teacher* Sue said she had:

- tended, at first, to organize in ways similar to those used by 'respected' supervising teachers;
- gradually developed her own form of organization as she came to know the children and responded to their needs;
- looked at the environment from the children's perspectives as well as her own.

As a more *experienced teacher* Sue said she had:

- begun to question familiar forms of organization and explore new forms (e.g. balancing time for different activities over a week instead of a day; leaving 'buildings' up so that play could be continued the next day);

- closely observed and analysed children's responses to new forms of organization;
- come to visualize ideals for children in terms of the types of learning environment she wanted them to experience.

After considering your own experiences, Sue's comments, and those made by the student teachers in the tutorial, you will have realized that organizing the physical aspects of the environment is a far more complex task than it may at first appear. Not only are there all the dimensions of the use of space and time and the nature of resources and their presentation to think about, but there are also their possible effects and messages to consider. The organization of the physical environment is further complicated by the fact that, in early childhood settings, unplanned events can occur which change the nature and organization of that environment. For instance, paint can be spilt; a child can fall and need attention; there is an unexpected birthday celebration to fit in; or children can become so involved in an activity that the time schedule changes. Although you cannot control or prevent some of these 'happenings', you can recognize the need to be flexible and be prepared to adapt and change aspects of your organization.

BEING PREPARED

There is also another vital element relating to the organization of the physical environment that needs to be highlighted. This is the teacher's ability to be sufficiently prepared and organized to present activities and experiences in ways that challenge children's learning and thinking at appropriate moments. As a student teacher you must show that you are thoroughly prepared for any learning experiences that you present. You need to recognize that your own organization – or lack of it – also affects the smooth running of the classroom, as well as the children's behaviour.

Have you ever had that dreadful feeling of being totally disorganized? Most of us have. Our disorganized moments are generally memorable occasions, but memorable for the wrong reasons. Marietta had such an experience during her last teaching practice with a Year 1 class, which she has agreed to share. She wrote in her journal:

> This afternoon was the last straw. I am just about ready to throw it all in! After the chaos of yesterday I thought the children might benefit from a 'fun' Friday afternoon activity. I had planned to read the book about bubbles and afterwards engage the children in a bubble-blowing

activity. A simple enough plan ... but I hadn't taken into account a series of stuff-ups. First of all I was rostered on playground duty. I was not aware of this until Mrs F., my supervising teacher, came to find out why I hadn't come out to do the duty. This was unfortunate because I had been planning to set up the equipment during this break. 'Well', I thought, 'it doesn't really matter. I will still have time to prepare when we return to class because Mrs F. has to finish off the maths lesson.'

Think again, Marietta! When we returned to class Mrs F. settled the children down, and I thought, 'Great! I'll go and set everything up now.' Instead, she told the children to go and get their hats because Miss T. had a special activity planned for this afternoon. I nearly dropped dead! I looked at her and she must have read the look of panic on my face. I approached her feeling more and more anxious and confessed that I had nothing prepared yet. Oh! It was an absolute nightmare. Mrs F. was not very impressed, and basically said, 'Well then, what are you going to do?'

I ended up running madly around from classroom to classroom trying to collect containers and then racing up to the staff room to make up the bubble mixture. This made me feel so embarrassed and humiliated. After a week of feeling pretty confident, I had landed flat on my face! Meanwhile, Mrs F. was reading a story while the children waited for me.

I finally returned to class and rushed through explaining what we were going to do. We were running out of time and I didn't even think to mention safety or behaviour expectations. My only thoughts were on getting through this experience. We got outside and I thought, 'OK, everything's fine now.' Was I wrong! From the moment we made it into the adventure playground, chaos reigned supreme. The children were running around and wouldn't listen to my instructions. They were climbing on equipment and fighting over the containers. I tried to implement calming strategies – hands on heads, clapping rhythms, but they would not pay me any attention. Tahlia got some of the bubble mixture in her eye and Dominic tripped while running around chasing bubbles. By this stage I was a nervous wreck and nearly out of my mind with despair. I couldn't control the children and Mrs F was standing over near the fence, watching, but not becoming involved in my 'fun' afternoon. Finally she walked over to me, and the children reverted to their normally sedate behaviour. By now the thought of someone else being in charge had me almost weeping with relief.

Discussing the afternoon's events later with Mrs F. helped me some-what, but as I write this story now I feel so utterly stupid. I recognize that it was a good learning experience, and I will endeavour never to repeat this mistake, but the event has diminished my early confidence and, as I am expected to take whole days in the next two weeks, I feel more nervous than I had thought I would.

At the end of her teaching practice, some weeks later, Marietta reflected on her experience this way:

For many this story might seem meaningless – you made a mistake, Marietta – get over it. But for me, it was a crisis point affecting my confidence in becoming a teacher. I can so vividly recall my feelings of frustration and helplessness as the children completely ignored my requests to settle down. At the time I recall thinking, 'What is wrong with these children? What a terrible, horrible bunch of children!' Looking back it would have been so easy to just blame them and justify the whole experience by pretending that these children had no self-control and were complete and utter ratbags. Had I done that I would have learned nothing and I really would have been a failure. Instead I chose to grasp this opportunity and benefit from it ... to give myself a chance to learn something about teaching.

I believe the absolute chaos stemmed from my lack of organization and preparation. This neglect, in turn, led to feelings of anger, confusion and failure, emotions that generated further *Angst* as the children intuitively picked up on my feelings of inadequacy and frustration. By the time I got home that afternoon I was ready to throw it all in. A chat with a teacher friend over that weekend helped to change my perspective. She called it a learning experience, and reminded me that the ultimate failure would be not to learn something about the value of organization and preparation.

If I were to be faced with the same situation again, I would immediately terminate the activity so as to avoid any further accidents and return the children to the classroom. It is not advisable to take a group of 25 Year 1 children into an adventure playground, give them bubble-blowing equipment and *then* try to explain safety rules and behavioural expectations. These should be made very clear beforehand. While my first mistake was being unprepared, and my second was to fail to explain any safety or behaviour rules, my third mistake was to lose all control and confidence in my role as a teacher. By remaining relaxed, calm and confident in manner it is easier to take hold of a situation and diffuse it, rather than let it continue to gain momentum and eventually reach crisis point.

Marietta has told her story so clearly, I'm sure you will be able to learn from it too. For me, Marietta's story exemplifies how events can intertwine and snowball in classroom situations. Marietta's story also illustrates how closely interwoven the social and physical aspects of the environment are, with the lack of physical organization resulting in the breakdown of the social organization of the class. It is vital, then, that in thinking about the creation of learning environments you also consider the social aspects that contribute to the learning process.

SUMMARY

The discussion in this chapter has focused on the physical factors that are seen to contribute to effective learning–teaching environments. A number of steps for building your understanding of these factors and their effects have been suggested. These include:

- noting similarities and differences in how early childhood settings are designed and organized in terms of space, materials and time;
- considering possible reasons for particular organizational decisions;
- becoming aware of the messages conveyed to children by organizational decisions and teachers' actions;
- observing the ways in which the behaviour of children and teachers is influenced by organizational factors;
- developing an ability to predict children's responses to particular organizational decisions and consequent messages;
- evaluating the physical aspects of the setting in the light of your beliefs about learning and teaching.

During teaching practice there are few opportunities for you to make or trial major organizational changes because schedules, routines and room arrangements are generally established. There will be opportunities to assess your own organizational and decision-making skills, however, as you fulfil some of your teaching practice requirements. For example:

- when planning and taking an activity with children;
- when settling and taking a larger group for a lesson, story or music session;
- when assisting children to make a transition from one activity to another;
- when in control for a certain period of the day.

It is important that you are frank and honest in your appraisal of your own efforts as you reflect on such situations. Ask yourself some questions:

- Did I explain my expectations clearly?
- Did I look at the physical set-up from a child's perspective?
- Did I closely observe the effect of the room arrangement on the children's behaviour?
- Were the children able to see and hear each other when asked to discuss ideas?
- Was my use of 'time' appropriate?
- What physical changes could I make to improve the experience?

Ask your supervising teacher, too, for suggestions as to how you could have prevented difficulties arising or for some alternative strategies that you could have used. It is important to acknowledge the problems you may experience as you develop your organizational abilities and learn from your mistakes. By talking or writing honestly of your experience and seeking reasons for its success or otherwise you are able to develop and refine your strategies and skills.

SUGGESTED ACTIVITIES

- Design and sketch your 'ideal' physical environment for a particular age group (for example, babies to three-year-olds; three- to five-year-olds; five- to eight-year-olds). Indicate some of the design features, such as natural lighting, landscaping and fixed equipment. Show how you would arrange your selected indoor and outdoor furniture and equipment and how you would store materials. Be prepared to discuss the reasons for your design and choice of resources.
- Develop a resource file in which you keep examples of the use of space and equipment, the selection and storage of materials and the daily schedule that you have observed. Jot down the messages you felt were being conveyed to children by these particular forms of organization and explain how the organization was contributing to these messages.
- What recyclable materials would you want in your storeroom for the under threes; three- to five-year-olds; five- to eight-year olds? Where would you get these supplies and how would you store them? What are some of the best storage ideas you have seen?
- Imagine that you are about to begin teaching in a Year 1 classroom. Decide how you will position desks/tables; where you will place the

whiteboard; whether or not you will keep a large area for group discussions; where you will position the computers; and whether or not you will have particular learning centres. After deciding on your priorities and the room arrangement, consider what these tell you about your teaching approach. What beliefs about learning and teaching are reflected in your arrangement of the physical environment?

• Think about where you would prefer to be – in a suburban shopping centre or walking through a national park. What are the features of your preferred environment which attract you? In thinking about the reasons for your own preferred environment, draw some implications for the planning of environments for children.

Chapter 5

Creating socially secure environments for learning and teaching

The new understandings stemming from neuroscience are highlighting the importance of the provision of enriching and emotionally warm and supportive environments for children's learning and development. Children need to feel accepted and secure, to have trusting relationships with adults and a developing sense of confidence in themselves as being capable and competent if they are to learn effectively (Catherwood, 1999; Goleman, 1995; Landy, 2002; Kostelnik *et al.*, 2002; Wolfe and Brandt, 1998). In this chapter we will focus on a number of aspects of pedagogy that can contribute to the development of socially secure environments for young children. These are:

- welcoming and celebrating cultural diversity;
- building caring and cooperative relationships;
- promoting independence and a sense of responsibility;
- engendering a sense of fairness;
- fostering problem solving and conflict resolution;
- guiding behaviour.

Since 11 September 2001, recognition of the need for a socially secure environment has become greater, but so too have the challenges in ensuring children experience peaceful, caring communities. While this provision is a societal responsibility, teachers, parents and children working together can contribute to the creation of safe, secure and socially responsive environments for learning and teaching. In developing such environments we must focus as much on 'prevention (i.e. teaching young children how to live peacefully) as on intervention (i.e. helping children make sense of and work through the violence in their lives)' (Levin, 2003: 8). Such prevention and intervention require an integrated approach to the curriculum with problem solving and social skills not being taught as isolated skills but being integrated into subject learning and explored in the everyday experiences of 'living' with others.

WELCOMING AND CELEBRATING CULTURAL DIVERSITY

During your teacher education course you will probably have opportunities to undertake studies that will assist you to teach in classrooms that reflect our diverse society. It is important that you are familiar with relevant literature and research and take steps to increase your own understanding so that you can help children to respect and celebrate difference. Particular aspects you would be wise to study include: teaching in a multicultural, multilingual society; building relationships with all families in ways that are sensitive to social class, religion and family circumstances; promoting gender equity and respecting gender difference; and promoting inclusion by supporting children with disabilities. (Texts you may find helpful in this regard include: Ashman and Elkins, 2002; Barrera *et al.*, 2003; Copple, 2003; Dau, 2001; Kostelnik, 2001; MacNaughton, 2000; Paley, 1997.)

As you undertake teaching practice in a range of locations you will encounter children and colleagues with languages, culture, religions, ethnic backgrounds and ways of living that are different from your own. It is vital that you take every opportunity in these situations to consider your own cultural beliefs, behaviours and attitudes in the light of those shown by others with different backgrounds and perspectives. At the end of the practicum ask yourself, 'What have I learned? How have I changed?'

Mandy had a very positive introduction to working with children from diverse backgrounds during her teaching practice at an inner-city childcare centre attended by many children whose home language was not English. The centre was preparing for accreditation and during her teaching practice the staff were reviewing their practices relating to 'respect for children' which is Quality Area 2 in the *Source Book*, provided by the National Childcare Accreditation Council (NCAC, 2001b). After Mandy had read the principles and key concepts outlined in the *Source Book* and talked with staff about their practices, she found herself thinking more deeply about the various ways in which respect could be shown. She wrote in her journal:

> I hadn't realised that *how* I communicate with children can convey so much. I want to listen and encourage children to discuss their ideas so that I can show them that I really 'value' them and their thoughts. This is harder with the children who have little English but now I'm

convinced that it is worth trying to learn key words and phrases in their home language to show them that I want to communicate and that I value *their* language. I can also see the importance of getting information translated for families and using translators and resource people where possible as this shows families their communication and the information they give is valued too.

When I was looking through the centre's posters and picture sets the other day, for a display, I realised that there were many I wouldn't want to use. This was because they seemed to reinforce stereotypes – all white skinned, physically perfect children, and pictured with mum and dad, brother and sister and the family pet. I must admit I used similar posters in a previous prac without thinking what message was being conveyed. Nor did I think how children who had 'different' family structures might feel. The centre has just purchased some picture sets that are terrific as they show men and women in non-traditional roles and portray different types of families. I'm going to select storybooks much more carefully in future, both in terms of their pictures and the story line. Issues of gender, equity, fairness and inclusion can be so easily glossed over but they need to be handled sensitively.

When I talked with the director about how she promoted respect with her group she said that if you were 'attuned' there were many opportunities that arose naturally. She told me how one day some children decided they needed security cards to show at their 'airport'. They discussed how they would make them and, after looking at her driver's licence, they decided they needed to draw a picture of themselves, 'but just the head and shoulders'. The director said she stressed how important every detail was. They had to match eye, hair and skin colour exactly. This led to much observation and discussion of each other's features and inevitably led to discussions about Keiko's and Sonnie's 'different' coloured skin. The director said she recalled an aboriginal friend sharing with her how, as a child, she had longed for someone to tell her that her brown skin was 'beautiful'. So she said she went on to do just that. They talked about Keiko's beautiful creamy brown skin and Sonnie's beautiful smooth black skin, and David's beautiful freckled white skin, and how everybody's skin colour is just right for them.

The director also shared with me how wanting to show respect for the child-rearing practices of families can lead to real dilemmas for staff. For instance, what is a respectful and appropriate response to families where gender equity is not practised or valued at home and where families hold different expectations for their son's and daughter's experiences in the centre? Similarly, how important is a consistent approach to behaviour management for children who experience very different management strategies at home from those used in the centre? I must admit I hadn't even thought about such issues, let alone connected them with 'showing respect'. I can see that I'm only just at the very edge of understanding diversity and helping children value it!

Have you thought about some of these issues and considered how your attitudes and actions are culturally based? How will you work with families and children with different cultural backgrounds? Gonzalez-Mena (2003: 23) suggests that a major goal for these children 'who are grounded in one system and end up in another' should be 'that they do not experience conflicts that interfere with their growth, development, attachment to family or self-identity'. What are your goals for these children? What strategies will you use to help you achieve them?

BUILDING CARING AND COOPERATIVE RELATIONSHIPS

Just as the physical organization of the classroom sends messages to children about what they are expected to do, so the social climate of the classroom also sends messages to children about who they are, how they are valued and what they are capable of doing and being.

As you spend time in classrooms and group settings you will quickly sense whether the environment is warm and caring or rather cold and impersonal. Just as you can observe and record features that contribute to positive physical environments, so too can you become attuned to the actions and interactions that contribute to a socially supportive environment. As you observe the teacher and children interact, alert yourself to 'a moving set of relationships within which different groups and individuals are constantly in negotiation' (Woods, 1990: 17). You will also notice that these relationships generate feelings among children, as well as among children and teachers and that there are many different ways of handling these feelings.

It is important that you think about the kind of relationships you want to foster in your group or classroom and the skills that you and the children will need to promote their development. Your own skills are particularly important for, as Goleman (1995: 279) says, 'how a teacher handles her class is in itself a model, a *de facto* lesson in emotional competence – or the lack thereof.' In your pre-service course you will most likely undertake studies that will assist you to guide children's behaviour and to develop caring

Plate 5.1 Building the castle provided many opportunities for the children to share ideas, negotiate and help each other. (Photo courtesy of Kelvin Grove State College, Preschool Campus.)

cooperative relationships. Many student teachers comment that while they have felt they were familiar with steps outlined in textbooks for managing particular behaviours, they have found the actual implementation much more difficult, particularly if a child responds in an unpredictable way. This is why you want to take every opportunity to observe and talk with experienced teachers about how they develop cooperative relationships.

Liz is one of those skilled teachers. I asked her to share some of her strategies for developing a sense of community in her multi-age classroom for five- to eight-year-olds in a lecture with a group of final-year pre-service teachers. I found it interesting that in the following year when I spoke with a number of beginning teachers who had attended this lecture, they spontaneously said they had used some of Liz's ideas in their own classrooms as they developed their own strategies. You may find some of these ideas useful too.

Developing 'living together' skills

Liz said she thought of her multi-age class as 'a family' with people of different ages. In the first week she talked with the children about being 'a family' and in this way introduced the notion that, just as families have some 'rules', so their class would need rules too. She asked the children to think of what some of those rules might be and they made suggestions such as 'listen to each other', 'speak nicely to each other' and 'ask the teacher if you want to leave the room'. Liz said that as the children came up with their ideas and they discussed what these rules might mean, she categorized them under headings such as safety rules, movement rules, talking rules and respect rules (Rogers, 1989). In the following weeks Liz said they explored the skills needed in keeping these rules using games and Y charts ... What does listening *look* like? When you're listening how do you *feel*? When you know somebody is listening to you how do you feel? What does listening *sound* like?

Liz said that she was surprised at just how much help the children needed in becoming aware of what was involved in building these 'living together' skills and how frequently they revisited them throughout the year. The hand puppets, Hush and Mem who became loved classroom identities, were also used to model cooperative skills and make them explicit.

Developing confidence and self-esteem

As the year progressed Liz observed that the use of put-downs by some children was quite distressing for others and decided to open up a discussion on the topic using the puppets. Liz said she was saddened that all the children could so easily come up with examples of put-downs ... 'You're an idiot', 'You're a loser', 'Shut-up stupid', 'That's dumb'. After talking about how put-downs made them feel, they closed their eyes and tried to think of build-ups ... things they could say that would make them feel great and happy. This list was built more slowly ... 'I like what you do', 'You're a very good friend', 'Great idea', 'That's brilliant', 'Good on you'. Together they decided that their classroom was going to be a 'put-down free zone' and made appropriate signs. They also practised giving each other build-ups using a variety of games from books such as those by Hill (1992) and McGrath and Noble (1998).

Other strategies that Liz used for promoting self-esteem and helping each child feel special included individualized welcome back notes that she placed on each child's desk at the start of terms 2 and 3. At the beginning of term 4 she posted a letter home to each child, sharing her holiday experiences and foreshadowing term 4 learning experiences. Liz said this led to a spate of letter writing both to her and other children and as a result she introduced the 'writing bag' which contained assorted stationery and pens. The children took turns at taking the bag home and using it to write letters, and to share favourite recipes, jokes and stories.

Liz also sent an 'end of year' letter to each child that coincided with their report card going home. Liz said she wanted each child to see that they had learnt a lot and to be able to see that growth in learning in meaningful words, alongside their report card. She shared a number of these letters in the lecture (see Table 5.1 for an example).

In discussing some of the points Liz had made in her lecture some student teachers commented that, while they knew that it was important to value and respect children, they had not realized that this valuing and respect could be shown in so many different ways – even in assessment. They also commented on the introduction of the writing bag, which followed from the children's interest in writing, which in turn had been spawned by the teacher's letters to them. They said this had clearly illustrated the motivational benefits for children when their interests were acknowledged and their learning supported in a context that held meaning for them.

Others recalled personal experiences from their own school-days or observations from teaching practice experiences which, for them, highlighted particular aspects which contributed to, or in some cases, worked against the creation of caring and cooperative relationships.

Peter recalled a 'put-down' incident from his own school days and later reflected on how that experience was influencing his own approach to teaching, and why he felt so strongly that all children deserved respect. He wrote:

Table 5.1 Teacher's letter written in words that are meaningful to a child to accompany a more formal school report

---

Dear Jonathon,
I am writing to you because I want you to know how pleased I am with what you have done this year. At the beginning of the year remember how you cried a lot because you were not sure about reading and writing … but look at you now! You are reading books and what a great story you wrote about the 'Lion King'.
Your maths are improving too and you are working on base ten games much more easily. Most importantly, you have really improved in solving problems that happen in the playground and the other children really like the way you help them with this because you have such good ideas.
When I spoke to you the other day, you said you knew you had to learn more of your number facts. Yes, you CAN practice your count-on 1s (e.g. 12 + 1); count-on 2s (e.g. 12 + 2); and double facts up to 20 (e.g. 6 + 6, 7 + 7). I have really enjoyed having you in class this year because you have such great ideas and you are so helpful to other children. Have a great Christmas and a wonderful holiday.
Love from Mrs Irwin (and Hush and Mem).

(Perry and Irwin, 2000: 43)

If there was one incident from my own schooling which has helped to shape my philosophy and approach to teaching, it is what happened to me in Year 2. My teacher, Mrs K., was quite a good teacher who made learning fun for us. I was a very bright and inquisitive child and I was nearly always first to put my hand up in order to ask or answer a question. Mrs K. got to know that I knew the answers and asked the others instead of me. Even when I wanted to ask questions Mrs K. would say, 'Put your hand down, Peter. You know the answer, now stop being silly.' This type of treatment continued until the day of our maths exam, when I fell from grace. The question that I remember vividly was on measurement. It was, 'how many feet tall are you?' I had no concept of the linear measurement so I looked at the size of my foot and proceeded to approximate just how many feet tall I thought I was. I came up with thirteen and wrote it down. The teacher laughed as she read my answer out to the whole class. The other children laughed too and I cried. The one positive to come from this experience was that Mrs K. started to ask me to answer questions again.

Although it was a very traumatic experience for me at the time, I now see it as a very valuable one as I develop my thinking about teaching. I continually reflect on my teaching practices and interactions with children in an attempt to ensure that I provide a warm and supportive environment that encourages exploration and approximation.

Peter's story highlights the importance of valuing each child's contribution and appreciating the nature of the thinking that underlies it. There is no place whatever for ridiculing or putting down a child's effort. Such actions indicate a total lack of respect for the person concerned and work against the development of self-confidence and self-esteem. Teachers' actions must send the message that each child's effort and contribution is valued even if they do not result in the 'right' answer, and that it is natural that when we do our own thinking we will sometimes make mistakes.

PROMOTING INDEPENDENCE AND A SENSE OF RESPONSIBILITY

There are many ways in which teachers send messages to children that they are competent and capable. By encouraging the under fives to develop self-help skills so that they can dress, feed and toilet themselves, for example, a teacher is showing respect, not only for a child's ability and competence, but also for their right to feel independent and responsible when this is appropriate. The ways in which routines such as morning tea and lunch, tidy-up and rest times are handled in your teaching practice situations can also provide you with many insights concerning the amount of respect paid to children. For instance, when preparing to make the transition between playtime and lunch, are children given some notice that it will soon be time to finish their game or activity? This allows them to bring some 'closure' to their play and, in a subtle way, gives the message that their activity is valued. When making the transition, are the children lined up and kept waiting with nothing to do, or are children able to contribute and take some responsibility for tidying the setting before moving independently to the next activity? Is sufficient time allowed for nappy changing and toileting toddlers so that they are unhurried and can delight in warm interactions with adults who respond to their babbles and engage in peek-a-boo games? These leisurely, caring interactions all help to build a child's sense of being valued and respected.

Cassie was distressed by the way in which rest time was handled in one of her preschool teaching practice settings. She wrote:

> No matter how frustrating or difficult a child is, no adult has the right to 'pin' a child to their bed. Surely there must be better strategies such as giving a child a book, for example, or letting them sit quietly in book corner. Do all the children need to be doing exactly the same thing at one time ... lying like statues on their stretchers for one hour? Do they all need to be covered by their sheet? At any other time of the day the teacher encourages individual children to make choices. What is so different about rest time? Why does it need to be so regimented? I tired of listening to my nagging voice – 'sheet bags under your beds', 'lie straight on your bed', 'shut your eyes'.
>
> Perhaps I was particularly distressed by this situation because 17 years ago I was one of those 'wrigglers and disrupters' during rest time. I distinctly remember my stretcher being placed under the keyboard of the piano so I could not move my stretcher about or sit up without bumping my head. Although I believe that some routines are important in order for children to feel secure, unnecessary control will cause continual pressure on both the children and staff. To me it seems just as important to respect the individual needs of children during routine times such as lunch and rest as it does at other times of the day.

Rosanda had a much more positive experience of rest time during her preschool teaching practice. At her centre, after a short period of quiet rest, children were able to have drawing boards on which to draw while they rested.

One day, however, a number of children were restless in spite of having their drawing boards. Rosanda described in her journal what happened:

> After observing that the children were having difficulty settling (it had been a very exciting morning with a visit from a theatre group), the teacher said that there really seemed a problem at rest time today and she would need everyone's help to solve it. This group just love dealing with problems and they quickly came together to discuss some ideas. The children decided they needed some rules and came up with several. The teacher wrote down the rules and the children illustrated them (see Figure 5.1).

What different messages children in these two settings were receiving. In Cassie's preschool, children were expected to conform to a certain standard of behaviour, set and controlled by the adults with no allowance being made for individual differences or needs. In contrast, in Rosanda's preschool, the teacher was sensitive and responsive to children's needs and involved them in setting reasonable limits. This enabled children to experience self-control and to participate in a shared responsibility.

Figure 5.1 The children's rules for rest time

ENGENDERING A SENSE OF FAIRNESS

Ruth undertook a teaching practice in a preschool where her supervising teacher was keen to promote respect for the rights of others. Her teacher regarded the notion of social justice as being equated with fairness (Milne, 1997). She wanted children to treat each other fairly, to value difference and diversity, to respect the rights of others and to be able to resolve conflict in a fair way. Ruth observed many discussions that occurred during play where children were challenged to think about what would be fair. She detailed one of these discussions in her journal:

> Two groups of children had built their houses from large hollow blocks and pieces of cardboard, side by side in the middle of the room. They had been quite amicable neighbours until Karen picked up Charlie, the favourite toy dog, from a nearby shelf and claimed that Charlie lived at her house. Jane, who lived in the other house, immediately disputed this and said that Charlie lived in her house. The teacher listened to the argument from a distance but, seeing that feelings were running high and that the argument was not going to resolve itself, came over and said, 'What can we do about Charlie? We've only got one dog and two households that want him?'

KAREN We could make another one.

JANE And we'll have the real Charlie.

TEACHER Well, what do you think? Would that be fair? (*Neither Karen nor Jane thought it would, so the teacher asked them again what they could do.*)

JANE We could share him.

TEACHER How will you do that?

JANE We could join our houses together.

KAREN Yeah! You could live with me and I could live with you.

JANE You come to live with me first.

KAREN No! I'm not going to live in your house first.

TEACHER Oh dear! What are you going to do?

JANE We could both be mothers.

KAREN We could sleep together ... in bunks.

JANE And if we have two dogs one could sleep on the top bunk and the other on the bottom bunk.

TEACHER But you've only got one dog.

KAREN You could have a ring-tailed possum. My sister goes out at night looking for a ring-tailed possum.

JANE No, I want Charlie.

At this stage the teacher suggested they go to the storeroom to see what materials they could use to make their beds. They came back with cushions, large pieces of material and a small mattress, and made their beds with Karen still clutching Charlie under her arm. As they got into bed, however, Charlie was placed between them and, as the play developed, Charlie was forgotten as they had to care for their very sick daughter.

Many discussions like this one seemed to occur during the children's play. There would be real conflict but there would also be talking about how the problem could be overcome. I realized that the way in which the teacher intervened enabled the children to do most of the problem solving for themselves, although the teacher did keep bringing them back to think about whether what they were suggesting would be fair.

In this preschool, the teacher was sending a clear message that if there was a problem, then children were capable of solving it in a fair way. In order to do this, however, children had to listen to and consider other people's suggestions for solving the problem and to think about whether the suggested solution was a fair one. The teacher supported them in this task.

Plate 5.2 Puppets can become much-loved 'members' of the group. For children they can be participants in play and a source of emotional comfort. With a little imagination teachers can use them to model behaviours, contribute ideas and present different perspectives. (Photo courtesy of Kelvin Grove State College, Preschool Campus.)

FOSTERING PROBLEM SOLVING AND CONFLICT RESOLUTION

When I visited Liz's multi-age classroom for five- to eight-year-olds following her lecture I became very aware of the emphasis Liz placed on problem solving. There were opportunities to create and solve problems in all of the key learning areas. I heard children make comments such as 'Hey, let's make a pattern of a hundred' and saw them link a hundred things together, solving many 'space' problems in the process. I saw documentation of their solutions to some of the problems in a technology unit which included designing a tool to retrieve a metal toy car that had fallen into a grate-covered drain. Their interest in problem solving also extended to social concerns and they often discussed conflicts that had arisen in the playground.

The morning I visited, a situation had arisen on the soccer field during recess as the children from Liz's class played with some older Year 5 children. The children were concerned because the principal was going to come at lunch time and talk to them about bullying (the class had recently seen a video on bullying and the school was refining its policy, so bullying was a topical issue). When the children came in from recess Liz agreed that those involved could discuss the problem to see if they could come up with some fair solutions. Their proposals were that the Year 5 children could play in their own area, that they could bring their own ball and that they should not be allowed to borrow equipment from the sports shed. When Liz asked whether these solutions were fair for the Year 5 children there was general consensus that they were, although, as Liz presented the Year 5 perspective, some conceded that perhaps they did have to work out other ways to play together. A major problem had been that the Year 5 children got to pick the teams and chose the older 'good' players, while the younger children – the 'bad' players, did not get picked. In the process of the discussion that I was able to tape, some interesting insights into the thinking and experiences of five- to eight-year-olds regarding social conflict and bullying were revealed. Here is an excerpt from the discussion:

> CINDY Mrs Irwin, Brian was calling a lot of kids bad players and saying they couldn't play. (*Outburst of agreement ... 'Yeah and he's in Year 5.'*)
> TEACHER But that's bullying and that's not allowed in this school.
> JOE No. It's not tolerated.
> TEACHER That's right Joe. None of the teachers will tolerate it.
> ANDY (*coming close to the teacher with tears in his eyes*) Mrs Irwin, Brian called me a crap player.

TEACHER How did you feel when he said that? (*Andy couldn't answer as tears rolled down his cheeks.*)

JOE He got really angry.

TIM He got really upset.

TEACHER (*putting her arm around him*) Andy, what did you say when he said that to you? You must have felt terrible! (*Andy is crying and still can't talk.*) What a terrible put-down. What did all of your friends do?

JONO We were just listening.

JOE I was just waiting for him.

CINDY I saw it. ... I saw it but I couldn't stop it.

TEACHER Were you a bit scared to say something? (*Cindy nods.*)

TEACHER Joe, were you a bit scared to say something too?

JOE Yeah! If I'd said something he would have said the same to me too.

TIM Yeah! Just because he's older he thinks he can say those things.

TEACHER He thinks he's stronger and more powerful does he? (*Children agree.*)

TEACHER Andy, what would you have liked your friends to have done when you were feeling so terrible?

TIM I would have liked them to face up to my enemies.

TEACHER Would you?

JONO No! I would never face up to my enemies ... especially if they're real old. No! There's no way I'd face up to a Year 5'er.

TEACHER Joe, if it had happened to you what would you have wanted your friends to do?

JOE I'd like them to come up and say 'Are you all right?'

MIKE I'd like them to say 'Stop bullying. It's bad.'

SALLY In the Brady Bunch there's this boy ... the middle one ... and he's in this class and he says 'I want you to start leaving him alone. You're just a big bully.'

TEACHER So he actually stands up for his friends does he? Is that what you would have liked, Andy ... to have your friends stand up for you? It takes a lot of courage to do that though.

CINDY Yeah! Because he might say, 'I'm going to bash you up now.'

JONO Yeah, you get paranoid they're going to bash you up.

TEACHER You get so scared you mean?

JONO No. You get paranoid and ...

ROB ... and they might tumble and trip you down.

JOE Yeah! It could make them even angrier.

TEACHER So what are you saying? If your friend's in trouble and being bullied …

JOE You face up to them once and that's it!

SALLY No. You don't stand up to them … you tell the teacher … and they'll get into trouble.

TEACHER So Andy, what did you do?

ANDY I told the teacher.

TEACHER (*with some anticipation*) And what did the teacher do?

ANDY Nothing.

TEACHER (*in disappointed tone*) Oh! (*There is a silent pause.*)

JONO We need more thinking teachers … teachers don't do anything … they don't.

JOE Yes they do.

JONO They just go and say 'You can't play.'

CINDY The teachers don't ever believe us.

JONO We need someone … like to really hear us … who wants us to tell them those things …

(The conversation ended at this point as a child from another class entered the room with a request for the Year 1s to go to singing.)

(Perry and Irwin, 2000: 45–7)

Have you experienced a discussion such as this with children? You may find it helpful to analyse what Liz said and did which made for such open and honest discussion. For instance, in order to facilitate such discussions you will need to acquire skills that help children to focus and refocus on the topic, to clarify issues, to summarize thinking, and engage in deeper thinking when appropriate. Timing is essential. Knowing when to introduce new ideas and when to give children time to do their own thinking and connecting is also important.

You may also want to consider this discussion in the light of Liz's other strategies for developing a caring community in her classroom presented in a previous section relating to building cooperative relationships. Children will only share their thoughts so openly with an adult they trust and respect and whom they know listens, respects and values them.

GUIDING BEHAVIOUR

If you have spent any time with young children you will know that there are moments when you may see a child grab something from another child, push over equipment in apparent frustration or begin to run wildly in a way that might cause harm. As a responsible adult you will have recognized that in some of these moments it is necessary for you to intervene. From your studies you will be aware that there are many different ways to make this intervention – the management approach and the guidance approach are just two examples. The guidance approach, for instance, aims to teach children to think about their actions and be considerate of others, while the management approach seeks to control behaviour by teaching children to do what adults tell them to do (Porter, 2003).

It is important that you think about your approach to discipline so that you can decide upon your goals in this regard as you undertake teaching practice. Merryn did this as she prepared for her final teaching practice in a preschool. In particular she related to the guidance goals outlined by Porter (1999: 38). These were to encourage children to become self-disciplined, express their feelings appropriately, cooperate with other people, develop integrity and empathy and be orderly when being disorderly would interfere with other people in the group.

Merryn wrote:

> From my pre-practicum visits I have learned of one particular four-year-old who is causing difficulty for both staff and the children. Because of my lack of experience I see this as a challenging opportunity to learn more about guiding children's behaviour. My specific goal for this situation is to reduce the amount of disruption and physical and emotional upset caused to other children by children with behavioural problems.

To help herself to achieve this goal Merryn had decided to read further on the topic, and be prepared with some strategies so that she could try to reduce the disruption and upset that Jason was causing. She wrote in her journal:

> From what I had been told about Jason I must admit that I had some preconceptions of him even though I didn't know him. After researching the topic I realized I needed *to develop a positive attitude towards him* if I was going to help him. It gave me confidence to know that I had gathered a number of strategies I could try in order to interact with him positively. At the beginning of my first morning at the centre I heard a terrific yell. When I went to investigate the problem, Alex was crying and told me that Jason had hit him over the head with one of the trucks. When I asked Jason if this was true, he yelled, 'But he was annoying me and I wanted the truck.'

In this situation I was able to use one of my strategies, which was *to encourage Jason to use his words to express how he felt, rather than using physical force*. I explained to Jason that words let people know how we feel and that it is better to use words rather than hurt people. I encouraged Jason to talk about what had happened but he was very uptight and found this difficult. I continued with this strategy, however, speaking to him individually and using a calm, soft voice until he began to relax. I talked about the consequences that would follow if he went on hurting other people. The next day Jason seemed to want to test me out. In one specific incident, after talking about the behaviour that was expected and the consequences that would result if he chose not to do as he was asked, Jason hit Aaron over the head with a book. I acted immediately and withdrew Jason from the situation. I told him that when he felt he could act properly we could talk and he could rejoin the group, but until then he was to remain by himself sitting on the step.

I also became aware of the need *to remind Jason of the rules ahead of time*. For instance, I found that it helped when I said, 'When you have tidied up your area, please sit on the cushions for story time.' If I did not give this reminder Jason got very distracted and confused about what to do next and often lashed out, whereas knowing what was expected of him seemed to minimize his aggression. Similarly, I could not say, 'Tidy up time', and expect Jason to tidy up on his own initiative as many of the other children were able to do. I found, however, that if I allocated specific jobs to all the children this worked well, and that with some encouragement and supervision Jason could fulfil this responsibility. I also realized how helpful it was *to give Jason positive feedback*. I'd say, 'It was great you helped John take the ladder to the shed. Now we've packed up we can have our special snack.' On these occasions it seemed as if he did want to please.

In reflecting on her experiences, Merryn said:

I learned an incredible amount from my experience with Jason. In building my relationship with Jason I became aware of just how different each child is. Even though textbooks suggest particular strategies, I had to discover just how Jason would respond to my particular ways of using them. I saw that getting to know Jason by observing and talking with him had to be a priority if I was to come to know his reasoning and understand how I could help him. Although I was only at the centre three weeks I feel I did get to know him and was able to help him reduce his negative behaviour.

This experience sparked some more questions for me. I wondered whether it would help if parents and teachers used the same types of discipline strategies and how a more consistent approach could be established: I realized that I need to seek advice about how to approach parents to talk about the difficulties their child might be having. I also decided I needed to find out about agencies or resource staff who can assist teachers and parents in such situations. Another issue I felt that I hadn't resolved related to how to provide for the other children in the group if my time is taken up with children like Jason.

Merryn's reflections reveal the importance of doing your own thinking about your teaching actions. Although she was using recommended strategies, she had to discover how she herself put them into practice and what effect they would have on a particular child. The questions that Merryn raised as part of her reflections are important and may provide you with a valuable framework for extending your understandings and skills in guiding behaviour.

SUMMARY

In this chapter the rights of all children to feel accepted and secure, to have a trusting relationship with adults and a developing sense of confidence in themselves as capable and competent have been recognized and strategies for promoting such socially secure environments for this learning were highlighted.

From the narratives of experienced and pre-service teachers that have been presented you will have noted that there are both personal and professional challenges to be met in developing effective strategies. For instance, in welcoming and celebrating cultural diversity, there is a need to clarify one's personal values while appreciating the different values of others. In building caring and cooperative relationships it is vital to demonstrate caring and respect in one's own relationships with others while fostering similar skills in children. Promoting independence and a sense of responsibility in children challenges you to examine whether opportunities for choice and taking responsibility are available in all aspects of the daily programme not just in 'free choice' or 'free play' time. Similarly, engendering a sense of fairness, fostering problem solving and conflict resolution and guiding children's behaviour effectively takes time and effort and a commitment to a number of underlying moral principles. These principles require you to:

promote the good of others – by using effective measures to correct disruptive behaviour and promote self-control;

do no harm – by avoiding strategies that are punitive or humiliating and unnecessarily restrictive;

demonstrate justice – by treating families and children fairly and equally and balancing the rights and interests of one individual with those of the group;

intervene competently – by ensuring you are adequately trained, skilled in supervision and continue to learn from your experiences in behavioural intervention.

(Adapted from Porter, 2003: 5–6)

Maintaining a commitment to such principles may seem a little overwhelming as you set about creating socially secure environments for young children. Just remember, however, that big things grow from small beginnings. As you consider your actions and interactions ask yourself, 'What are the children learning from what I am doing, saying and being?' Above all, think about the many small ways in which you can show children that you value and respect them. This attention to the small things, together with consistency and a willingness to seize the teachable moment, will assist you in creating a caring community for your children.

SUGGESTED ACTIVITIES

- Select five children's books that in your view break gender role or cultural stereotypes. From your review of children's books develop a checklist that will help your selection so as to avoid stereotyping in the future. For example: males and females are engaged in similar activities; cooperation rather than competition is shown between the sexes.

- Write down ten strategies you could use in a childcare, preschool or lower primary setting that would convey to the children that you value and respect them.

- How would you organize transitions in order to send the message that you want children to be as independent as possible and that you trust them to take some responsibility for their actions? Outline some specific actions you would take.

- If you believe that it is important for children to have opportunities to make choices, how would you organize your environment to maximize choice? List and describe at least five things you would do.

- Reflect on a conflict situation you have observed between young children. Was it resolved in a fair way? Consider the steps you could take in future conflict situations to ensure that they are resolved in ways that are fair to all.
- Develop your own list of positive ways of handling difficult or inconsiderate behaviour. Keep adding to it as you read further, gain experience and observe skilled teachers in action. It will be a handy reference as you begin teaching.

Chapter 6

Becoming a teacher and a researcher of teaching

Because teaching is such a complex and challenging process with no 'best way' to teach young children, it requires that teachers actively involve themselves in the process of seeking solutions to the problems and issues that continually arise. This active involvement can be regarded 'as a form of *action research*' (Stremmel, 2002: 62).

In this chapter we will think about how you can engage in this form of teacher research during teaching practice. In particular, we will focus on methods that can assist you in:

- developing your own knowledge about teaching;
- acquiring and refining your practical skills
- using research to grow as a teacher.

DEVELOPING YOUR OWN KNOWLEDGE ABOUT TEACHING

An important aspect of becoming a teacher is to develop your own knowledge and theories about teaching. Although this may sound a difficult thing to do, you are more than likely developing your own theory without even being aware that you are. Whenever you talk with friends about teaching, reflect on your own school days, undertake readings and assignments and think about your observations and experiences of teaching, you are, in fact, building your own personal construct of what teaching is for you at that particular time. If you have shared your ideas about teaching with friends, you have probably discovered that your 'theories' vary from those of others. This is because you have not only had different personal experiences, but your thoughts about teaching and your perceptions of your experiences will have been influenced by your particular beliefs and values.

Developing your own theory of teaching is important, because it serves as a background against which you make decisions about the practical actions you can take. In fact, Handal and Lauvås (1987: 9) argue that it should be termed a 'practical theory' because it is 'the strongest determining factor in [a teacher's] educational practice'. It influences not only what you do but how you do it. It is important, then, that in developing your theories about teaching you develop your knowledge, not only of what teaching is, but also of how teaching can be undertaken. Some teachers refer to their theories and knowledge of teaching as their 'teaching approach'.

Don't feel too concerned if, at this stage, you are unable to write or talk about your teaching approach in a coherent way. Even experienced teachers have difficulty doing this. What you need to do, as a pre-service teacher, is to become more conscious of your thinking about teaching. You can develop your awareness of the nature of teaching in a number of ways during teaching practice. Think of it as teacher research – a form of *action research* in which you set out to develop your understanding and seek practical solutions to issues you may face (Stringer, 1999). Here are some methods you can use:

- Describe situations and ask questions about the teaching actions of your supervising teacher and yourself.
- Explore the reasons as to why you feel particular learning–teaching experiences were successful or otherwise.
- Challenge and extend your existing knowledge about teaching.
- Consider ethical issues associated with teaching.

Describing situations and asking questions about teaching actions

From your very first visit to an early childhood setting try to form a picture in your own mind of what is happening. Such a setting can seem confusing at first, with children and teachers continually on the move and engaging in a wide variety of activities. One starting point for building this picture is to write brief descriptions of particular situations. As you write these descriptions you will probably begin to ask questions about the teacher's actions and interactions with children. If you are able to participate and interact with children you can also ask questions about your own actions. At first you may find that you are focusing on the 'what' question. If you are writing descriptions of what the teacher did, or what you did and how the children responded, it is helpful to add the 'why' question. Why did the teacher act in a particular way, or why did the children respond in the way they did? The 'what', 'how', 'where', 'when' and 'why' type questions always provide useful prompts. These descriptions and questions will help you, not only to become more aware of what is happening, but also of what is likely to happen if you do certain things in a certain way. This awareness develops your ability to anticipate and predict, which is a fundamental aspect of teaching.

Tricia made progress in building her knowledge of teaching during her last teaching practice, when she looked closely at what her supervising teacher did when preparing and presenting a lesson and compared these observations with her own approach. Tricia wrote:

> During this prac in a Year 1 class I focused on what the teacher did. I noticed that the teacher seemed to have so many resources and ideas to draw on and I basically had nothing. I had many discussions with my teacher about this and she had many comments to make. Her main concern was that I seemed ill-prepared in the management part of teaching. And honestly I could see her point. During the first week of prac, before this discussion, I hadn't thought about the resources that were vital when I planned the experiences. They were such little things, like having a pen ready when I was about to mark the roll … or making sure there were enough crayons and scissors available for everyone. I just hadn't thought of having a box of tissues within easy reach … and making sure that I knew where the book was that I planned to read. The list went on and on and, as I started to consider all the little things, my stomach sank. What type of teacher would I be if a great deal of the valuable learning time was lost due to my incompetence?
>
> From then on I wrote every single resource down on my plan … from the scissors needed … to the glue for sticking the parts of the plant on to the poster. To my surprise these new plans ran like clock-work. Even though it took a little more organizing in the morning, I had everything there. When I have my own classroom it will be my responsibility to provide these resources and to know where everything is.

By researching why the teacher's lessons seemed to flow so much more smoothly than hers, Tricia discovered the value of preparation and organization. This became an important aspect of Tricia's teaching approach at this stage in her understanding of teaching.

Julie also began to ask questions about her own teaching actions in her very first teaching practice. She wrote:

> When I entered this course in teacher education I had very little idea of what a teacher did. During my first teaching practice I fell in love with

the notion of being a leader in a group of three- to four-year-old children who willingly built me tall towers out of blocks, painted pictures of their favourite thing, brought me flowers and looked cute in the dress-up clothes. The first activity I planned was balloon painting, because we had to plan and present an art activity as part of the teaching practice requirements. Although this was a lot of fun, I found it frustrating to have to tell a child what to do in order to 'succeed' in this activity. I continued to carry out my set, planned activities during prac, but I began to wonder what exactly teaching was. What was I doing when I sang a song with Lisa in time to her rhythm as she learned to push herself on the swing or went and got the hose when I saw that David and Luke had built a dam in the sandpit? Were just my planned set activities teaching – or were these spontaneous actions based on my observations part of teaching too?

Even at this early stage in her experience, Julie was beginning to identify some of her own values; namely, her preference for a child's own creative expression rather than conformity to an adult's view of success. She was also trying to figure out in her own mind what teaching is. Does teaching mean making the most of each moment – the planned and the unplanned? Can the unplanned, spontaneous responses or activities that result from a teacher's observation be regarded as teaching? These questions were very important ones for Julie in developing her understanding of teaching. She needed to do more research, however, and find answers to them. This is not an easy task. One way to approach it, though, is to consider the effects of these spontaneous teacher actions on children. If you can see that children's experiences are being enriched and their thinking challenged by such responses, it seems reasonable to regard these actions as an essential part of teaching.

Clarifying reasons for particular responses

Researching the reasons as to why particular learning experiences appear successful or otherwise is another useful means of building your knowledge of teaching. Graham found it helpful to think about why an experience that had begun in rather difficult circumstances worked so well. He wrote in his journal:

I had just set up the obstacle course outside this morning when it began to rain and I had to rush and bring the equipment on to the patio. Mrs G. said we would still break up into our small groups and, as I was

Plates 6.1 and 6.2 In discussing the problem posed by robbers taking things from the castle the teacher asked 'How do you think you could find the robbers?' The boys decided to draw and put up pictures so that others might identify the robbers. Would you say this was teaching in the context of play? (Photo courtesy of Kelvin Grove State College, Preschool Campus.)

to take the children at the obstacle course, I wasn't sure what to do. My eight children arrived on the patio and there I was with my jumble of boards, hoops, tunnel, trestles, mats, rope and balance beam. I told the children what had happened and suggested that they could help set up the obstacle course. They had some great ideas ... so many that they all wanted to talk at once. After we worked out that they each would be able to make a suggestion, we soon had a terrific 'course' with more obstacles than I had set. They worked out that they would need the mats under the higher boards 'so they wouldn't get hurt'. Some of the children who had difficulty explaining their ideas verbally were able to show the group what they meant by arranging the items themselves. Some of the ideas seemed rather dangerous so we talked about these and considered what might happen if ... The children were able to see and talk about the reasons for the concern and suggest some safe solutions. We spent so long setting up the course that the next group arrived after the children had only had one turn.

The second group was not nearly as interested in overcoming the obstacles as the first group had been. Observing the lesser involvement of the second group compared with the enthusiasm of the first group made me realize just how important it is for children to have some say in what they do and how they do it. I also realized that, in setting up the course, the children were talking with each other, solving problems and seeing something come from their ideas. I think they learned far more than they would have done if it hadn't rained!

In describing what had happened, Graham was able to identify the features of the experience that in his view provided worthwhile learning. His experience with the second group provided him with a basis for comparison in terms of children's responses, and enabled him to think about why there was such a difference in the degree of involvement. When I talked with Graham about this experience he indicated that, whenever possible in the future, he would try to empower children by encouraging them to express and share their ideas for what they could do. He also said that he had realized just how much the way a teacher does things affects the number and nature of the learning opportunities children have. It is this type of critical reflection or research that leads you to incorporate certain types of actions into your teaching approach.

Neridah discovered the value of clarifying the reasons why things can go wrong. She described her discoveries this way:

I felt confident entering the book area to prepare for the story. The children responded immediately to my initial attempt at seeking attention when I sang 'Hello everybody'. It was straight after this that the problems began. Cameron got up and wandered over to the book-shelf and picked up a book. When I asked him to come back and sit down he ignored me. I decided to ignore him, but, just as I started to introduce the story Samantha jumped up and said she wanted to do a puzzle. (I guess she thought if Cameron could get away with it she could too.) By the time I'd talked Samantha into sitting down, all the other children were restless. Even when I began the story I never really regained their attention. As I read the story, I realized that it wasn't all that interesting. I kept stopping and reminding different children to 'tuck up their legs' and 'keep their hands to themselves', but while I did this the other children totally lost interest and also became fidgety. A couple of times I just put the book down and waited for them to be quiet, but this had no effect either.

I hadn't dreamt this would happen so I hadn't prepared any strategies to deal with this situation. There I was in front of a group of preschoolers trying to make sense out of nothing! Interestingly, I didn't become frustrated. If I had, I might have been more direct with the children who needed it. So here I am writing an evaluation of a group time I hadn't sufficiently planned ... a major blunder! After a long discussion with my supervising teacher, who witnessed the whole disaster, I've come up with these ideas:

- establish my leadership role right from the beginning;
- settle the children and gain their attention with a song or clapping game;
- avoid pauses;
- state expectations clearly and expect responses;
- limit all possible distractions before beginning the story;
- if the story is not holding the children's interest be prepared to shorten it, or tell it in another way – by discussing pictures;
- if a child doesn't respond to a request, give a warning which contains a choice – 'If you are not going to sit on the mat with us and listen to the story you will have to sit on the chair near Mrs J.'s office. What are you going to choose to do?' If the child does not choose to sit with the group I must follow through on the consequence.

In thinking about the reasons for her lack of control, Neridah was able to clarify how she could have handled the situation more effectively. Researching the *how* of teaching is an important part of developing your practical knowledge. Knowing how to do something, however, doesn't necessarily mean that you are able to do it. You have to use that 'how to' knowledge in order to develop your practical skills. Neridah had a chance to do that the next time she took the group for a story.

> Following last week's disaster I tentatively entered the story area today. I mentally went through the strategies I might need to use during the session and sat down. The initial settling period went smoothly and I only needed to speak to Kia and Jay about remembering what they needed to do during storytime. The story about a teddy bear was one I knew would interest the children after our teddy bears' picnic, so it was relatively easy to maintain their interest. I put a lot of effort into the reading of it and involved the children in parts if their attention started to stray. I avoided long pauses and getting caught up talking to individual children. The children seemed to see me as being in control today, perhaps because I felt that I was.

Neridah's experience is a great example of the practical skills that can be developed if you are prepared to research why a situation was not successful and identify alternative strategies that are likely to be more successful. Although Neridah had read about group management skills and watched her supervising teacher manage the group, it was only after she experienced the situation herself that this previous knowledge began to be 'personalized' and incorporated into her own teaching approach. To be a skilful teacher you have to be a thinking teacher – a researcher. You also have to develop skill in putting your 'how to' knowledge into practice.

Challenging and extending your existing knowledge about teaching

Accepting that your existing knowledge about teaching is subject to challenge and possible change is one of the most difficult yet rewarding aspects of being a teacher. Challenging or extending your teaching knowledge requires you to search continually for new meanings and understanding, to consider them in the light of your existing knowledge and, perhaps, be prepared to change your views. For example, just as you feel you have come to understand what it means for children to 'learn through play' you may see a different teaching approach which presents some new ideas about the meaning of that term. Are you willing to think about these new ideas and perhaps incorporate them into your teaching approach, or are you going to say, 'No! I've just found out what "learning through play" means and I'm not prepared to consider any new notions about play at this stage'? This is a decision you have to make and there may be circumstances where you need to consolidate your thinking before taking on board some different ideas. Be aware, though, that if you frequently decide to ignore new information, you are in danger of having one teaching practice five times over rather than experiencing and benefiting from five teaching practices.

In an assignment focusing on play, Rhyll's reflections show how she was prepared to have her thinking challenged as she sought to understand 'play'. She wrote:

> I continue to search for answers to the question, 'Why is play so important to young children?' In seeking answers I was first confronted with the problem of what I meant by play. In an earlier assignment I defined play in terms of activities done for the enjoyment they give. I feel I have created a more complex picture of play since then. I now think of it as behaviour that has a number of characteristics. Play is intrinsically motivated, is free from externally imposed rules, has an 'as if' or pretend element, focuses on the means rather than the ends, and is controlled by the players who are actively involved (Bodrova and Leong, 1996). These characteristics provide me with a very different picture of play from the so-called play activities which teachers provide and expect children to undertake. I have seen these characteristics most in children's pretend play.
>
> During my last teaching practice in a preschool I was with a teacher who encouraged pretend play. I was fascinated by what I saw and heard. I recorded this conversation as Tim and Mike were preparing to go 'scuba diving'. Tim had finished making his air tank and was waiting for Mike to finish his. The teacher was helping Mike in this task.

> TIM to MIKE I might do a drawing while I'm waiting. (*He gets crayons and draws lines all over his paper.*)
>
> TEACHER to TIM and MIKE I wonder what the weather will be like for scuba diving?
>
> TIM to TEACHER I know what the weather's like 'cos I'm drawing what the weather map's like.
>
> TEACHER to TIM (*looking at map*) Goodness, that looks like bad weather.
>
> (*Tim keeps on drawing.*)
>
> TEACHER to TIM What does the weather map tell us?
>
> TIM to TEACHER Just look at it and you'll see.
>
> TEACHER to TIM It looks as though it will be a wild, rough sea. I don't think it will be safe enough to go down.

MIKE to TEACHER We'll just stay in the water by the shore.

TEACHER to TIM and MIKE Are you going to stay in the shallow part?

TIM to TEACHER Yes – and then we'll go round to the deep part.

TEACHER to TIM and MIKE Well look, the water currents are going this way. (*She draws arrows in a circle on Tim's drawing.*) They're going around and around and they're making the water very rough.

TIM to MIKE and TEACHER O-Oh! It's going to be a whirlpool and we'll go here. (*He marks a spot in the circle on the map.*) Right there.

TEACHER to TIM and MIKE Look, I don't think you'd live if you went in there. I think you'd drown.

TIM to TEACHER No, we can swim out of them.

TEACHER to TIM No. Whirlpools are very dangerous.

TIM to TEACHER On Boris [*a television show*] these baddies got blasted out of a whirlpool in his rocket.

TEACHER to TIM But that's not possible for you because you're not in a rocket.

TIM to TEACHER But our boat can turn into a rocket.

TEACHER to TIM But all you've got are your air tanks.

TIM to TEACHER And our boat!

As I thought about this conversation, some of the benefits of pretend play became very obvious to me. Tim and Mike were representing their ideas in a variety of forms – through constructing air tanks, drawing a map, as well as expressing their ideas verbally. They were accessing their 'scripts' of scuba diving, and prior knowledge of oceans, weather maps and television shows, and were being challenged by the teacher to assimilate information into their scripts and adapt them to make sense of new information. They were being challenged to imagine consequences and come up with solutions to possible problems even before their pretend game had begun.

As time has progressed, I have become more convinced about the benefits of this type of play. I have also had to think more about the teacher's role in play. The notion of 'scaffolding', as proposed by Bruner (1986) and Vygotsky (Bodrova and Leong, 1996) which highlights the idea that a child's existing knowledge base forms a framework from which new knowledge may be learned has been helpful. I have come to view part of the teacher's role as helping children to tap into their existing knowledge and supporting them in building on this knowledge. I have also come to see that this can be done in the context of children's play as the teacher was doing with Tim and Mike. Although my thinking concerning the role of an early childhood teacher has only just begun, my present hope is that I will help children build personal meaning and understanding as they engage in play and express their own ideas. It is from this base that I believe they will come to understand the wider world, and it is for these reasons that I have come to see the value of play.

From these comments it would seem that Rhyll actively sought to challenge and extend her own thinking and understanding. In moving towards a deeper understanding of play, Rhyll had been influenced by some particular theoretical notions derived from her readings, as well as by her observations of practice. As a consequence of her research into play, Rhyll was also thinking further about her role as a teacher and beginning to articulate her approach to teaching more clearly.

Considering ethical issues associated with teaching

In considering ethical issues associated with teaching you will ask yourself questions relating to the right and proper ways to conduct yourself when teaching. Although the early childhood teaching profession in a number of countries has developed codes of ethics which are helpful in providing guidelines in this regard, occasions arise in daily teaching experiences which require a teacher to make a personal decision concerning how a particular situation will be handled (Berlak and Berlak, 1981; Stonehouse,1998). Often the decision revolves around the teacher's use of power in relation to a child. David witnessed such an incident during a practicum which he found particularly disturbing and which led him to think deeply about the ethical issues involved. He wrote:

> One morning before class my supervising teacher realized that there was money missing from his desk. (The class had recently been fund-raising for an excursion.) He suspected two children who had stolen money previously and called them up to the classroom. One of the children, Darren, was taken inside while the other was told to wait outside. The teacher talked to Darren, and asked him if he knew anything about the missing money. Darren said that he didn't. The teacher, however, said that he knew Darren had taken the money because Byron, the child waiting outside, had told him he had. Darren began to cry and insisted that he had not taken the money. The teacher then talked to Byron, telling him that Darren had told him that he, Byron,

had stolen the money. This upset Byron, who became very angry and insisted that he had not taken the money. The teacher then talked to both children telling them they were thieves and that they should own up to their mistake. Later that afternoon the teacher found the missing money under a pile of books on his desk. He did not say anything to the children.

This incident upset me terribly and made me reconsider the teacher's role. To me the role of the teacher is to provide children with new knowledge and understanding and to provide support for children in this process. In my view the teacher did not provide support for children in this incident. He jumped to conclusions and assumed the two boys were involved in stealing again. I believe that children should not be continually punished for past misbehaviours and should always be given the benefit of the doubt. The way in which the incident was handled caused anger between the teacher and the boys and between the boys themselves. The boys refused to be near each other for the rest of the day and this tension between them continued for the remainder of my prac.

I have learned what not to do from this experience. I have realized that teachers are human and make mistakes, but that it is important that when we do make mistakes we apologize for them. In this case an apology was definitely needed. The children needed to know, and had a right to know, that the money had been found and that they were no longer accused of stealing. I believe this would have lessened the anger.

I have thought about how I would handle such a situation. I think I would talk to the whole class and discuss the problem with all the children. I would talk about how other people are affected when money is stolen. I definitely would not accuse anyone of stealing unless I had witnessed something myself, and I certainly would not lie to children. It was obvious that the two boys were very hurt by the thought that their friend would say such things about them. Having seen the appalling effects of a teacher's unethical and unprofessional conduct I will always try to act ethically.

While it is unlikely that you will witness the type of unethical behaviour that David did because teachers' high standards of professionalism make these types of instances rare, it is useful to reflect on David's experience. This is because, in building your teaching approach, you need not only to understand reasons for actions based on theory and observations of practice, but you also need to be able to justify your actions on moral and ethical grounds. In examining his supervising teacher's behaviour in this instance,

David highlighted behaviours that appeared to break an accepted moral code. These behaviours included making accusations without evidence, falsifying the situation, failing to admit his own error and to apologize for perpetrating a hurtful act without justification. While such an incident clearly demonstrates a gross misuse of adult power, you need to be aware that many other 'smaller' incidents can occur which may be counter to an accepted moral code. Issues relating to justice and fairness, labelling children and suspected abuse, for example, can challenge you to deal with some difficult ethical dilemmas.

From reading of the experiences of other pre-service teachers and reflecting on their research it is hoped that you will have gained some ideas for the way in which you can set about enlarging your own knowledge of teaching and formulating what your approach to teaching will be. As your experience and knowledge of teaching increases you will gain deeper insights from your research. As Ros said: 'When I look at the observations I made in first year I'm embarrassed at how little I seemed to see ... and yet at the time I felt I'd made detailed observations.' It is important to note, though, that while you may develop quite a sophisticated knowledge of the 'what' and 'how to' of teaching, unless you use that knowledge in practical ways and develop your practical teaching skills it will be of little value to you in teaching situations.

ACQUIRING AND REFINING YOUR PRACTICAL SKILLS

What comes to mind when you hear the term 'practical teaching skills'? Some pre-service teachers I asked saw practical teaching skills in terms of 'how to'. They gave as examples: how to take a group for story or music; teach a language or maths lesson; help the toddler group make the transition from play time to lunch time; and talk with children in ways that challenge their thinking. Others, while agreeing that these were important practical skills, wanted to add different types of skills. These included knowing when and how to intervene, and deciding what to do in a particular situation. Felicity gave as an example an incident in which two boys were struggling over who would have the use of the one reel of masking tape in the dispenser on the making table. She said, 'I sat there and watched them and I thought, 'Should I say something, and if I do, what will I say?' She said she spent so much time thinking about the situation that by the time she'd decided she would say something the moment had passed. For Felicity, knowing when and how to intervene was an important practical teaching skill that she wanted to develop. Similarly, Katrina said she wanted skills for managing situations where three or four children wanted her attention at the one time.

There are many ways in which practical skills can be developed. For instance, you can read about and then practise applying particular teaching techniques such as open-ended questioning, modelling, positive reinforcement, and directive and non-directive statements (MacNaughton, 2003). You can undertake a micro teaching course and have your teaching videotaped so that you can evaluate your skills and have others comment on and discuss your teaching, and you can observe an experienced teacher in action and try to emulate that teacher's actions. Each of these methods can help you become more skilful in particular teaching techniques.

Having a high degree of practical skill in teaching, however, demands more than just having a number of specific practical techniques at your fingertips. It requires you to 'read' situations, to make decisions and to act or respond in the most appropriate ways in order to promote learning. If these teaching decisions and actions are to be consistent, meaningful for individual children and relevant to particular situations, then you cannot rely on an isolated skill or technical proficiency. You must draw on your broader knowledge of teaching and learning. Developing this higher level of teaching skill is a gradual process that comes through critically reflecting on your experiences. A few experiences shared by pre-service teachers may

Plate 6.3 Knowing when and how to intervene is an important practical skill. (Photo courtesy of Northgate State Preschool.)

help you get a feel for this process. Their stories illustrate ways in which you can research and refine teaching actions.

Coping with numerous demands simultaneously

When I visited Katrina during her teaching practice she told me that she was feeling very pressured at times. She said:

> I feel I need to be with every child who wants my attention. This morning Ben wanted to make his sandwich for the picnic, Caitlin wanted me to be in their hospital, and Alex came up with his stickle bricks and wanted me to see the building he had made. I knew it was important for each of them that I focus on their needs. I've found that I have to make very quick shifts in my thinking so that I can respond to each of them.

When I asked Katrina how she decided to take the action that she did, she said:

> Well ... it helps that I know the children, and being aware of how they respond helps me decide what I'll do ... like Ben needs my immediate attention as he just can't wait, while Caitlin and Alex can cope with a little wait. So I knew I had to stay with the sandwich making with Ben ... and I told Caitlin that I had to make the sandwiches for the picnic then, but that I would ring her later at the hospital to make an appointment. And I was able to talk to Alex about his building while I helped Ben with his sandwich.
>
> I was wondering whether I was right to give Ben priority just because he was the most likely to make a fuss. When I talked with my teacher about this she said these children should learn that sometimes other children need your attention first. I think it would take Ben a while to develop that understanding, but one of these days I might try saying, 'Ben, I do want to be with you while you make your sandwich but Caitlin needs me in the hospital at the moment. I'll be here in the hospital for a little while and then I'll get the butter so you can make the sandwich.' ... I think I'd have to pick the right moment, though, for Ben to accept that.

In deciding on her course of action Katrina was influenced by her knowledge that it was important to value and attend to each child. On the other hand, she had to deal with the practicalities of the situation. She did this by using her knowledge of each child's behaviour in making her decision about how she would act. Even though her teaching action appeared to be effective, Katrina was questioning whether it was right for Ben always to receive her immediate attention. Again she was using her theoretical knowledge as a framework against which to consider and refine her teaching actions.

Clarifying teaching actions by reflection

Felicity discovered that she could draw on her knowledge of teaching in deciding how to act, although previously she had avoided taking any action at all. As indicated in her example of the tussle between two boys over the use of the one reel of masking tape, Felicity had great difficulty in deciding whether or not to intervene in such situations. As we talked about incidents like this, Felicity indicated that she often felt she should intervene but didn't because she did not know what to say. In discussing this further Felicity agreed that, in relation to such situations, she needed to work out what she could say and why. Together we devised some questions that could guide her research, and help her decide on a particular teaching action. These questions were:

• What is my goal for this situation?
• What can I say or do that will help achieve this goal?
• How can I evaluate whether or not my teaching action was successful?

After some reflection Felicity decided that, in relation to the masking-tape incident, her goals could have been to get the boys to talk about their problem and try to come up with a fair solution. She decided that she could have intervened during the tussle by saying, 'There seems to be a problem here ...' and then asking the children individually what they saw the problem to be. Felicity saw this as a means of getting them to verbalize and accept the problem before asking them for ideas that might 'fix' the problem in a fair manner. She thought she could evaluate this teaching action in a number of ways: by the boys' willingness to discuss the problem and to come up with some ideas; the extent to which the ideas were fair; and the actual way in which the situation was resolved.

Even though this research occurred after the situation had passed, Felicity said that, having thought through a teaching action, she felt more confident to try it in a similar situation in the future. She also indicated that she was surprised to find that she could draw on her own knowledge, that she had this knowledge tucked away. Now that she knew this knowledge was there Felicity intimated that she might be more confident to step in and say or do something spontaneously if the need arose and reflect on those actions afterwards. Felicity said: 'I haven't done that before because I thought I might have too many negative experiences to reflect on at the end of the day!' Doing your own thinking and drawing on your knowledge of teaching not only helps you to develop your practical teaching skills, it can also give you confidence.

USING RESEARCH TO GROW AS A TEACHER

In this chapter we have considered the type of teacher research that is done individually or in discussion with another and uses mainly methods of observation and reflection. Reflection in this context can be defined as:

> … looking back on experience in a way that informs practice, learning in the midst of practice, and/or making informed decisions about what to do, when to do it, and why it should be done.
>
> (Jay, 2003: 14)

Many teachers see this type of research as a part of their everyday work. It is sometimes called practical enquiry, with practical knowledge of teaching being constructed through reflection (Schön, 1983, 1987; Stremmel, 2002). There are other types of teacher research – conceptual and empirical – that are done more systematically and on a larger scale. This type of research can also be a source of valuable information for teaching. No matter what form teacher research takes it is important that it is of practical benefit to teachers.

Some years ago I had an opportunity to instigate a research project that sought to compare two different approaches to teaching – the activity-based approach and the event-based approach – and to consider their effects on young children and the implications for teachers (Perry, 1988; 1995). The research was undertaken in a double unit preschool, catering for four- to five-year-olds. Although the teacher in each approach believed that the learning experiences provided should foster the children's active participation and be related to their interests, there was clearly a difference in the extent of child initiation and negotiation in the curriculum. The activity-based approach emphasized teacher-initiated activities, whilst the event-based approach fostered child-initiated play, supported by and negotiated with the teacher in which children re-created 'events' that were meaningful to them. The extent of teacher direction in the activity-based approach and child initiation in the other, and their consequences in terms of opportunities for learning, was revealed in many facets of the programme. Here is just one example.

I happened to be observing in the centre in the week in which the local fire brigade had agreed to visit as a follow-up to the children's interests in firefighting. I was fascinated to observe the different ways in which these two preschool teachers went about preparing the children for the visit, as well as the way in which the visit was followed up. Here are some of my observations:

> Cathy, the teacher in Unit One, told the children at the morning discussion group that the fire brigade was going to visit their preschool on Tuesday. The children seemed interested and John asked if they would bring their fire engine. The teacher said they would, and then proceeded to show the children some pictures of firefighters (all men) in action that she had previously selected. She asked the children what they could see happening in the pictures, and some of the children replied with the obvious answers, 'They're putting out the fire,' 'He's holding the hose,' 'They're wearing their helmets.' The teacher looked pleased when they gave their 'right' answers and often repeated what a child had said ... 'Yes, they're putting out the fire.' There was no further questioning once an answer had been given. After they had looked at the six pictures Cathy said she would put the pictures up on the wall so they could have a closer look at them later in the day. She then said she was going to read them a story about firefighters. The story was somewhat dated and stereotyped, with stylized illustrations of old-time fire engines. The children seemed interested, however, and listened attentively. There was no further discussion at the end of the story and I didn't hear any more comments from the children about the visit during their play, although I noticed two children individually pause to take a closer look at the pictures the teacher had pinned on the wall.

What are your initial reactions to such observations? In reflecting on the teacher's actions I thought here was a teacher who was well-organized, having the pictures and story ready, and who was keen to prepare the children for the visit by giving them information about what firefighters do and the equipment they use. I did wonder what the children got from the discussion. Did they discover anything they didn't already know? I wondered, too, about whether the outdated story and illustrations could have reinforced stereotypes and caused confusion in relation to the children's own knowledge of fire engines. The children had, however, appeared very focused as they listened to the story. When I talked briefly with the teacher about this session she said she had wanted to give the children some specific information about firefighting and that by 'discussing' the pictures, all the children had an opportunity to be involved. Overall, I thought this discussion and story time was like many I had taken and had seen other teachers take. I had cause for much more thought, however, when I saw how the teacher in Unit Two introduced the visit.

> Joan, the teacher in Unit Two, also told the children about the forthcoming visit of the fire brigade at the group discussion. The children were impressed. Timothy said, 'Wow! That's exciting,' and David asked, 'Will they show us the siren?' The group discussed David's question and decided that they would. The teacher said, 'I wonder what the firefighters will bring with them?' With that leading question, the discussion took off. The children suggested all kinds of possibilities ... 'hoses', 'their helmets', 'their axes' (what did they need those for?) 'their radios'. ... They also wondered about what they would wear and why firefighters needed to wear different clothes when they were fighting fires. Nearly all the children in the group contributed either a suggestion or comment to the discussion and each child's idea was listened to and treated with respect. Sometimes the teacher had to ensure that an idea was heard by saying, 'That's an interesting thought, Naomi. Did you all hear what Naomi suggested?' There were a number of 'I wonders' left hanging, with the teacher suggesting, 'We'll have to especially look for that,' or 'That's an interesting question. You'll need to ask the firefighter about that.' At lunch I heard a few children continuing to discuss the visit, with David saying, ' I hope they let us sit up the front in the engine part' and Martin replying that he didn't think they would.

What do you see as some of the main differences between Cathy's and Joan's approach in this introductory session? From my observations Joan seemed keen to build on the children's knowledge, but she needed to discover what knowledge they had first. A few key 'wonderings' concerning what the firefighters would bring and wear were sufficient to spark the children's thinking so that they began to access and contribute their own knowledge of firefighting. They seemed more actively involved than the children in the other Unit. I found it interesting that, at this stage, Joan did not seek to give information through pictures or reading a story. Instead she sought to establish what the children knew and what they wanted to find out. When I spoke briefly with Joan concerning her goals for this introductory session, she said that she wanted the children to do their own thinking about firefighting, to share what knowledge they had and to hear what ideas the other children might have. She also said that this type of discussion gave her glimpses of individual children's ways of thinking and understanding.

Would you agree that, at this point, there seemed to be some fundamental differences between these two teaching approaches? Cathy wanted to give the children information and Joan wanted the children to realize what they already knew, what they wanted to know, and how they could find out. I was not at the preschool the day the fire brigade visited, but I did observe the follow-up discussions on the day after the visit. The different ways in which these discussions were handled provided more challenges to my thinking.

> Cathy began the discussion with her group by saying, 'Well, did you enjoy the firefighters' visit yesterday?' All the children chorused 'Yes'. Cathy then said, 'David, what did you like best about the visit?' David replied that he'd liked the siren. Cathy said, 'Yes, I liked that too. Mark, what did you like?' All the children in the group were asked individually what they had liked and most came up with three- or four-word answers. ... 'I liked their helmets,' 'the hoses', 'their radio thing'. There was a deal of repetition as some children reiterated what others had said and there was no discussion or elaboration on the children's likes. It was a question-and-answer situation which ended with the teacher saying, 'Well, you might like to pretend you're firefighters during inside time today.' Cathy then explained the other activities that were available.

In contrast, the discussion in Joan's Unit was a real sharing of what both the teacher and the children had learned and had found interesting.

> Joan began the discussion by saying, 'Well, I learned lots of new things about firefighters yesterday. I didn't know that they sometimes wear masks, did you?' Nicholas said, 'Yeah, I did. But the mask felt funny when I put it on.' Joan responded, 'Did it? What did it feel like, Nicholas?' Nicholas searched for words, 'Well ... it felt ... all over my face.' There were many spontaneous comments. 'I liked ... sitting high up in the front part ... holding the hose ... seeing the axe ... the badge on the coat ...', with children being encouraged to express why they had liked particular aspects. During the discussion the teacher introduced some books and pictures which were used as a basis for comparison. Joan would say, 'In the picture the fire engine has the hose stored on the side here. Is that where the hose was on our fire engine?' 'This seems to be a different type of siren. What's different about this siren, from the one we saw?' The children quickly became engrossed in

pointing out similarities and differences, debating the finer points, not only with the teacher but also with each other. At the conclusion of the discussion when the children were talking about their games for inside time, several indicated that they were going to be firefighters. Joan discussed with them where they were going to build their fire engines and what materials they might need.

As I reflected on these two follow-up discussions I realized that they had provided very different experiences for the children in each Unit. Cathy's children certainly got to state their likes and hear other children's likes, but what other opportunities for learning were there? The question-and-answer format of the session afforded no opportunities for the children to express the reasons for their preferences or to share their wonderings. From being able to observe these two different approaches I came to realize how important it is for teachers to question critically whether their actions are achieving their goals. I recalled that when I was teaching, like Cathy, I had sincerely believed children should be actively involved in their own learning. Because I had led discussions in a way similar to Cathy's, however, I had probably kept the children's participation to a superficial level. It was only as I had the opportunity to observe and think about Joan's approach that I came to see a 'better' way of leading a discussion.

In Joan's Unit the children were able to build on their previous knowledge of firefighters. Because the introductory session had helped the children to organize their own thinking and to feel confident in their role as learners and questioners they were prepared to ask the firefighters questions and discover new knowledge. This excitement, which stemmed from these discoveries, was shared by the teacher and the children in the follow-up session as they communicated their thoughts and feelings. The introduction of the pictures after the children had clarified their own knowledge seemed to provide a further stimulus for discussion, encouraging children to make more connections as well as to search for similarities and differences. The building of the fire engines and the pretend play fire 'events' that followed reflected their awareness of detail and a clear understanding of the firefighters' role.

In trying to clarify why Joan's approach so appealed to me, an immediate reaction was to state my reasons in terms of the children's more active participation, the sharing and organization of their existing knowledge and their delight in the discovery of new knowledge. The observations seemed to provide 'evidence' of effective teaching and learning. As I thought about my reasons some more, however, I realized that my view of the 'evidence' was also being influenced by theoretical understandings of the benefits of promoting multiple learnings – assisting children to learn three or four things at the same time (Fortson and Reiff, 1995). Joan was not only furthering the children's knowledge about firefighting but also doing it in ways that enabled children to:

- communicate their own thoughts and feelings;
- make discoveries about what they did or did not know;
- work out ways to ask questions and gather more information;
- feel confident in their role as learners and questioners;
- share the excitement of making new discoveries;
- search for similarities and differences.

All these learnings were contributing to the broader competencies necessary for successful living. From my theoretical knowledge I recognized that today's children – tomorrow's adults – will not only require content knowledge but they also will need to have 'cope-ability', and to be flexible, resourceful, enquiring and responsible (Toffler, 1974). This theoretical knowledge, then, indicated the importance of teaching competencies that provide the foundations for success throughout life while at the same time teaching specific information. In thinking about the process that helped me decide why Joan's teaching approach so appealed to me, I was analysing the observed 'practice' and the children's responses and considering them in the light of my theoretical understanding. This type of research process led me to reconsider teaching strategies for leading discussion groups and building on children's knowledge. It was a process that challenged me to change and grow as a teacher.

I have shared those observations and that research process with many groups of experienced and pre-service teachers and from the comments that have followed, in some instances years later, I have realized the impact such research can have on practice.

SUMMARY

In thinking of yourself as a teacher and a researcher and undertaking research into your own teaching you will expand your practical knowledge of teaching. This chapter has highlighted a number of ways in which you can further your understanding of the 'what' and 'how to' of teaching. These include:

- asking questions about your own teaching actions;
- clarifying reasons for the particular responses of children to your actions;

- being prepared to challenge and extend your existing knowledge about teaching at a practical and theoretical level;
- considering ethical issues associated with teaching.

Although becoming skilled in particular teaching techniques such as questioning, modelling and positive reinforcement is important, teaching demands more than technical skills. It requires you to 'read' situations and make decisions that enable you to use the most appropriate strategies for individual children in particular situations. In order to make these types of decisions you must draw on your knowledge of the 'what' and 'how to' of teaching – on your practical knowledge.

It is important that you begin to think of yourself as a teacher and a researcher even as you undertake your teaching practice. This is because teacher research is, as Stremmel (2002: 69) argues, 'liberating and empowering'. It allows teachers to 'take their lives as teachers seriously, to generate knowledge and understanding that can improve teaching and create a more democratic and equitable community.' By making this research an integral part of your teaching you will also be giving yourself '... the possibility of transformation and renewal' throughout your teaching career.

SUGGESTED ACTIVITIES

- Describe some actions you have seen teachers take that for you exemplifies 'good teaching'. Analyse these actions and identify the aspects that make them appear to be 'good' teaching in your view.
- Select a topic related to teaching which is of particular interest to you (for instance, helping children problem solve; resolving conflict; bullying; the teacher's role in play; developing number concepts; emergent literacy). Prior to teaching practice undertake readings on the topic, and during teaching practice take every opportunity to observe, and extend your knowledge and experience in relation to it. After teaching practice, summarize what you have learned concerning the topic and indicate how your teaching practices have changed as a result of your new knowledge.
- Recall an ethical dilemma that you have experienced, or alternatively, an ethical dilemma you perceive or have heard talked about. Consider the factors that are contributing to the dilemma and write down possible ways of handling the situation including the people from whom you could seek advice.

- Describe a particular teaching strategy you use (for example, the way you settle a group, read a story, encourage problem solving). Observe another teacher's handling of a similar situation or talk with your peers about their particular strategies. Critically reflect on what you do in the light of these observations or discussions as well as your theoretical knowledge. Decide whether or not you want to make changes to your teaching strategy and give reasons for your decision.
- What are some of the most important aspects of your approach to teaching? Spend some time writing them down and then outline them to a friend and in the process explain why they are important to you.
- Identify an aspect of your own teaching that you would like to research during your next teaching practice. Consider and list your aims for this research and the methods you will use.

Chapter 7

Gaining the most from the teaching practice experience

In this chapter we will consider a number of actions you can take that will assist you to gain the most from your teaching practice experiences, as well as prepare you to begin your first year of teaching. These actions include:

- building effective working relationships (e.g. with your supervising teacher);
- getting to know the organizational structures, roles and relationships;
- promoting partnerships with families;
- setting personal goals;
- developing professionalism.

BUILDING EFFECTIVE WORKING RELATIONSHIPS

Because teaching is a collaborative process, teachers are required to develop and maintain effective working relationships with colleagues, families, volunteers and other professionals associated with their school or centre, as well as with the children. Teaching practice gives you the opportunity to observe these relationships in action and enables you to become familiar with the organizational structure of a variety of settings. This structure has a bearing on working relationships as particular people will occupy particular positions to which expectations are attached. The principal or director, for example, is expected to provide overall leadership, while aides or assistants support classroom teachers. Beside this more *formal* organizational structure there is also a more *informal* network of social relationships developed by staff, regardless of their positions, as they chat in the staff room, exchange 'news' in the corridors or participate in school activities. Becoming aware of both the formal and informal organizational structures of your practice teaching setting will help you to understand better the nature of the relationships and the factors that contribute to their effectiveness.

Teaching practice gives you the opportunity to gain skill in developing your own effective working relationships. For instance, it is important that you establish a positive relationship with your supervising teacher. Depending on the type of setting you are in, there may also be opportunities for you to establish collaborative relationships with an aide or other members of staff. Although your supervising teacher will be as keen as you are to develop an effective relationship, other staff members may not have the time to be as collaborative as they may wish. If the teaching practice is short, be realistic about the type of relationships that can be established in a limited time. Sometimes, in some teaching practice situations, you have to be content to observe 'relationships' from the sidelines. You can learn a lot from such observations, just as you can learn about building professional relationships in general, from developing your relationship with your supervising teacher.

Wondering how you will 'get on' with your supervising teacher is likely to be uppermost in your mind as you make your initial contact with staff in the centre where you will undertake your teaching practice. Often that first meeting is the hardest hurdle to overcome. Sarah described her experience this way:

> The memory of my first visit to the school where I was to do my final teaching practice will linger throughout my teaching career. Those moments of introducing myself to the Deputy Principal, administration staff and supervising teacher seemed to last forever. My mind charged ahead of me as I tried to envisage what might happen next, what people might say and how I could respond in a professional way. I so wanted to be seen as a keen, industrious and pleasant student.
>
> I had thought about what I wanted to learn during this prac. I needed to sift through my developing knowledge base and apply the strategies in practice that looked so good in my assignments. I wanted to reflect on my own philosophies of teaching, be able to take risks, experiment with ideas and explore personal ideologies about children and learning. I also wanted to interact more with other staff members, to learn about their experiences, feelings and attitudes and gain some helpful advice. I felt ready to involve myself in extra-curricular activities so I said 'Yes' when these opportunities were offered, and agreed to umpire school netball, attend school meetings and assist in the organization of the cross country race.

The importance of communication in building relationships

Sarah had prepared for her initial visit by thinking about the image of herself as a student teacher that she wanted to communicate. She had also clarified what she hoped to gain from her teaching practice and was able to share these goals with her teacher. Fortunately for Sarah, her supervising teacher was happy to support her in working towards her goals.

The relationship Sarah and her supervising teacher built was a very positive one. There appear to be a number of factors that contributed to its development:

- they each were aware of the importance of clear communication;
- they prepared for the teaching practice by clarifying their own expectations and possible actions;
- they shared common goals;
- they each expressed ideas as to how these goals might be achieved;
- they respected each other's contribution to the relationship (e.g., the teacher respected Sarah's keen attitude and her willingness to take on challenges, while Sarah appreciated the teacher's confidence and trust in her abilities and the opportunities to make her own discoveries).

Because pre-service teachers and supervising teachers have different personalities and communicative abilities and experience so many differing needs and pressures, the student–supervising teacher relationship does not always develop effectively. Sometimes your supervising teacher may perceive a particular problem or weakness, or you may feel that your teacher's expectations or demands are unreasonable. Although when looked at objectively it seems that it should be relatively easy to talk with each other about these problems, in practice it is quite difficult. It is useful to think about why this is, because by understanding the reasons for the difficulty, you will be in a better position to overcome it.

Sometimes, even though you may sense there is a problem it is hard to identify what the problem is. Even when you are able to clarify the nature of the problem, it is not always easy to admit your part in it to yourself, let alone to another person. This is because we tend to look at problems in terms of 'failures' rather than seeing them as a means of learning. Even some supervising teachers find it difficult to talk about students' problems because they see themselves 'failing' to help the student. Frequently, discussion of the difficulties gets left until a third person, such as the principal or director, intervenes or the liaison teacher visits. Probably because this third person is outside the working relationship, both teacher and student find it easier to discuss their concerns with this outside person. I recently experienced this type of discussion with two supervising teachers, who, in talking about the progress of their students, also expressed some concerns. For example:

- Miss T. said that Dale seemed to ignore her suggestions for planning a lesson.
- Mrs S. indicated that Angela managed time poorly – the children's time and her own.

When I spoke with Dale and Angela about the particular issue their supervising teacher had raised, they agreed that a problem did exist. I was fascinated to discover that in talking about the problem with me, each could see possible ways of working through the problem or of resolving it. Neither of them, however, had discussed these possible solutions with their supervising teacher. For instance, Dale said:

> I know Miss T. thinks I'm not taking notice of what she says when she tells me how to plan a lesson, but honestly ... I don't know what she's talking about half the time. There's so many things she says I should do ... my mind just shuts off. She keeps mentioning these words ... like 'orientating' and 'enhancing phases of the lesson' ... and because she thinks I know their meaning, I'm not game to ask her what she means. If she'd just focus on one or two things I should do each lesson ... I think I could cope with that ... or if she gave me a sample lesson plan ... that might help.

As we talked further, it was evident that Dale's supervising teacher expected her to plan her lessons in a particular way and to incorporate more into her lessons than Dale felt able to do. Her supervising teacher didn't ask Dale how she felt about what was being asked of her, and Dale felt unable to say she didn't understand or could only deal with a certain amount at one time. Because of this lack of communication, frustrations built for both Dale and her teacher. There was an obvious need for Dale to be more honest in communicating to her teacher about what she did and did not understand. We talked about how Dale could do this through her use of 'I' messages (Gordon, 1974), which would indicate to her teacher that she recognized it as *her* problem. We also discussed some possible 'I' messages she could use (for example, 'I don't understand some of the terms you use to describe the lesson phases. Could you explain them to me please?' 'I'm having difficulty including all the things you ask me to do in my lesson plan. For tomorrow, could I focus on just two of the aspects you've suggested?') Dale agreed to try this approach and later told me that, although she felt she still had not met the teacher's expectations, her more honest approach in communicating her difficulties had helped them to develop a more effective working relationship.

Angela, in talking about her difficulty in managing time, indicated that this had always been a problem for her. She said:

> All my life I've had trouble with time. I sit down to write my plans as soon as I get home ... and they just take me hours. I must spend a lot of time just thinking because I don't have that much on paper to show for it. Then, even though I plan a lesson carefully, when I actually give it, I find that something I thought would take ten minutes has only taken three, or something I thought the children would do quickly takes them ages. So I'm either finished way before the bell is due to go, or the children are just getting involved when it's lunch time. I know Mrs S. doesn't think I'm a very good organizer, and I can see why. I'm trying to plan extra activities so I've got something prepared if we finish early but I'm not sure how I can stop running over time.

We talked about the possibility of Angela asking Mrs S. to look at her plans and help her estimate more accurately the time needed for particular activities. At the conclusion of her teaching practice Angela told me she did this, and that Mrs S. had been very helpful. She said:

> Once I broke the ice we had some very helpful discussions ... and she gave me a lot of useful information. She even had some suggestions for managing my own time when planning ... like giving myself ten minutes to come up with three outcomes and strategies for a particular lesson.

From these discussions with pre-service teachers about the concerns raised by their supervising teachers, a number of aspects relating to the nature of verbal communication necessary in building effective relationships emerge. They provide some helpful guidelines for communicating in ways that will help you build your relationship with your supervising teacher.

- *Be open and honest in sharing your own thinking or perceptions of situations.* If you don't understand what is being said or asked of you, use 'I' messages to clarify meanings and expectations, or to indicate what you feel you can do.

- *Be prepared to talk about the realities or difficulties of your situation.* Provided that you do not use your difficulties to make excuses, talking about them will help your supervising teacher better understand what you are facing. Often, when difficulties are shared, they are more easily overcome because two heads are better than one in finding solutions.
- *Seek specific information and guidance whenever possible.* The more specific you can be in asking a question or seeking information, the more likely it is that you will receive a relevant and meaningful answer. Remember, too, that once you have broken the ice by asking a question or seeking advice, the easier and more natural this process becomes.

The importance of positive attitudes in building relationships

In some instances negative attitudes or emotions that have not been dealt with can be the cause of difficulties in developing effective student–supervising teacher relationships. This proved to be the case for Diane and Karley. Diane's teacher was concerned that Diane stood back and did not interact easily with preschool children, while Karley's teacher told me that Karley seemed to freeze in some situations, so that children quickly became out of control.

When I talked with Diane about her teacher's concern over her lack of involvement with the children, Diane said that she was feeling overwhelmed, not only by her first experience of teaching practice, but also because of some personal problems. She said:

> I moved out of home last week into a flat with some friends. I've never lived away from home before and I've had to get my furniture organized and ... I've been so busy thinking about all those things I'm having difficulty focusing on prac ... and anyway, I'm not really sure that I want to be an early childhood teacher. I can see my teacher is committed to what she does. When I came to this preschool I realized just how much a teacher has to do ... like be friends with parents ... be aware of home backgrounds. You must get a lot from doing that ... and that's the kind of job I *think* I want ... but I'm just not sure.

Diane was discovering that it is difficult to give your best effort to teaching practice when you are coping with personal problems. For Diane her personal difficulties were compounded by her uncertainty about whether or not she wanted to be a teacher. She was dealing with so many personal emotions that she was unable to focus on her teaching practice responsibilities and remained uninvolved. As we talked, Diane came to the view that, although sharing all her personal problems with her supervising teacher would be inappropriate, it was only fair that her supervising teacher should know something of her difficulties and her uncertainties about being a teacher. She felt this would help her teacher understand her lack of emotional commitment. She also wanted her supervising teacher to know that the difficulties preventing the development of a working relationship were not of the teacher's making. I don't know whether or not Diane shared her difficulties with her supervising teacher, but I learned later that she had deferred her teaching practice and was talking with the student counsellor before making any decisions about her future career.

When I talked with Karley about her teacher's concerns, she agreed that in some situations she just 'froze'. She said:

> I seem to freeze while I try to work out something to say that won't offend anyone. From Uni I've got all this information in my head that conflicts with my natural feelings, which stem from what I've been taught as a child. Like I was told 'be quiet' … 'go to the corner' which didn't make me think about what I had done wrong … it just made me cranky. And when a child is being difficult I go to do what comes naturally … and then I think about my lectures … and I know what I'm thinking of doing is wrong. Then I feel a bit nervous because I haven't reacted straight away because I have to think about those two things … and I just stand there. But I think I know my teacher well enough now to talk to her about this.

Karley did talk with her teacher about her difficulty. On her return to the University she told me that she had opened up the conversation by saying: 'I'm really confused about discipline … I don't know whether it does anything to send a child away from the group. … I can see that you can't have one child totally disrupting the class … but I was wondering is there something better?' By opening the conversation with this 'I' message, Karley was indicating that she wanted to think more about the purpose and nature of effective discipline. She indicated that her teacher had responded by sharing her thoughts about promoting self-discipline. Karley had written many of her teacher's comments in her journal:

> My teacher said that in any group situation you've got to have some sense of order and control and that what she was aiming for was for children to have self-control. She said there were many ways of helping children achieve this. Some of her suggestions were:

- to explain to children why some behaviours are acceptable and others are not;
- to encourage the children to help make rules ... but only to have a few, and to make sure they are reasonable and positive ones;
- to use praise effectively by stating the desired behaviour (e.g. 'That was thoughtful to move up to make a space for Joe in the circle');
- to warn children of the logical consequences that will follow if rules are broken but to do this in a way that allows the child to make a choice (e.g. 'Either you sit here quietly and keep your hands in your lap ... or you will have to sit over there by yourself');
- to follow through on the consequences if the child doesn't comply.

Karley said she had found this discussion very helpful. She had come to realize that, as a child, she had not been given any reasons as to why her behaviour was unacceptable. Nor had she been given any warnings or choice. Although she still did not feel comfortable about 'disciplining' children because of her own experiences, she was coming to see that achieving self-control was an important aspect of children's learning. Karley said that she recognized that the discipline strategies the teacher used seemed likely to help the children. She still felt her own stress levels rise, however, when she observed these situations and realized she would have to do a lot more reading and thinking about the topic in order to come to terms with her own past experiences, and use positive guidance strategies with children effectively.

Although this discussion about supervising teachers' concerns may suggest that supervising teachers are hard to please, this is not true. In my experience, in any round of teaching practice visits there are many more 'delighted' supervising teachers than 'concerned' ones. I recently asked three experienced supervising teachers what type of attitudes they valued in pre-service teachers. Their comments may help you look at the student–supervising teacher relationship from the supervising teacher's perspective.

Fay said:

> I enjoy having students who show me that they have a real interest in teaching and a real interest in children. I like students to ask me questions that show me they are thinking about what they are seeing ... or that help them build on the knowledge they have already gained. Another reason I like them asking questions is because I know that they're interested in what we're talking about ... and it's not just something that I'm interested in.

Jan said:

> I particularly value those who come with an open mind. I've had students who've come and said, 'On this prac I have to do this and I have to do that.' They haven't stopped to look at what the centre might have to offer them, nor have they thought about some of the additional things they might learn. They seem to have blinkers on and only attempt to meet the set requirements. I find it frustrating working with students who put limits on their own learning.

Gabriella agreed. She said:

> Yes. That's why I've really enjoyed having Lucy this prac. She's treated prac as a valuable experience in itself ... not as something to 'get through'. She's thought about her prac requirements but she's met the requirements in ways that have ensured that she has added to her understanding. She's been at a stage where she will notice something and can verbalize her thoughts about what she sees and I can talk about how I see that situation. We've had some interesting discussions. It's been a valuable experience for both of us.

These examples and comments, then, provide you with some guidelines concerning the types of attitudes that will help you build an effective relationship with your supervising teacher.

- *Aim to be free of personal problems during teaching practice.* Try to deal with personal issues prior to teaching practice. Should personal difficulties overwhelm you, seek help from a counsellor. It is not reasonable to burden your supervising teacher with your personal problems.
- *Be prepared to think through your own childhood experiences in the light of your new knowledge.* If, for example, you are going to give children positive guidance and support you will need to feel comfortable with yourself and what you are doing. Talk with your teacher about strategies that can be used and the reasons for their use. You may also need to 'confront' some of your more negative past experiences. Seek help from a student counsellor if necessary.
- *Enter teaching practice with an open mind.* Remember that your learning can go beyond meeting the set requirements. As you build different relationships with different supervising teachers, you will find that each

has particular strengths that may influence your own practice. Seek to discover a variety of perspectives on teaching issues and remain open to persuasive arguments.

BECOMING FAMILIAR WITH ORGANIZATIONAL STRUCTURES, ROLES AND RELATIONSHIPS

Because the organizational structure of each teaching practice setting will differ due to its size, type of administration and style of leadership, it is important that you seek advice from your supervising teacher concerning the particular aspects of your setting with which you should become familiar. In this way, as you gain experience in different early childhood settings you will be acquainted with various aspects of organization and a range of roles and relationships. In your first teaching practice you may find it easier to focus on roles and relationships within your own classroom. By your final teaching practice, however, you should be familiar with the roles of all members of staff as well as the administrative and organizational aspects of the school or centre. In this section a small sample of pre-service and supervising teachers' experiences will be presented to illustrate how your understanding of roles and relationships can be increased during teaching practice.

The teacher–aide relationship

Gabriella, an experienced teacher, indicated that she wanted her student to understand the role of the aide and the nature of the teacher – aide relationship because it was an important aspect of her preschool's organizational setting. She said:

I think it's important for students to realize that aides really do have to know what's going on ... even if some of the information you pass on seems trivial. For instance, if I don't pass on a telephone message about Jack's grandfather picking him up instead of his mother, then there could be confusion between the aide and Jack's grandparent at going home time.

I also think that students need to know that your aide is an important member of the teaching team. In this centre my aide, Anita, is constantly interacting with the children ... and I need to share my goals for the children with her so we can work together. I encourage Anita to share her perceptions of the children and how they have handled particular situations. I really value her observations. When my student plans a particular experience I ask her to explain her plans to Anita and how she would like Anita to assist her. I know she has found this difficult to do ... because Anita is so much older and more experienced than she is ... but I think it is important that a pre-service teacher learns how to do this ... in a collaborative kind of way.

Lucy, Gabriella's student, agreed that she had found it difficult to explain to Anita, the aide, what she planned to do and how Anita could assist. She realized, however, that an aide had to understand the teacher's goals if the assistance was to be effective. Lucy also said that she had to be 'extra clear' in her own mind about her plans if her explanations were to be helpful to Anita.

Plate 7.1　Aides are important members of the teaching team continually interacting with children. (Photo courtesy of Northgate State Preschool.)

The role of a child-care centre director

Although Bella, a final-year student, was doing her teaching practice with the babies and toddlers in a child-care centre, Helen, the director, suggested that Bella should also become familiar with the director's role. Helen assisted Bella in this by sharing with her some of her activities. Bella noted these activities together with some observations in her journal:

29 July
Helen demonstrated leadership skills as she oriented me to the centre, talking about the reasons underlying the set up of the environment. She lent me the Staff Policy Handbook and gave me a folder of information about the centre.

Helen works 'from' her office rather than 'in' her office. There is no desk – just chairs side by side to help people feel more relaxed.

12 August
Helen put up a notice to parents reminding them of the need for punctuality when picking up children. The notice board carried an additional large, red-lettered PLEASE READ sign that was effective. Jamie was discovered to have a sore eye, possibly conjunctivitis. Helen contacted his parent. Jamie was 'isolated' in his pram from other children but was comforted by a staff member until his mother arrived.

28 August
Helen came to the babies' room to settle a child who was very upset because the regular carer was away. Needs of the children take precedence over whatever else is on Helen's agenda.

29 August
Fire drill held today (occurs approximately once a month). Staff gather children and move to the gate in the over threes area. Babies are carried in arms. The roll is called.

Helen talked about staff–parent relations with a staff member who had experienced a confrontation with a parent recently. The staff member later commented in the staff room that she had appreciated Helen's support and caring attitude.

4 Sept
Staff have one-and-a-half hours for programming each week. Helen attends when possible. In the session I attended:

- Daily sheets from babies' room (solids, fluids, sleep, nappy care, etc.) were sorted into folders for each child. Parents can access these files at any time and receive them when child moves to another room or leaves.
- Previous week's programme was evaluated.
- Developmental records updated from joint observation notes. (This information is used as a basis for parent interviews.)
- Action plan developed from issues.
- Weekly programme developed from action plans.
- Weekly programme displayed on wall for parents to see.

Attended staff meeting 6 p.m.–7.45p.m. (Pizzas ordered in!) Helen chaired it. The agenda had been on view in the staff room.

- *Health issues*: medical supplies to be ordered ... ice packs, digital thermometers. Staff asked questions re sterilization of thermometers, putting babies down on backs.
- *Workplace health and safety issues*: Video on back safety available for staff to view at home. Safety Officer to visit. The Health Handbook for parents is to be updated – staff asked for suggestions. New medication forms to be developed.
- *Enrolments*: Parents to be reminded that forms are due in for next year. Start to 'transition' toddlers to D.'s group from November, rather than all at once after the Christmas break. Comments indicated that staff felt older children's visits with younger children were working well. Discussed ideas for rainy days ... set up one room with climbing equipment, use staff area as TV room, share morning tea (e.g. older children with toddlers).
- *Professional development*: Forms to fill in re. goals/needs for professional development plan ... where staff want to be in five years' time. Helen discussed orientation of new staff members. Was anyone interested in being a mentor? Discussed sharing of resources and articles.
- *Parent subcommittee*: Staff member who attends this committee reported on meeting. Plans for staff Christmas function are in hand.
- *General business*: Two staff members shared their thoughts on transitions – from home to centre as well as the transitions within the centre. This led to an interesting discussion about children having choice. Some staff saw the benefits of choice in terms of greater contentment and less conflict for children. The group felt that the centre atmosphere was much more positive.

I was impressed with the climate of the meeting. There was lots of laughter and a good feeling as the staff shared the pizzas and the discussion. I also noticed that matters raised at the meeting were followed up the next day.

These brief observations helped Bella build her understanding of the many facets that are a part of the director's role in a childcare centre. From her range of teaching practice experiences Bella was able to see that the larger the staff and parent body, the more complex the task becomes for the director or coordinator. The building of relationships among colleagues can also be more difficult where there are many members of staff.

Braving the staff room

In large institutions such as primary schools, the staff room often takes on a life of its own. It can become an 'institution' within the institution. Spending time in the staff room is often anticipated with fear and dread by some pre-service teachers. Cherryl wrote:

> Prior to this prac I found staff rooms to be stressful places that made me feel uncomfortable. My peers did too. We talked about their special type of infrastructure which makes a newcomer stand out or feel foolish, particularly if you attempt to sit on the one spare chair which unbeknownst to you is 'owned' by the Year 7 teacher. Our shared experiences suggested that, as student teachers, we were either pressured to conform to the staff room community and its entangled web of rules or were segregated, making us feel that we had some social disease. In talking with other students I found I was not the only one to manufacture all kinds of reasons to stay in my classroom and thereby avoid the staff room.
>
> But after this last prac my fears of staff rooms have diminished. Instead of counting down the minutes until I could leave the staff room I was counting the minutes until I could get there. Thanks to a mixed bunch of zany, fun-loving people I was able to rise to the challenge of the staff room. My practicum was at a school in the country where the staff room was warm and cosy and everyone sat around one table. Although at first I was apprehensive of its intimate nature, the small staff room made it easier to get to know everyone. All the staff made me feel welcome and included me in conversations. I now feel more empowered and more able to cope with the whole staff room experience. I am amazed at how one warm fuzzy experience can wipe out so many black spots.

In talking with Cherryl's tutorial group about their staff room experiences after their teaching practice there was general consensus that student teachers could be better prepared for some of the staff room realities. A number of suggestions were made for overcoming staff room fears. These were:

- to share some of your initial anxieties with your supervising teacher and ask if there is someone who could 'show you the ropes' or help you through the first morning tea or lunch break;
- to make the effort to go to the staff room frequently, and not hide in your classroom, so that others will come to see you as 'a regular';
- to contribute to the conversation if opportunities arise, or create an opportunity for conversation by sharing an experience;
- to join in other aspects of school life so that you get to know other teachers in their work context and have a common base for discussion in the staff room;
- to sit in different areas of the staff room from time to time so that you have a chance to talk with different members of staff;
- to make the most of the occasions when you are feeling isolated and alone by observing the informal networks among the staff and seeking to discover ways of joining the networks.

All these suggestions involve effort on your part. Most students agreed that when they had been 'brave' and had shown a positive, friendly attitude and a willingness to contribute and communicate, they had found teachers in the staff room who were prepared to reciprocate.

Collaborating with colleagues

The term 'collaboration' is sometimes used in a way that suggests that it is a natural phenomenon and that schools or centres are, by their organizational nature, collaborative enterprises. The experiences of some of the beginning teachers recounted in the next chapter illustrate that this is not necessarily so. Only those who have worked towards achieving meaningful collaboration with other teachers understand the effort needed. Many skills and abilities are required in order to collaborate: giving and receiving advice, offering and accepting support, and providing and benefiting from feedback and criticism. Although these skills may seem relatively simple, you have probably discovered from your teaching practice experiences that acquiring them is not as easy as it first appears. Andrew and Steve had two very different experiences of collaborating with colleagues.

Andrew and another pre-service teacher from a different teacher education institute were undertaking their teaching practice in an environmental education centre. Because this centre catered for children of primary school age who camped at the site and explored the surrounding outdoor environment through a range of activities, a relaxed, holiday atmosphere prevailed. For Andrew and the other student, however, the atmosphere between them was anything but relaxed because they found their opinions about how to approach situations clashing. Andrew gave this example:

> As I was to read a story to the class I spoke to the children and told them to make themselves comfortable. I reminded them that if they wanted to see the pictures, they would need to sit up the front. Many of the children lay on the floor, some leaned against the wall and others sat at the front. I was just about to begin the story when the other student walked in and told the children to sit up, move to the front and cross their legs, which they did – but the relaxed informal atmosphere was gone. I did not want to confuse the children so continued with the story, but later I approached the student to talk about what had happened. I was promptly told that I obviously didn't know what I was doing. I wished to talk about this some more, but the other person did not. This infuriated me and I decided that I did not want to work with this person further.

Upon reflection, Andrew said he had realized that what had happened was not very professional. Ideally, they should have been able to talk about different approaches and respect, support, encourage and learn from each other. However, it is often difficult to give and receive feedback as our own feelings, emotions and confidence levels all play a part in our ability to give and receive feedback and criticism. It is also inevitable that conflict and anger will result if a person's competence or values are challenged (Meade-Roberts *et al.*, 1993). After sharing his experience with some of his peers, Andrew dealt with his anger and, in the process, discovered that it could be used to think further about the situation and to motivate change. Developing a collaborative relationship becomes almost impossible, however, if one party refuses to communicate. The lines of communication have to be kept open. Stacey (1991: 97–8) makes a number of suggestions for handling criticism that you may find helpful:

•   Listen carefully so that you are clear about what is being said. Remember that criticism is opinion and may not necessarily be fact.

- Take several deep breaths before responding and then reply as honestly as you can. If the criticism is valid this may be difficult, but it is better to acknowledge it. You may want to explain your actions but don't offer excuses.
- If the criticism is untrue say so but be short and focused in your denial.
- Show that you take the criticism expressed seriously and that you want to talk about the matter further.
- Although it is important to recognize the feelings of all those concerned, focus on the facts of the problem rather than getting caught up in the emotion.

Steve had a much more positive experience of collaboration when he was asked to contribute to a planning group discussion for the Family and Friends' Day to be held at the preschool. Steve described it this way:

This was the first time I felt on the same level as the other teachers. Because the day was to consist of activities that would involve the family and friends of the children, the planning was to focus on how these activities could be linked with the preschool children's interests. At the start of the meeting I felt a little nervous. First we discussed the format – how things would happen, the rooms to be used, the set-up outdoors and how family and friends would be greeted. The discussion allowed everyone to speak. When I spoke the teachers didn't look at me in a funny way or criticize what I had to say and that felt good.

Next we talked about the specific activities each teacher had planned and I talked about my planning. I found it great that, as we were talking about our planning, we were using the same language so that everyone understood what was being said. Working with other teachers like this also gave me a sense of how close I am to finishing my degree and what skills I have and can use.

I learned several things from this experience. It gave me confidence knowing that I can work with other teachers as peers – that I'm not the odd one out. I also realized that I can discuss my planning and ideas with other teachers and that these are respected. This experience also made me think about the value of regular discussions between teachers because I learned such a lot from hearing other teachers' thinking and explanations of their planning.

By being able to participate in a collaborative process, Steve was able to experience the benefits of collaboration firsthand. Some of you may be thinking that Steve's view of collaboration could have been very different if, like Andrew, he had experienced negative feedback. Andrew's and Steve's contrasting experiences highlight the importance of developing skill in giving and receiving feedback and criticism in a way that is beneficial to all parties. Maintaining effective communication, respecting the other's contribution and sharing in the decision-making process are essential if collaboration is to occur.

PROMOTING PARTNERSHIPS WITH FAMILIES

Building collaboration between teachers and families has been a priority in early childhood education for many years (Bredekamp and Copple, 1997; Gestwicki, 2000; Goldberg, 1997; Henry, 1996; Stacey, 1991). This is because teachers regard children's families as partners in the educational process. With young children so dependent on their families, parent support of the school and its programme is vital to the child's well-being and motivation, while the school's support and valuing of the child's home and culture is essential to the well-being of the family.

If you are like most pre-service teachers you will be keen to develop skills during teaching practice that will assist you in the future to build cooperation with families. There is a need to think carefully, however, about the reasons for developing these relationships, the particular skills you require and what you can reasonably achieve in your particular setting in a short period of time.

What is involved in developing effective family–teacher relationships?

From your readings and observations you will know that there are many practical steps a teacher can take to promote the parent–teacher relationship. For instance, in getting to know parents, teachers can gauge each parent's particular interests and comfort level in being involved in their children's education and care. On this basis many different types of involvement might be offered. For example, some parents may be happy participating in classroom activities and working with children. Others may prefer to contribute to committees, write a newsletter, design or update a web page or participate in fundraising efforts. Others may want advice and support in child rearing or social contact with other parents. A reciprocal, two-way sharing of information and support needs to be fostered in ways that are practicable for both parties if meaningful partnerships are to develop.

You will find it useful for future reference to note the forms of information exchange that take place in your particular centre. For instance, is information sharing done in formal ways such as through interviews, reports and newsletters, or is this done using far more informal means? Does the orientation process set the tone for future communications? Is the teacher available for a chat with a parent at arrival or departure times? Are there opportunities to request a meeting? Is use made of telephone conversations, e-mail contact or a parent–teacher notebook for parents who have difficulty

Plates 7.2 and 7.3 An artist dad sharing his love of painting inspires a child to paint. (Photo courtesy of Sue Thomas.)

getting to the centre frequently? Does the centre have a library of helpful resources available to families? Also note other ways in which the centre shows respect and support for families. For instance, is the centre 'family friendly' with hours suited to family needs? Do parents see the centre as a source for social contact with other people, or are they so preoccupied with other aspects of their lives that they have little time to spend at the centre? How does the centre 'include' busy parents? Does the centre provide translation/interpreter services if needed?

As you gain experience in different teaching practice situations and observe and participate in various approaches to building partnerships you will realize that the type of parent involvement will vary in different settings. Also, by talking with your teacher about why particular strategies are used or particular emphases are given to certain activities you can develop your understanding of your supervising teacher's goals for the parent–teacher relationship.

What skills can be developed for promoting partnerships with parents?

For many supervising teachers, finding ways to assist pre-service teachers to develop their practical skills in working with parents poses some difficulties. There are a number of reasons for this. If the duration of teaching practice is only three or four weeks, then there is really not enough time to come to know parents well or to develop a relationship. It is also important that you do not do anything that might damage the relationship that may only just be developing between a parent and teacher. Mary, an experienced supervising teacher, expressed her thoughts this way:

> I've found that a lot of students don't quite know what to do in relation to parents. Some will have a little chat with them because they feel they should ... but a few students I've had have wanted to become best friends with parents in a hurry ... and that really bothers me ... and I find it a difficult situation to deal with. I realized I couldn't say, 'I really don't want you to become too friendly with parents' ... because I really haven't got anything to hide ... but when I thought about it some more, I realized I was worried about how the parents might interpret what the student said about their child. It takes a long time to get to know children ... and parents ... and you have to have the really big picture ... and I don't think a student-teacher ... or anyone ... can get that in just a few weeks.

Against the background of the types of concerns raised by Mary, I talked further with supervising and pre-service teachers about the kinds of experiences students could reasonably undertake during teaching practice to develop their skills in working effectively with parents. Both teachers and students agreed that it was vital that before teaching practice began the students should discuss their goals and ideas for developing relationships with families with their teachers. The teachers in turn needed to outline their own approach to working with families and discuss how realistic the students' goals might be for a particular setting. Once the goals had been clarified and agreed to, the teachers were in a better position to support the students and provide opportunities in which the goals could be pursued, while the students were more confident because they knew they were working within the parameters of the teachers' expectations.

Some of the goals that were agreed pre-service teachers could pursue in most early childhood settings were:

- to observe the teacher's style of communication with parents and families, the strategies used and the activities emphasized – and to discuss these observations with the teacher;
- to introduce yourself to parents – through an introductory poster, a note sent home or a social conversation with individual parents;
- to get to know parents by being available to talk with them at the beginning or end of sessions – a general comment about the day or about something a child enjoyed doing was seen to be a useful 'opener';
- to listen to what parents have to say – informally seek their views on topical issues;
- to join in activities designed to foster family participation – such as grandparents' day; a 'special person's' night; a sausage sizzle for all the family;
- to chat with parents who may be visiting or on roster and help them feel at ease;
- to explain how parents could participate or assist in an activity or routine;
- to invite a parent to contribute to the programme (e.g. play a musical instrument, bath a baby, share something related to their occupation);
- to make posters or create displays for the notice board that communicate information to parents;
- to write a newsletter or send home a note about 'our' week at the school or centre – children can be encouraged to contribute to these newsletters with comments or drawings;
- to attend meetings organized for parents if appropriate;

- to participate in a parent meeting by sharing information or contributing to a discussion on a particular topic;
- to communicate with families through children by having the children make invitations or write thank-you notes;
- to thank parents personally for their participation in events or for their contribution to the programme.

Chloe had the opportunity to develop many of these practical skills during her last teaching practice. She wrote:

> With each of my pracs the interaction I have had with parents has gradually increased as I have become more confident. As I began to believe in myself as a 'teacher', the roles I carried out became more like those of a teacher. I casually talked with parents about their child and what they had done that day. If certain resources were needed for an activity later in the week, then, with the teacher's permission, I wrote a note home to parents asking for their cooperation. I was still hesitant in approaching parents, though, and I must admit that most conversations were spontaneous and initiated by parents.
>
> Before my last prac I shared with my supervising teacher my need for more experience in interacting with parents and she gave me lots of opportunities. During the weeks I was 'in control' I greeted children and parents at the door. Some children were a little confused by this, and I had to reassure them that their teacher was inside the room. Most parents were open and friendly and made me feel more confident and comfortable. Because they knew I was a student, however, they still went to the teacher with any 'real' issues. Where appropriate, the teacher referred them back to me so that I had to deal with the information ... that Uncle Tom was picking David up instead of his Mum ... or make a decision about whether Sally could bring her new dog to show the children. I enjoyed this responsibility and found my personal philosophy coming into play. For example, if I believed having a pet at preschool was unhygienic, I would have explained to Sally's Mum that it wouldn't be appropriate for Sally to bring her dog. Because the children had set up a vet's surgery in their play, however, I thought it would be a valuable experience for Sally to share how she looked after her dog Tex.
>
> My experiences this prac have shown me that it is essential to be outgoing and approachable and that not all parents will approach me first. I also saw the value of using a variety of communication strategies because it increases the chance of the message being received by parents.

Chloe was fortunate that she was in a situation where her teacher felt comfortable for her to have as much contact with parents as she did. In Chloe's situation the parents recognized that any 'real' issues were to be discussed with the teacher, and the teacher was able to decide whether they were appropriate for Chloe to handle. This meant that the teacher knew what Chloe was talking with parents about and felt comfortable with how Chloe would respond. Chloe also knew that she must refer the parents to the teacher if they did want detailed information about their child.

SETTING PERSONAL GOALS

Throughout this book emphasis has been given to the fact that learning to teach is a very personal process. As you talk with peers about teaching practice you will find that you each have had different experiences. This is because, in undertaking teaching practice, you are drawing on your own unique past experiences, as well as your current understanding of specialized knowledge. Your teaching practice experience is also being influenced by your particular setting, as well as your own expectations, learning style and personality. For these reasons, then, it makes sense to set yourself some personal goals to achieve during your teaching practice, in addition to those set as part of the course requirements. If they are thoughtfully devised such goals can provide you with deeper insights and skills that will help you when you begin teaching.

Tara decided to set a personal goal. She wanted to discover more about building relationships with both children and their parents. Because she was undertaking her teaching practice in the babies' and toddlers' group of a long day care setting she knew that there would be opportunities to explore this goal. In thinking about the nature of her interactions she wrote:

> Although I have found interacting with children to have been one of the most satisfying aspects of past teaching practice experiences, I would like to move beyond 'interactions' to 'building relationships'. For me interaction implies the mutual engagement of two parties – that something is happening. Interactions are a state of doing. Relationships, on the other hand, are a state of being. They refer to the connection, or tie, that exists between two persons. I want to enter into a caring relationship with each child that will enable me to understand each child better and consequently foster holistic development.

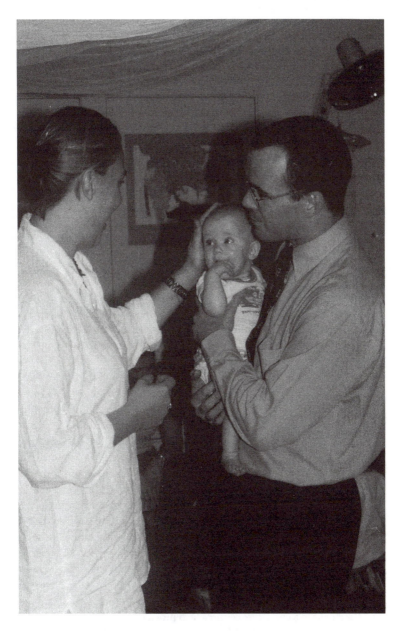

Plate 7.4 Building caring relationships involves positive interactions with children and their parents. (Photo courtesy of Lady Gowrie Child Centre, Brisbane.)

Tara began to think about how she would enter into caring relationships by reminding herself of the strategies likely to promote positive interactions with babies and toddlers. She also reviewed strategies for interacting with their parents. In her reflective journal she wrote:

> I believe I was more successful in building caring relationships with the children than their parents, although I sensed a ready acceptance in those parents who saw that I had an effective relationship with their child. For instance, at the close of nine-month-old Lachlan's first visit he clambered from his mother's lap to mine. When she next brought him in she called, 'Where's our friend Tara?'
>
> In building relationships I was reminded of how important it is to be sensitive to how children feel at different times of the day. This was brought home as I tried to accommodate 18-month-old David's irritability after he had experienced an upsetting lunch and sleep routine. I also saw the value of seeking information on home child-rearing practices. Having noted that Anna's mother had said 'Twinkle, twinkle, little star' was Anna's favourite song, I used the melody to soothe her to sleep. My experience with the triplets reminded me how differences in temperaments can influence relationships, with Yvette being reserved, Caitlin placidly accepting, while Izabella reached out to me at our first meeting.
>
> I also became aware that there is a reverse side to relationships. Kathryn (13 months) arrived as an emergency enrolment early in my time at the centre. A medical crisis had turned life upside down for her out-of-town parents. There was an instant rapport between her parents and me and, as Kathryn was not accustomed to other staff members she became my responsibility. Although she initially explored the playground with glee, separation anxiety set in on her second visit and, on this and subsequent occasions, she looked to me for comfort. Her father's course of treatment was extended, and it became apparent that I would be leaving the centre before Kathryn. This meant she had to adjust to yet another change during a difficult period in the life of her family. I realized the importance of looking at all aspects of a situation and not relying on rapport alone in deciding what is best for a child.

In reflecting on her experiences in building relationships, Tara said that her placement in a child-care centre which provided for children on a regular as well as an occasional basis had convinced her that, in order to be responsive to family needs, the provision of occasional care was important. She wondered, however, whether at a personal level she was suited to this task. She asked:

Am I sufficiently dedicated and patient to soothe and support children continually as they separate and settle into a new environment? I found the constant changes to be my greatest challenge. The dynamics of the group are not only changing day to day, but also during the day. When David awoke from a nap he could have lost or gained several playmates. Am I adventurous and energetic enough to relish each day being on an uncharted sea? Am I perceptive enough to discern a child's interests and needs quickly and sufficiently organized to provide appropriate resources and activities so that the children's time in care also has a clear educational benefit?

In reflecting on her experiences in building relationships with parents and children, Tara became more aware of the characteristics of child-care settings that impacted on those relationships and the demands and opportunities they placed on teachers. In the process she also began to think about her own suitability for working with children in that particular context and her abilities to meet those demands. The personal goal that she had set for the teaching practice had helped her not only to deepen her knowledge of building relationships but also had helped her come to know herself better.

DEVELOPING PROFESSIONALISM

In Chapter 1 it was suggested that becoming an early childhood professional involved developing specialized knowledge, using that knowledge to assess and make decisions and acquiring high standards of practice (Katz 1995a). Each of these aspects has been discussed throughout the book and suggestions made as to how you can develop these professional skills as you undertake your pre-service education course and engage in teaching practice. As the stories of the beginning teachers presented in the next chapter highlight, you will certainly rely on these skills as you make the transition from being a pre-service teacher to being a teacher of your own group of children. You will also draw on all your inner strengths as you seek to present a professional persona in situations where you feel far from confident. Developing a quiet, yet well-founded, confidence during your teaching practice experiences is an invaluable achievement that can make such a difference, particularly in your first year of teaching.

Christina decided that as part of a broader goal to develop her professionalism she would focus on gaining confidence in speaking with adults. She wrote:

Feeling confident in talking to other teachers, administration staff and parents has always been an issue for me. I have often talked to friends and lecturers about ways in which I could build my confidence. It is not that I don't know how to do it or what to say. It is just that I am shy when I have to talk to people I don't know. Over the last one-and-a-half years I have really tried to work on building my confidence with adults as I realize that a teacher must be able to communicate easily. My goal is to feel comfortable and confident as I speak with adults whom I don't know well.

Having decided upon this goal, Christina was rather taken aback when she found she had a male supervising teacher. She wrote:

I was delighted when I found I had been allocated a Year 2 class, which was what I wanted, but my confidence took two steps back when I found out I had a male supervising teacher. This was really going to test my confidence as I had never worked with a male teacher before and I thought that there would be a different communication style. I decided that I still had to be confident and deal with everything in a professional way. As I got into the first week of prac I realized just how wrong my initial reactions had been. Having a male teacher was just like dealing with any new person in my life. He was a teacher, too, and had a lot to offer me as he was working on a mentoring programme. His goal for himself was to assist me to be as independent and self-reliant as possible. I'm not sure whether he realized just how much he was helping me by setting this goal for himself. It really did help me to go one step further in my ability to communicate effectively with other teachers and parents within the school. The process began gradually, with John introducing me to everybody whom we came across. This was his way of showing me the ropes and making sure I knew who everybody was. Then it was up to me. Each day I would set myself little goals that I needed to accomplish. My diary looked like this:

Monday talk to Neil (teacher librarian) about resources for topic 'fairy tales'; check with John about cooking with the children.

Tuesday see deputy principal about the risk management policy in relation to cooking;
spend time in the staff room at lunch;
book the Creative Skills Centre for art.

These goals helped me see what I was doing and that I was making progress. I became sufficiently confident to access resources from the library and storerooms without going to my supervising teacher first. I also invited the other Year 2 teachers to watch a video that related to the topic we were doing and this resulted in more sharing of the resources between classrooms. With parents who came into the room before or after school, I would introduce myself and try to make some small talk. I found that everyone was very friendly and after the ice was broken they readily approached me at a later stage.

In reflecting on her experiences, Christina said:

I felt my professionalism grow as my confidence with people grew. As I became confident in communicating with other teachers I found it easier to talk with parents and the administration staff in the school. As I begin teaching next year I will set myself similar goals and reach out to as many people as I can.

From this experience Christina found that success leads to more success and that, as she gained in confidence, contacts could be made more easily with other adults occupying a range of positions within the school setting. Christina knew that gaining this confidence in her own ability to communicate was important if she was to be effective as a beginning teacher.

SUMMARY

In order to gain the most from your teaching practice you not only have to develop trusting relationships with children, you also have to build effective working relationships with adults. Your teaching practice experiences can enable you:

* to develop and refine your skills in building working relationships with your supervising teacher and other colleagues;
* to become familiar with a range of formal and informal organizational structures and roles and the ways in which they influence relationships;
* to consider how partnerships with families can be developed and gain confidence in communicating with families;
* to set personal goals that will help you build your sense of professionalism.

In developing your relationship with your supervising teacher it is important to consider how best to communicate so that you can achieve your goals. Being open and honest in sharing your thinking, talking about your perceptions or difficulties and seeking specific information and guidance will help your supervising teacher understand your reality, assist your teacher to focus on your key issues and provide opportunities that are most likely to meet your needs. Having a positive, enthusiastic attitude and demonstrating that you are open minded and ready to learn and accept criticism also contribute to effective working relationships with colleagues.

These same communication skills and enthusiastic attitudes will help you begin to build relationships with families. If your teaching practice is of short duration, the development of collaborative relationships may not be a realistic aim. Nevertheless, you may have the opportunity to observe such collaboration in action and to identify the factors that contribute to its achievement. Children and their families, as well as teachers, benefit when effective relationships are established.

Setting goals for yourself relating to aspects of teaching that you feel require you to gain further knowledge, understanding and skill before you begin teaching are vital to the growth of your professionalism. Recognizing the need to continue to extend your ability to reflect on and critically analyse (i.e. research) your own teaching is also fundamental in developing your professionalism throughout your career.

SUGGESTED ACTIVITIES

- Imagine that you are a supervising teacher. What characteristics would your ideal pre-service teacher have? List them. Think about what you could do to develop some of those ideal student characteristics.
- Recall some experiences you have had in developing relationships with supervising teachers. If they have been positive ones, list the things you and your teacher did that promoted their success. If there were difficulties in the relationship, try to identify their causes and consider some strategies that you might use to overcome them if faced with a similar situation in the future.
- Describe the formal organization of a school or centre with which you are familiar. Outline the roles you perceive to be taken by people occupying particular positions. (If you are describing the setting where you are undertaking teaching practice, you may be able to check out your perceptions with the people concerned.) Describe how you see

the form of organization contributing to the functioning of the school or centre.

- Imagine you are working in a team-teaching situation. Your colleague wants to give the children rewards (jelly beans, gold stars and stamps) when they achieve at a high standard. You want to foster the child's sense of achievement and satisfaction without offering external rewards. Write the script of the discussion that you would have in order to negotiate some workable arrangement that you could both 'live' with. Note what you learned from this activity

- Interview some parents who have children in early childhood settings – preferably parents not associated with your current teaching practice setting. Ask them about their experiences with early education, the concerns they may have and school/centre practices they have found helpful. Using this information formulate some goals and strategies for developing cooperation between parents and teachers.

- Develop a resource file of practical ideas for involving parents in centre activities and for developing partnerships with families. Become familiar with resources that may be suitable for a parent lending library and develop a list of referral agencies that may be of help to families.

- Look back over journal entries, programme folders and observation and planning records you have made during previous teaching practice experiences. Examine them critically and identify areas that you feel you need to develop further if you are to be a successful beginning teacher. After this consideration write down some goals and actions you could take which would enhance your professionalism.

Chapter 8

Stories from beginning teachers

What is the reality?

In this chapter some beginning teachers whom I had worked with during their pre-service course share more of their teaching stories. (Other brief extracts of these stories were included in Chapters 3 and 4.) In thinking how to present their narratives in this chapter, I have decided to offer them in the style they were shared with me as we chatted over coffee during the Christmas holidays at the end of their first year of teaching. Unfortunately their stories have had to be cut drastically to fit within this chapter. This has been done by focusing on the key issues and joys experienced by each teacher. The names of the beginning teachers and others mentioned in the stories have been changed for reasons of confidentiality.

As you read this chapter you will no doubt be alerted to teaching contexts, situations and experiences that you may not have anticipated. The stories revolve around such topics as:

- providing leadership in a community-based centre;
- taking up the responsibilities of teaching in a government school;
- surviving professionally and personally in a tough teaching situation;
- promoting the transition between preschool and Year 1 in an independent school;
- developing professional relationships and knowledge;
- coming to terms with the challenges of putting ideals into practice.

All the beginning teachers I talked with had been keen, high-achieving pre-service teachers, enthusiastic about commencing teaching careers. They were, however, surprised by and, in some instances, unprepared for many of the experiences encountered in their first year. Their willingness to share their stories was prompted by the hope that you can learn from their experiences and better prepare yourselves for the realities of teaching. As you read their stories ask yourself, 'What would I have done in that situation?'

'What knowledge and skills do I need to acquire in order to manage such situations?'

KYLIE'S STORY: 'WORKING IN A COMMUNITY-BASED CENTRE IS REALLY FOR ME'

Kylie is a director of a community-based kindergarten in a relatively large rural town. Each unit has a four- to five-year-old group that comes from 9 a.m.–2.30 p.m. three days a week and a three-year-old group that attends two mornings a week.

I'd always thought I'd teach in the state system, but no job offers came. People kept asking, 'Have you got a job yet?' and I'd say 'No'. I started to panic and then this job came up at the kindy where I'd done my prac … so I put in my application. There were actually two jobs going – one for the teacher's job and one for the director's. I thought they would just interview me for the teacher's job … so when they told me I had the director's job it was a surreal experience. I said 'WHAT?! … Oh well OK.' The person who got the teacher's job was a first year teacher too. I'm so glad that I took it because now I know that working in a community centre is really for me.

I enjoy working with a parent committee although there was a lot to adjust to … I had no idea of committee procedures and I had to get used to things being moved and seconded. At the first couple of meetings the parents would suggest that we do certain things and, because the other teacher and I were new to the centre, we had no idea what this meant … and we'd just say 'OK'. But having Maxine, the aide, was really excellent because she would say, 'Well when we do this, this happens' or 'if we go there you'll have to do such and such.' At the third meeting the parents said, 'We want the children to plant seedlings.' Maxine had told us this happened every year and that sometimes it wasn't very meaningful for the children because generally it was the aide who ended up planting and looking after the seedlings. So when this suggestion was made, I was prepared … and explained why it might be better to do something else that the children were interested in at the moment. This was a real turning point. From then on the parents knew that they couldn't just tell us what to do all the time … and they seemed more willing to respect our ideas. It became more collaborative.

I've also had to learn about running staff meetings. There are five people on the staff. At the first meeting last year I wasn't sure what to do so I said 'I don't know what to do ... what do we talk about here?' And so we talked it through and I realized I would have to be prepared for the next one so I had this agenda. I still find it hard to follow the agenda, particularly if the others say they don't want to do something. But towards the end of the year I could feel myself becoming stronger in the staff meetings, and for my first staff meeting next year, I've already worked out what I want to say.

At the start of the year we were aware that there was quite a bit of gossip in the town with people saying 'Why send your kids to that Centre? They've got two first year teachers there!' But our parents were really supportive and said their kids loved coming to us. The other teacher and I really worked with the children. It was funny because we'd say, 'It's like we're friends of the children. Fancy being friends with four- and five-year-olds!' ... The parents seem like friends too, because we see them twice a day. Because we're young and most of the parents are young it's been easy to establish that friendly relationship. But I've had to work at developing a professional relationship too.

At the beginning of the year parents would come and tell me things – gossipy things really, and I didn't know how to respond. But now I can handle it and help them see what's important to talk about and what's not. And we talk a lot about their children's development. I've got more confidence in doing that.

At the end of the year break-up we were crying and they were crying. We gave each child a book with photos and some of their work ... and in the book I wrote about how they'd developed during the year. When the parents opened up the books they were thrilled. One parent came up to me and said, 'I can't believe that someone else thinks this of my child.' This mum had been through a rough patch during the year and had been very depressed. She'd said 'I could have just dumped my child on your doorstep and run away.' And we'd helped her through that and at the break-up she was smiling and coping. Our Centre's like that ... everyone comes in and they relax ... and it is a happy, friendly situation.

We're a bit unorthodox. When I started teaching I had some dream goals ... like having a float in the town's annual festival ... which did happen. It was something that was special to me ... and I felt it put the Centre 'out there' in front of the community. When I mentioned this goal at the interview I could see the parents liked the idea. And when it came time to do it ... because it was The Year of the Outback ... we said, 'Why don't we have utes (traybacks), a number of them with each one decorated with a different theme – cotton, cattle, sunflowers, Australian animals.' The kids really got involved. We had eight utes in the end, so straight away we had eight families, then those families had special friends to help. The day before the festival I had such a warm fuzzy feeling because we had forty families working on decorating the utes. Everyone still talks about the warm fuzzy feelings they had that day. I found I became the organizer of the day … 'OK Ute Number Three in you come.' From that point on I could see that parents saw me more as the person responsible … and it was a change … but back to the utes …

Before that day we'd had the flutterers … 'But how are we going to do this?' 'Can you do that?' (It was like when I started I was asked so many questions I didn't have a clue about and I'd think 'Oh gosh, you're asking me?' Even little things like 'There's a washer missing from the tap outside. Where do we get a washer from?' 'The sprinkler system isn't working so how do we fix that?' All these questions kept coming … and I just had to get used to it because that's part of a director's role.) On the day when we were decorating the utes all the questions kept coming to me, but this time I felt I could handle them. Although it was a bit stressful to begin with, it did all work out. There were so many parents and brothers and sisters that got involved. It brought everyone together … and even afterwards I had so many phone calls from people saying how great it was. It just seemed to spark the spirit of the Centre and for the rest of the year everyone was involved and we felt we'd proved ourselves in the eyes of the community.

For Kylie, being employed as a director by a community-based kindergarten committee gave her many opportunities to provide leadership. She offered leadership to other staff members, a parent committee who also employed her, as well as children and parents and the broader community. There were many unexpected challenges – chairing staff meetings, working out how to be 'friends' with parents and children while also being 'professional', negotiating curriculum content with the committee and taking the risk of following a dream and having the centre 'out there' in the town's festival.

Kylie was fortunate. She was ready and able to take on those leadership responsibilities and found she enjoyed the challenge. She appreciated the opportunity to work in a context that was closely linked to the community as was evident in her comment – 'now I know that working in a community centre is really for me' and revelled in 'sparking the spirit of the Centre'.

JANINE'S STORY: 'THAT FIRST DAY I REALIZED I WAS TOTALLY RESPONSIBLE'

Janine is a teacher of a Year 1 class of 22 children at a large outer suburban state primary school where she had previously undertaken teaching practice.

> I had a great range of children in my class. I had two very challenging children – Bradley and Zoe. Then I had about ten children who were very high achievers and the rest needed a great deal of support. There were very few average children. There were two aboriginal children who had teacher aide support and there was also a number of children who had speech and language difficulties.
>
> With behaviour management I had very little support from the administration. I got hit a couple of times and I felt there were occasions when I should have been able to ring for support but I found it would take about 40 minutes for someone to come, and by that time I'd had to manage the problem. Sometimes no one came at all. I understand administrative staff are busy but I think I was expecting a little more support.
>
> Bradley was from an abusive background and he would just explode for no apparent reason. I felt I could never have a day off because he would react very badly to any new person coming into the classroom. Zoe was a foster child who had reactive attachment disorder. It's to do with not forming attachments in the first years of life. These children tend to sabotage any relationships after that. We did have a honeymoon period with Zoe and then we had all sorts of problems ... stealing and swearing. She spent a lot of time on her own because she couldn't form any friendships. Fortunately I had a good rapport with both of these children's parents ... having had my own child helped. The guidance officer was supporting both families too.
>
> At Uni I thought parents would play a very big part in my classroom. That was part of my teaching philosophy. But I found it very hard to get parents to come. I had four parents to start with but by the end of the year that was down to two who came regularly. After they settled their children into Year 1 they went back to work. I communicated regularly through a newsletter and invited them to participate but I got a very limited response ... so that didn't pan out as I thought.
>
> I know this sounds negative but there were highs!
>
> The rapport I had with the children was wonderful. I really liked all the children. A couple of mums said to me they were worried at first when they heard they had a first year teacher ... and then they were

worried because they heard I was a mature age student ... then they realized I was the mothering type. Looking back I can see that helped to develop the rapport. The children liked coming to school so that made the parents feel better too.

I guess I hadn't understood just what a responsibility it is to have your own classroom. On prac there was always someone else if things started to get out of hand. On that very first day I realized I was totally responsible ... for the ones who tried to run out of the classroom ... and the one who was crying.

There are lots of things I'll do differently as a second year teacher. I remember saying at the beginning 'OK let's say that a little bit louder' and then there'd be this screaming response! I'm sure I'll still be enthusiastic but I'll probably temper things a little more. And I'll put much more emphasis on teaching discrete skills ... and be quite explicit ... 'If you wind your glue stick up too high it won't wind down again' ... 'If you sharpen your crayon too much it will snap off.' I had one little boy crying on the first day because he'd 'lost' his work. He'd done his tracing of the letter S and then he thought he'd lost his S because he'd actually glued it in his book upside down, so to him it had disappeared. I had no idea of the levels of dependence and independence of the children in my class. I had one child who needed to sleep every afternoon ... and did ... on the carpet. On the first day she just nodded off ... and I thought 'What do I do?' I decided she needed her sleep. But there were lots of times I wasn't sure what I should or should not be doing.

I was a high achiever at Uni and I think I put more pressure on myself because I was very aware of what I wasn't achieving. I had this ideal in my mind of what my classroom would be ... learning centres ... big cushions ... and I had those things, but then the children would use them and they'd misbehave, or I'd have to remove a barrier so I could see what was going on. I wanted to do a lot of cooperative learning ... and I found that was just so hard to achieve in the first few terms of Year 1. I found I had to slow down, and introduce things gradually, and teach the children how to use things. By the end of the year I had achieved cooperative groups but it was hard work.

Another thing that makes the first few weeks so overwhelming is that not only do you have your teaching load but you also have playground duty, staff meetings and induction meetings, as well as just getting to know the culture of the school ... and even just finding your way around. That was something I hadn't realized ... like finding the science resources ... and who was the computer technician. Then trying to remember when I was on duty ... even the little things like remembering to put out the tuckshop basket.

My husband and son were a real part of the class. My teaching did encroach on my family life. In first term it was like a 200-hour-a-week job and my husband said this couldn't go on. So then I tried to leave Saturday and Sunday free from schoolwork. But teaching is a big commitment. I wanted my room to look beautiful and inviting. I put a lot of work into displaying the children's work ... and making the lessons interesting ... and I did a lot of science experiments, and that involved my husband in making some equipment. I guess that was why I was disappointed when the back up from the administration just wasn't there. Because I was giving it 100 per cent, I was expecting that back.

I remember my husband and I had an argument because we had been going to the movies but I had talked with Bradley's dad for a long time on the phone. Bradley had tried to set fire to something at home that day ... and his dad wanted advice and support. I stayed talking to him and we missed the movie and that caused a bit of dissension at home. So I was talking about it in the staff room next day ... and one teacher was saying that you really have to distance yourself and switch off at three o'clock. The guidance officer came to me afterwards and said 'I think it is very hard to switch off. I can't do it. If your job means so much to you then you can't just cut a parent off.' But I guess I will have to try to find a happy medium ... balancing family commitments and the workload.

When I did my job interview I had a picture of my son on a poster and it had 'Wanted: A teacher for this child' ... and I'd written all the things I would want in a teacher for my child. They were all my values ... and I try to aspire to them ... kind, flexible, caring, and creative. I think I had a successful year. The children were happy and the parents were happy. I was happy too.

In reflecting on her first year of teaching, Janine acknowledged the negatives as well as the positives. The lack of support from the administrative staff within the school was particularly frustrating because of the huge commitment she herself was making. Janine realized that she was putting pressure on herself by trying to live up to her 'ideals' in terms of her class and her family and said she would have to 'try to find a happy medium ... balancing family commitments and the workload'. It is interesting that at the end of her first year of teaching this statement is phrased in the future tense. For many beginning teachers the focus of this first year is on 'keeping going' with little time given to seeking solutions, even when issues such as time management are recognized. It is also interesting to note that for Janine, the happiness of both the children and parents was an important criterion for assessing the success of her first year. It is important to acknowledge the emotional aspects of teaching. Promoting the well-being of all those involved in school contexts – children, parents and staff members – has many positive spin-offs. For first-year teachers, particularly, the happiness of children and parents boosts confidence and self-respect and assists in building a positive approach to professionalism.

SUZANNE'S STORY: 'A MAJOR HIGH FOR ME WAS THAT I SURVIVED!'

When the school year started Suzanne had not received a job offer from the state education department. In the third week of the first term, however, she was asked to do relief teaching with a Year 4–5 class at an inner suburban school. This was to be for just a few weeks. Before she had completed her initial contract, however, Suzanne was offered a long-term contract and remained with that class until the end of the school year.

> Getting a middle primary class was a huge shock, although my early childhood training helped me cope. I had quite a different class … I had eight children who had learning difficulties … they actually went to special classes … and then there were five children with real behaviour problems. Of the 28 children nearly half had real problems and were very dominant in the classroom. As a consequence we spent a lot of time on social development and building up each other's confidence … and focusing on listening and being patient, learning to help each other through … and not becoming frustrated and switching off.
>
> When I found out I would be with this class until the end of the year … after being their relief teacher for two-and-a-half weeks, I felt I'd wasted valuable time, particularly in relation to behaviour management. I decided to focus on behaviour management and I said 'Right, this is how it's going to be.' We set up class rules together. The children wanted 20 but I said about eight would do! … things like listening; put your hand up to speak; no 'put downs'; encouraging each other; waiting in turn, and how to enter and exit the classroom. And then we went through what would happen if people didn't keep the

class rules … and everyone signed them to say they agreed with them and would try their best to keep them. We didn't present it as a list of rules. We made a poster which said, 'In our classroom we ___.' Everyone decorated it and signed it … and we put it up where everyone could see it. Then we went through the consequences. How many times do you think Miss N. needs to remind you about that behaviour?' They wanted only one warning but I said they might really need more than that … so we agreed on three, then it was time out for five minutes outside … and then to the office. That worked but there wasn't one day during the year that we didn't spend some time on behaviour management issues.

I went to a workshop on behaviour management and they reminded us about how kids don't understand the meaning of words we use … words like respect … and effort, trust and safety. So we put all the words up and the children wrote sentences about what they thought they meant. And we discussed these and designed posters about what they meant … and then we went into what that word meant for them personally … and for Miss N. … and for the community. And we also talked about what we wanted our classroom to LOOK like, FEEL like and SOUND like. After that we did up weekly charts of our successes for the week … whether it was our assembly performance, walking quietly, or fire drill … and we discussed what we needed to improve on the following week. 'Listening' kept coming up … and 'sitting quietly'. I found it interesting that the children were often harder on themselves than I was … but other weeks I'd think 'Oh no! There was nothing we were successful at this week!' I did a lot of looking into behaviour management. Although I did a behaviour management unit at Uni I really wasn't prepared for what some classrooms can be like. When you're in the classroom you just can't remember all the steps they tell you to work through.

Looking back on the year a major high for me was that I survived! In term two I was an emotional wreck. I was really fragile and coming home in tears … mainly because of the difficult behaviour. There was no support in place … I literally had to crumble before I got any support at all. Looking back perhaps I should have been more up front in asking for help … but the admin staff knew I was struggling. It wasn't till I said 'Look, I just can't come back next week. I just can't cope with the children's behaviour … and the lack of support when I do send them to the office.' I just felt I was shoved in my classroom and it was up to me whether I would sink or swim. That just seemed to be the school's attitude. Even when I was promised help and we put a plan in place for one of the boys, after three days the admin wanted to throw it out because they didn't want him in the office … and it was back to square one.

I survived mainly because of Lara, who was another first year teacher. We had each other and Edwina, the teacher next door to me. She gave me strategies … not just for dealing with the kids … but also how best to talk with the principal. Without them I wouldn't have survived.

Term two was the worst. That was when I realized I wasn't going to get any support from admin and it was all up to me. Edwina, the teacher next door said, 'OK this is what you need to do.' She said she'd had the same experience in her first year and even when she went to a guidance officer for help she'd come to realize that she was the one who would have to do something, and do it in her classroom. So I started going down that track. And then at the end of third term I realized a transfer was possible so that kept me going! Both Lara and I look back on this year and think 'Well it could have taken us five years to experience what we've experienced in one … and we've learnt so much.'

I've learnt about school politics too. As a student teacher I didn't even realize they existed … let alone how they impact, not only on you as a teacher, but how they affect your class as well. As a class we decided we'd like to do some fundraising for a special cause. We wanted to have a sausage sizzle and a cake stall. But it was just so difficult to organize. The avenues I had to go down and the people I had to ask just to get approval amazed me. I thought cake stalls were part of school life … but someone said it was the first cake stall at the school in 10 years. The kids from my class made patty cakes at home and brought them and we sold them for 20 cents. And the rest of the school just flocked to buy them … and the 200 sausages just disappeared. We raised $400. But then the issue arose that the money raised was school money. But we said, 'No, the money was raised so that it could be given to an organization that worked with endangered animals' … and that became another struggle … because we had to really research the organization and prove that it was a worthy cause.

The kids just loved the fundraising and choosing who they wanted to give the money to … and every week after that they wanted to raise more money for something else … but I was too scared to go and ask if we could have another fundraiser. And in the end I said 'No' to the kids, and they said 'Why?' … and I just had to say that we'd had our one fundraiser for the year. But inside I felt frustrated because there in the school motto was the emphasis on citizenship, and to me citizenship is all about what we were trying to do. And there were a lot of kids in the class that had not experienced that sense of giving ... so I thought it was my role to show how, if we work hard, we are able to give to others and help them. It was just so disappointing to have to say 'No' to the kids because they had lots of other ideas. But I guess those things happen.

Suzanne, like Janine, experienced lack of administrative support as she learned to cope with children with difficult behaviour. Coming to terms with her perceptions that the school's attitude was that it was up to her whether she was going to sink or swim, was very difficult and resulted in Suzanne not asking for help until she became 'fragile' and 'ready to crumble'. It was only the collegiality with another first-year teacher and support from a more experienced teacher who had gone through a similar 'beginning' that enabled Suzanne to survive.

The barriers Suzanne experienced within her school as she sought to facilitate the children's understanding of citizenship also added to her frustration. Her concluding comment, 'but I guess those things happen', whilst being a comment of acceptance that enabled Suzanne to survive, can also be read as failure in a form of school governance that is inconsistent with its goals. If a school aims for the children to thrive and to become contributing members of a learning community then teachers must also be enabled to thrive by being respected and having their requests for advice and support met.

Many schools offer comprehensive induction programmes for beginning teachers while others provide additional support or mentoring. Successful mentoring programmes are not easy to achieve, however, because of their complexity (Kochan, 2002). They require time for the mentor and mentee to identify their needs and goals, clarify their roles and responsibilities and work out ways to ensure confidentiality. It is also vital that the mentoring process remains supportive and not evaluative. Successful mentoring has been described as

> having two or more individuals willingly form a mutually respectful, trusting relationship focused on goals that meet the needs and foster the potential of the mentee, while considering the needs of the mentor, and the context in which they both must function.
>
> (Kochan, 2002: 284)

It is interesting that Suzanne set up an informal mentoring process similar to this definition of successful mentoring, with two of her colleagues in order to 'survive'. In this process, born of necessity, there seemed to be reciprocal benefits that encompassed collegiality, a sense of progress and mutual respect. It enabled both Suzanne and Lara to say at the end of a difficult year, 'We've learnt so much.'

AMY'S STORY: 'WE ARE LIKE A PREP CLASS SO THERE IS EMPHASIS ON TRANSITION TO SCHOOL'

Amy obtained a position as a preschool teacher in one of four preschool units in a recently established independent school overseen by a board. The preschool groups, or preparatory classes as they were sometimes called, had their own curriculum planning team as did the junior college (Years 1–4), the middle college (Years 5–8) and the senior college (Years 9–12).

> Right from the start I was made aware that because parents are paying fees, there are very high expectations. I had high expectations of myself too. In those first few weeks I really wanted my children to want to come to school and to be happy and to feel safe. I guess my ideals were influenced a little by the school situation I was in. If I'd been in the state system I think my ideals would have been a little different. I had to take on the ideals of my school … but most of them fitted with my own … with what I believe teaching is … so I didn't have too many issues there. My main goals were to try to live up to the expectations … and try something different if what I was doing wasn't working. And there were examples of that!
>
> Because we are very like a preparatory class, throughout the year a lot of emphasis is placed on transition to school. First term we have a group time where we might read a story and sing some songs … then we have our indoor session. That session is quite structured in that I set out activities on tables although I do try and keep the activities open-ended enough so the children can add their own ideas. I also involve the children in the planning of some table activities. For planning I have a little chart with six spaces … and I fill in four of them which highlight specific skills … like for scissor skills I might put out magazines on the table and we might plan to find red things, or animals, or a particular letter. But then I ask the children for other things we could do and we fill in the other two spaces. We do this planning at the end of a session for the next day. I don't plan for a whole week … just day by day so that it matches their interests. The children come up with great ideas … like making masks or making

clothes out of paper. We have other areas like blocks and puzzles and home corner and computers, and the children are always free to use those areas as they choose. We have inside time for an hour, then morning tea, then outside time for an hour and then we finish off with a story and planning. The outside area is huge and we share it with another group.

In second term the programme is basically the same with slightly extended times and with lunch included. In third term, two or three times a week, I'll have an hour block where half the group will do some literacy or numeracy activities with me for half an hour and the other half will do it with the aide, and then we'll swap groups. The activities are very basic … hands-on … like patterning, measuring, counting. I plan these sessions and they're focused on a particular concept. This is part of the curriculum we use so all classes would be focusing on a similar concept … but how we go about teaching it is entirely up to each teacher.

Right through the year we have specialist teachers (for music, technology, drama, and health and physical education) who come in and take half-hour lessons. In first, second and third terms they just take small groups while the rest of the children are involved in the normal programme. In fourth term they take the whole group … so that's where we get our non-contact time in fourth term. Because they start off with small groups, that helps them and the children get to know each other. The specialist teachers are all familiar with preschool-age children and we liaise about individual children, but the specialist teachers plan their particular programmes. On the end-of-the-year report the specialist teachers also have a section they fill in.

We do reporting at the end of first and second term as well. A lot of it is related to the Foundation Learning Areas and then we look at categories within those. In first term we focus on things like 'Can look after own belongings' … 'Can interact well with other children' … 'Joins in group times' … as well as basic literacy and numeracy skills, although there's really more focus on the social and emotional aspects. On the final report there is greater emphasis on literacy and numeracy … such as where they're at with their reading and writing. There's no set levels of achievement. We report on where the child is at … the emphasis is on the child's progression. At the end of the year I had three or four readers, some who were just starting and others who had no idea.

We pass this information on to the Year 1 teachers. We send profiles up with samples of the children's work. We asked the Year 1 teachers what would be helpful to them. They said things like 'knowing where they are with their writing, patterning ... whether they can draw a picture of themselves ... whether they can use scissors ... what letters, sight words and numbers they know' ... things like that.

Time management was my biggest challenge. I know all first-year teachers work exceptionally hard but it was difficult to create any sort of boundary for my own personal time. That's one thing I want to work on next year. An awful lot of time was spent working on the children's portfolios that go out every term with observations and photographs and work samples. You have to mount them and label them and it just takes hours. I think the parents appreciated the portfolios ... some more than others. Certainly some parents expressed their appreciation more than others did. The children could have a look at their portfolio too – so I think it meant something to them. It is an efficient way to gather information and the portfolios do chart a course of development across a year.

This year has confirmed for me that I just love working with young children. Every day they come out with these amazing comments. It's great! The last day for me was a real buzz because they were my first group of children and for me they'll always be special.

Amy enjoyed the challenge of meeting her school's high expectations because, in general terms, they fitted with her own values and beliefs. She appreciated the opportunity to participate in an innovative preparatory programme that involved liaising with specialist teachers and sharing information with Year 1 teachers. Amy also enjoyed coming to understand more of the transition process for children moving from preschool into Year 1. This involved promoting links in terms of curriculum content as well as helping children gradually become accustomed to the different organization of a primary school.

Although time consuming, Amy regarded the extensive reporting and portfolio presentations that were required as providing opportunities to assess many aspects of each child's progress. She seemed a little ambivalent, however, about some parents' appreciation of the portfolios and the work entailed. Like Janine, Amy saw time management and the creation of some boundaries to allow for personal time as a priority for her second year of teaching.

KATE'S STORY: 'WHAT I LEARNT MOST ABOUT THIS YEAR WAS HOW TO WORK WITH OTHER PEOPLE'

Kate was appointed as a teacher in a suburban preschool where the school population was growing quite rapidly. She was asked to establish a second preschool group although there was no designated preschool unit. This required her to utilize a small classroom in the primary school.

> During one of my pracs I'd been advised by my supervising teacher to get in with other teacher groups when I began to teach ... and I was lucky that there was a preschool teachers' network in our district that met once a month. That was just the best thing! One school would host the meeting and when they came to my classroom they just couldn't believe what I had done in such a small school room ... to turn it into a preschool. One of my previous prac teachers who was in the network, said she couldn't have done what I had ... making it so welcoming and bright. That was a real buzz for me ... to hear experienced teachers say they couldn't have done what I had ... and to have them asking me questions. The network was really great. I found it strange though, that some teachers were not willing to share their ideas ... but then others were really open and sharing. We'd share practical ideas ... ideas for transitions ... different ways to plan ... looking at what they did and how I might adapt it. That was helpful. I realized that I did a lot more observation as part of my planning than other teachers were doing. I think I will always include observation because it's the only way I know to establish where the child is at and where I can go with that child, particularly as a lot of my teaching revolves around the children's interests.
>
> My observations were similar to what I did at Uni although I did more running/event records with three or four children this year in order to understand them better. I had to plan time to do those recordings. My main observations were on small pieces of paper ... I'd write what I saw and then at rest time or at the end of the day I'd try to analyse what I thought they meant. I'd write a lot about social interactions ... because I believe preschool is very much about social development. Then I'd observe all the other things that come into that ... tracking who they were friends with, what they were doing, what they were saying ... and then I focused on the mathematical concepts – conservation, one to one correspondence. That's a particular interest of mine. I looked at language more with children who had some speech problems. My language observations tended to be more in the group

… what kinds of things they talked about. They loved innovating on a text so we would take a story and act it out … and I was able to observe the ones who just loved doing that and had real language skills.

Most of the values I had when I left Uni were confirmed … flexibility … spontaneity. I'm very flexible … in the first half-hour of the day we would discuss what we were going to do that day. I know my aide found that a bit difficult having previously worked in a situation where she was told what activities would be done and how many elephants to cut out. I had to help her follow through on the children's ideas and show how we could extend their play. We had a situation where the children built a whole set of shops. We had dress-ups and props that turned into the David Jones Store … and then there were shoe shops and a police station … so around our very small room we had these shops for nearly four weeks. The children really wanted the cash register and the telephones that the other group had. I said that we could make our own … but they didn't want to do that. They said, 'That wouldn't be the same.' Even though they were into box construction it wasn't used to make things for their play … but that did turn around during the year. After the 'shops' they did start to make things for their play and it was interesting to see my aide develop those skills too. She really helped kids see how they could make things for their play and use them … often by modelling. My aide changed from being very structured and telling the children what to do, to asking them about their ideas and helping them achieve. She started off doing all the sticking and taping when they made things and I'd say, 'They can do it. Let them do it and work out how things work.'

Previously my aide had never done any observing of children. I have a little tape recorder I use … or I write on 'stick it' notes that I just put straight into the children's folders … and she'd never seen anything like that before … so as she was so interested, she became involved. She really got into it. She'd say, 'Well I've observed this … what do you think that means?' and we'd discuss it and interpret it … and then she'd come up with ideas about how we could follow it up. And I'd say 'Fine, you set that up tomorrow.' I learnt a lot from working with my aide.

What I learnt most about this year, though, wasn't to do with children … It was more about how to work with other people. I came into teaching as a mature age student. I'd worked in retail for nine years before that … and I had to call on all that experience to get me through this year … What do I know about working with people? How do I establish a working relationship with my aide? How much do I share with parents? What kind of a relationship should I develop with the

Plates 8.1 and 8.2 The children made an elephant for their zoo and created a bed for their bird who was sick. (Photos courtesy of Sue Thomas.)

principal … and other colleagues? I even had to deal with changing relationships with my Uni friends … because some of us had jobs and others didn't. It didn't seem right, somehow, to be sharing the excitement of my teaching experiences with those who were still waiting for job offers. I really felt for them.

I had a great relationship with the children … but I had to work a lot harder at building relationships with adults to ensure that those relationships worked for the benefit of the children in my room. I had to accept that some parents didn't really value preschool … it was just a place where their children could go three days a week. I had to not let that bother me … in fact, in the end I think it empowered me. Next year I'll take up a preschool position at a new P-12 Catholic school. I am really looking forward to setting up the preschool in this new environment. My new principal believes that preschool is important, and he has already started to involve me in the planning process. This year I have learned a lot about teaching, a lot about relationships, a lot about children, and a lot about planning and implementation … and I have learned a lot about why I selected teaching as a career. I know that teaching is what I want to do.

Although her first year of teaching had its challenging times, Kate's experiences convinced her that teaching is what she 'wants to do'. Learning how to work with other adults was one of her biggest challenges. Contacts with other teachers through a network group brought a sense of collegiality and a pooling of ideas, although she was surprised by a few teachers who were not so willing to share. Developing a working relationship with her aide enabled Kate to support another in seeing children as competent learners and resulted in them both devising strategies for assisting children to express and represent their own ideas in a variety of ways. Building a relationship with her principal, as well as maintaining contacts with friends from university, also brought new and unexpected insights.

Coming to accept that some parents didn't place the same high value on preschool education that she herself did, somewhat surprisingly 'empowered' Kate and made her even more determined to assist children to gain the most from their preschool experience. Clearly, learning to work with other people had many positive spin-offs for Kate herself and others.

BRITTANY'S STORY: 'FIVE YEARS DOWN THE TRACK I MIGHT BE WHERE I WANT TO BE – AT A PLACE WHERE MY PHILOSPHY AND PRACTICE MEET'

Brittany was appointed to a Year 1 class in a large suburban school in the non-government sector.

I really feel that my personality affected the way I coped as a first year teacher. I'm the kind of person that likes to keep things on an even keel. I make suggestions in a quiet way. ... I tend to go along with everyone else, even if I really don't agree. I am going to make changes next year, though! I have to get a better balance between school and home commitments. Teaching this year has been a huge commitment ... and trying to be a parent, a wife and a teacher ... that's been hard.

There have been great times though. Watching some children mature ... I developed an amazing relationship with one little boy, Adam. It began with the writing programme ... I wasn't sure how to start ... and I didn't feel confident in my ability to teach the children to write because I hadn't done it before ... so I followed the guidance of the other teachers on the year level. They all got the children to draw a picture and then they would get the parent helpers to write a story. I felt quite comfortable with that ... their picture ... their story. When some teachers introduced a dictionary in week four I started to become uncomfortable. The school dictionary gave them the word that the children copied ... whereas I wanted them to have a go for themselves. I referred to the developmental writing continua and began to feel comfortable with my decision not to do the same. I discussed my decision with the other teachers and we all agreed that we needed to be comfortable with our own teaching practice and that there were different ways of approaching writing in Year 1. I started letting the children have a go and I modelled back. I wanted the children to feel that they were successful writers. If they'd written 'I wnt n a bot', the parent helpers or I would model back 'I hope you had fun when you went on a boat.' In this way we did not interfere with their writing by correcting it directly. I talked with parent helpers and gave them a copy of the section of the continua where it encourages parents to value children's attempts at writing.

I still felt that the writing programme in the classroom was not what I wanted though ... so ... to give the writing programme a boost I set up this letterbox in the classroom. This was an idea I'd gained from going back to the developmental continua documents. I said to the children that if ever they wrote to me I would write back. At the end of the year I'd written 75 letters! I kept them all as a memory of my first year.

(Brittany had brought a sample of the letters to show me.) She continued:

The first letter was challenging ... some yellow scribble ... so I wrote back

Dear Peter,

Thank you for sending me a drawing. I was so pleased to receive the first message in my letterbox from you.

Yellow is one of my favourite colours.

I wonder how you knew.
Yellow reminds me of the sun.
I am looking forward to your next message.
From

Mrs Robbie

The children wrote the letters at home and I would reply within two days.
Adam's parents helped him write his first letter. It said:

I left the house to fly on a plane.

Love Adam.

I wrote back

Dear Adam,
Thank you for your letter. I was so pleased to receive it. It must have been very exciting to leave your house and to fly on a plane. I noticed that you drew a pilot at the front of the plane. Where did you go? Who went with you? Was it Mum, Dad or Ally? Or was it someone else?
I look forward to finding out where you went.
Keep writing Adam. I can see you are trying very hard. Well done.
From

Mrs Robbie

His next letter came:

We went flying to Adelaide. We stayed with my grandma. We had seven sleeps. Thanks for your letter.

Love Adam

Adam wrote a series of letters over the next few months and so did other children. The replies took hours. But writing these letters also helped me because I could relate to the children one-on-one in my own time and my own way. If Adam wrote in the last week of the holidays I'd send an answer to his home. He wrote about his visit to the zoo and about when he moved house. Over time his letters changed because he began to write them on his own. One day he wrote 'I'd like to set up a toy shop in the class.' So I had to do it ... and we did ... eventually.

In June he wrote:

The thing I liked best about school is playing in the playground. I can't wait to learn about dinosaurs. We're going to the beach.

In October another letter came:

Dear Mrs Robbie,
Thank you for your letter. Sorry I have taken so long to write to you. This will be my last letter because I don't want to write any more. I really like Year 1. I loved learning about dinosaurs. My mind works like this. My angel gives me a tape everyday to help my mind remember everything that I have learnt. She puts the old tapes beside my bed so that I can remember still. Then my angel rests waiting for my tooth to get wobbly so when it comes out she can turn it into a gold coin. Can we play shops this term?
Love

Adam

(His mother said it was totally his idea to tell me how his mind worked.) I put a footnote on Adam's end of year report:

Adam, the letters you wrote to me this year have been among the highlights of my beginning teaching year. Remember I will always write back!

(Adam did write again early in Year 2.)

Looking back, I can see that it was important for me to do something like this because it made me feel good that I was achieving some of my goals. For me the gap between my early childhood philosophy and the

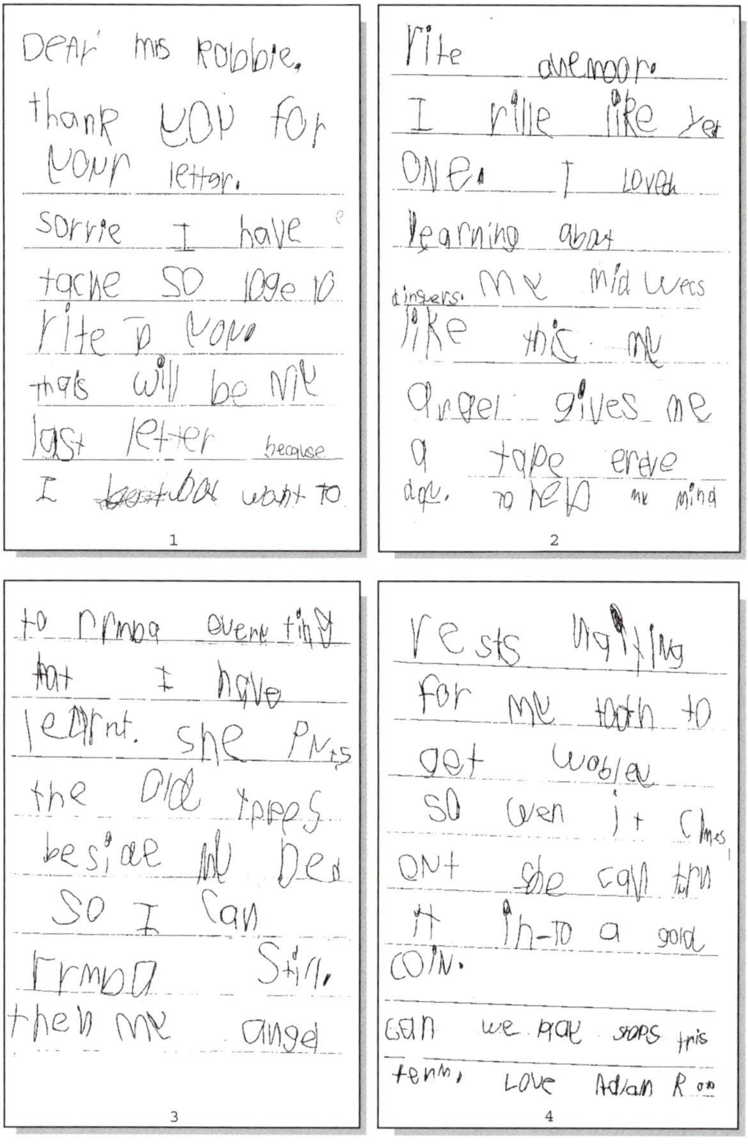

DEAr mis robbie,

thank UOU for
UOUr letter.

sorrie I have
tache so loge to
rite TP UoU
thas will be NIL
last letter because
I ~~teentbar~~ wont to

1

rite anemoon.
I rille like yer
ONe. I Loved
learning abut
dinosurs. Me mid wecs
like this. me
argel gives me
a tape erave
dqu. to hel me mind

2

to rmba every ting
that I have
leArnt. she puts
the old tapes.
besiae my bed
so I can
rmba still.
then me angel

3

rests lighling
for me tooth to
get woblee
so wen it cms
ont she can trn
it in-to a gold
coin.

can we plae stops this
term. Love Adam R ◦◦

4

Figure 8.1 Adam's letter. (Courtesy of Jane Roneberg.)

demands of the syllabus was a challenge … thinking I knew how to put that philosophy into practice and then finding that was more difficult than I thought.

This year when we did 'P' everybody did 'pretty polly parrot' and everyone hung them up around the room … all the same. Next year I'm going to encourage the children to be creative … and let them be things … not just colour-in worksheets. We'll be pigs … of course Ps have to be pigs, but because of my experience, I'll be able to control the situation better next year … and we'll do more collage. We'll use different symbolic modes. And we'll play more number games. I'll still use some work sheets but they will be far more creative and open-ended.

I want to let the children have more input into the curriculum and my classroom. At Uni I wrote in my philosophy how I believed the curriculum should emerge from children's interests. I know I have to get through all the set content. But I'm going to do more interesting things with the content. When we learn about dinosaurs I'll inspire the children to want to set up our own class dinosaur museum. I know my teaching approach has to evolve slowly. Five years down the track I hope to be where I want to be … at a place where philosophy and practice meet.

Brittany's account of developing her teaching skill is in keeping with the career of the expert who, according to Bereiter and Scardamalia (1993), progressively advances 'on the problems constituting a field of work.' This approach is in contrast to the non-expert who 'gradually constricts the field of work so that it more closely conforms to the routines the non-expert is prepared to execute' (Bereiter and Scardamalia, 1993: 9). Brittany did not want to let go of her ideals – to constrict her work, although she realized that the task of achieving all her ideals was impossible given the work context, syllabus expectations and her own inexperience. Her decision to work through a different approach to the teaching of writing and to initiate the letterbox was a manageable task that still encompassed some of her ideals. Brittany was prepared to 'push boundaries' in order to do this and in this process gained personal and professional satisfaction. She also recognized, however, that it would take time as well as effort before her philosophy and practice would 'meet'.

SUMMARY

There are many themes, similarities and differences running through these stories of beginning teachers. A major theme in each is the search for skills and strategies in order to master the craft of teaching in its many facets – in guiding behaviour, in time management, in transitions to another year level, in assessment and syllabus expectations and in communication. For each of the teachers a strong commitment to developing their own expertise is evident. Alongside this commitment, however, there is a very real caring and a desire to do their best for the children and families with whom they are in contact. For each one, their first year brought a confirmation that teaching was 'for them', although for some this confirmation came in spite of difficult and less than supportive work contexts.

Another chapter could be written on the very different work situations each of these beginning teachers experienced. For some there was support from administrative staff, colleagues and communities. For others, this formal support and induction was lacking. Some were able to share with interested families, others struggled to involve families and gain their appreciation of the educative process.

In reading and reflecting on the experiences of these beginning teachers you will have been asking yourself some questions. These questions will, no doubt, be different for each of you. Did the different experiences of these teachers help you clarify your preference for a particular type of setting in which you would like to teach, or a preference for a particular age group? Did you ask 'What would I have done if I had been faced with that particular situation?' Were you alerted to areas in which you may need to gain more knowledge if you are to feel 'prepared' to begin teaching? For example you may have decided that you need to know more about:

- working with management committees, administrative staff or management boards;
- providing leadership in a centre, school and even the wider community;
- building partnerships with parents;
- working collaboratively with teacher assistants and colleagues;
- finding out more about mentoring programmes and how you can be pro-active in seeking support and advice;
- implementing the practical aspects of curriculum documents and philosophies;
- handling school politics;
- easing the transitions for children as they move between groups, classes and settings;
- establishing a professional persona;
- developing your strengths including time management skills.

You will probably want to add other aspects that are of particular interest to you.

Don't leave it until the final teaching practicum to seek knowledge in these areas. Be pro-active. Develop an 'I want to know more about ... list' in the first year of your course and keep adding to it. I know a number of pre-service teachers who do this. In following up on topics of particular interest they talk with visiting guest lecturers and arrange to visit their classrooms in their own time. If they hear of teachers who are well respected for co-operative teaching, play-based programmes or other innovative curriculum approaches they plan to visit these classrooms also. Aim to be as well prepared as you can be for the realities of your first year of teaching.

CONCLUSION

This book has been written in the hope that you will develop your understanding of teaching and use your teaching practice experiences to develop competence in teaching skills and curriculum work. In exploring the nature of teaching young children, this book has also highlighted the fact that children have a right to expect not only a competent teacher, but also one who is caring and trustworthy. In this postmodern world filled with uncertainties, children need a teacher who can 'extend a firm but gentle guiding hand' and in so doing offer them a reason for hope because 'hopefulness is the only morally appropriate response to uncertainty' (Elbaz, 1992, cited in Bullough and Baughman, 1997: 24). As you undertake teaching practice give thought to how you will prove to the children you teach that you are not only competent but that you are caring and trustworthy too. As you prepare to commence a teaching career, continue to reflect on statements such as this one.

> Teachers have to 'prove they can be trusted' and 'that justice will be served because they are adults who serve it.' They have to prove themselves to be 'worthy guides' who respect and take seriously 'genuine human standards' and apply them 'sensitively and intelligently, as demanded by an abiding concern for the individual child's future and particularity.'
>
> (Adapted from Bullough and Baughman, 1997: 25)

These are the responsibilities and opportunities that are yours in becoming a teacher of young children.

SUGGESTED ACTIVITIES

- Reflect in depth on one of the beginning teacher's experiences. What can you learn from it? Consider and describe what you would have done in a similar situation.

- Think about making the transition from being a pre-service teacher to a teacher with your own class. Consider the added responsibilities that will be involved. List the type of information you can gather and the skills that you can develop in your teaching practice experiences to help you in this regard.

- Talk with parents of young children who are attending childcare centres, preschools or primary schools about what they want from and expect of their child's teacher. How do these expectations compare with the goals you have for yourself as a teacher?

- Select five objects that you feel represent you as a teacher or that symbolize your approach to teaching. (I have a little yellow rubber duck that, for me, represents the fact that on the surface I appear to be swimming smoothly but underneath I'm paddling crazily!)

- Imagine you are chatting with a friend over coffee about your practicum teaching experiences. Jot down what have been some of the issues, as well as the joys for you so far.

- Prepare a plan for your first week in an early childhood setting of your choice. Consider how you will welcome and reassure children and parents; handle parent departures; introduce routines and some expectations; and offer activities that may provide you with information concerning the children's abilities. Also start a 'beginning box' in which you can collect particular resources, posters and ideas that will be helpful in your first weeks of teaching or if you are asked to do relief teaching.

References

Abbott, L. and Nutbrown, C. (eds) (2001) *Experiencing Reggio Emilia: Implications for Preschool Provision*, Buckingham: Open University Press.

Alcock, S. (1999) 'Documentation: pedagogical or pathological?' *Conference Proceedings*, Seventh Early Childhood Convention, Nelson, New Zealand, volume 11: 1–10.

Almy, M. and Genishi, C. (1979) *Ways of Studying Children*, New York: Teachers College Press.

Ashman, A. and Elkins, J. (eds) (2002) *Educating Children with Diverse Abilities*, Frenchs Forest, NSW: Pearson Education Australia.

Barrera, I., Corso, R.M. with Macpherson, D. (2003) *Skilled Dialogue: Strategies for Responding to Cultural Diversity in Early Childhood*, Baltimore, MD: Paul H. Brookes.

Beaty, J. (2002) *Observing Development of the Young Child*, Upper Saddle River, NJ: Merrill.

Bentzen, W.R. (2000) *Seeing Young Children: A Guide to Observing and Recording Behaviour*, 4th edn, Albany, NY: Delmar.

Bereiter, C. and Scardamalia, M. (1993) *Surpassing Ourselves: An Inquiry into the Nature and Implications of Expertise*, Chicago, IL: Open Court.

Berk, L.E. (2001) *Development Through the Life Span*, 2nd edn, Needham Heights, MA: Allyn & Bacon.

Berlak, A. and Berlak, H. (1981) *Dilemmas of Schooling*, London: Methuen.

Bodrova, E. and Leong, D.J. (1996) *Tools of the Mind: The Vygotskian Approach to Early Childhood Education*, Englewood Cliffs, NJ: Prentice Hall.

Bredekamp, S. and Copple, C. (eds) (1997) *Developmentally Appropriate Practice in Early Childhood Programs*, revised edn, Washington, DC: National Association for the Education of Young Children.

Bredekamp, S. and Rosegrant, T. (eds) (1992) *Reaching Potentials: Appropriate Curriculum and Assessment for Young Children*, vol. 1, Washington, DC: National Association for the Education of Young Children.

—— (eds) (1995) *Reaching Potentials: Transforming Early Childhood Curriculum and Assessment*, vol. 2, Washington, DC: National Association for the Education of Young Children.

Bronson, M.B. (1995) *The Right Stuff for Children Birth to 8: Selecting Play Materials to Support Development*, Washington, DC: National Association for the Education of Young Children.

Bruner, J. (1986) *Actual Minds – Possible Worlds*, London: Harvard University Press.

Bullough, R.V. and Baughman, K. (1997) *'First Year Teacher' Eight Years Later: An Inquiry into Teacher Development*, New York: Teachers College Press.

Carr, M. (2000) *Assessment in Early Childhood Settings*, London: Paul Chapman Publishing.

Carter, M. and Curtis, D. (2003) *Designs for Living and Learning: Transforming Early Childhood Environments*, St Paul, MN: Redleaf Press.

Catherwood, D. (1999) 'New views on the young brain: offerings from developmental psychology to early childhood education', *Contemporary Issues in Early Childhood*, 1(1): 23–34.

Cochran-Smith, M. and Lytle, S. (1993) *Inside Outside: Teacher Research and Knowledge*, New York: Teachers College Press.

Cochran-Smith, M. and Lytle, S. (1999) 'The teacher research movement: a decade later', *Educational Researcher*, 28(7): 15–25.

Cohen, L., Manion, L. and Morrison, K. (1996) *A Guide to Teaching Practice*, 4th edn, London: Routledge.

Cooper, C. (1998) *Learner-Centred Assessment*, revised edn, Launceston, Tasmania: Global Learning Communities International.

Copley, J.V. (2000) *The Young Child and Mathematics*, Washington DC: National Association for the Education of Young Children.

Copple, C. (ed.) (2003) *A World of Difference. Readings on Teaching Young Children in a Diverse Society*, Washington, DC: National Association for the Education of Young Children.

Cross, T. (1995) 'The early childhood curriculum debate', in M. Fleer (ed.) *DAPcentrism: Challenging Developmentally Appropriate Practice*, Watson, ACT: Australian Early Childhood Association.

Curtis, D. and Carter, M. (2000) *The Art of Awareness: How Observation can Transform your Teaching*, St Paul, MN: Redleaf Press.

Danielson, C. and Abrutyn, L. (1997) *An Introduction to Using Portfolios in the Classroom*, Alexandria, VA: Association for Supervision and Curriculum Development.

Dau, E. (2001) *The Anti-bias Approach in Early Childhood*, 2nd edn, Frenchs Forest, NSW: Pearson Education Australia.

Department for Education and Children's Services (1996) *Foundation Areas of Learning*, South Australia: Department for Education and Children's Services.

Doyle, W. (1990) 'Classroom knowledge as a foundation for teaching', *Teachers College Record*, 91(3): 347–60.

Eaton, J. and Shepherd, W. (1998) *Early Childhood Environments*, AECA Research in Practice Series, No. 3, Canberra: Australian Early Childhood Association.

Education Department of Western Australia (1998) *What is Good Early Childhood Education?* Perth: Education Department of Western Australia.

Edwards, A. and Knight, P. (1994) *Effective Early Years Education: Teaching Young Children*, Buckingham: Open University Press.

Edwards, C., Gandini, L. and Forman, G. (eds) (1993) *The Hundred Languages of Children: The Reggio Emilia Approach to Early Childhood Education*, Norwood, NJ: Ablex.

—— (eds) (1998) *The Hundred Languages of Children: The Reggio Emilia Approach – Advanced Reflections*, 2nd edn, Norwood, NJ: Ablex.

Elbaz, F. (1992) 'Hope, attentiveness, and caring for difference: the moral voice in teaching', in *Teaching and Teacher Education*, 8(5/6), 421–32; cited in Bullough, R.V. and Baughman, K. (1997) *'First Year Teacher' Eight Years Later: An Inquiry into Teacher Development*, New York: Teachers College Press.

Fortson, L.R. and Reiff, J. (1995) *Early Childhood Curriculum: Open Structures for Integrative Learning*, Needham Heights, MA: Allyn & Bacon.

Garbett, D. and Yourn, B. (2002) 'Student teacher knowledge: knowing and understanding subject matter in the New Zealand context', *Australian Journal of Early Childhood*, 27(3): 1–6.

Gestwicki, C. (2000) *Home School and Community Relations*, 4th edn, Albany, NY: Delmar Thomson Learning.

Goffin, S. (1994) *Curriculum Models and Early Childhood Education: Appraising the Relationship*, New York: Macmillan College Publishing Company.

Goffin, S. (2003) 'NAEYC Commission seeks comments on early childhood program standards', *Young Children*, 58(3): 78–80.

Goffin, S. and Wilson, C. (2001) *Curriculum Models and Early Childhood Education: Appraising the Relationship*, 2nd edn, Upper Saddle River, NJ: Prentice Hall.

Goldberg, S. (1997) *Parent Involvement Begins at Birth: Collaboration Between Parents and Children in the Early Years*, Boston, MA: Allyn and Bacon.

Goleman, D. (1995) *Emotional Intelligence*, London: Bloomsbury Publishing.

Gonzalez-Mena, J. (2003) 'Bridging cultures with understanding and sensitivity', Keynote Address Abstract, presented at the 8th Early Childhood Convention, 22–25 September, Palmerston North, New Zealand.

Gordon, T. (1974) *TET: Teacher Effectiveness Training*, New York: Peter H. Wyden.

Gronland, G. (1998) 'Portfolios as an assessment tool', *Young Children*, 53(3): 4–10.

Handal, G. and Lauvås, P. (1987) *Promoting Reflective Teaching: Supervision in Action*, Milton Keynes: Open University Press.

Helm, J.H. and Beneke, S. (2003) *The Power of Projects: Meeting Contemporary Challenges in Early Childhood Classrooms – Strategies and Solutions*, New York: Teachers College Press.

Helm, J.H., Beneke, S. and Steinheimer, K. (1998) *Windows on Learning: Documenting Young Children's Work*, New York: Teachers College Press.

Henry, M. (1996) *Young Children, Parents and Professionals*, London: Routledge.

Hill, S. (1992) *Games that Work: Cooperative Activities for the Primary School Classroom*, Armadale: Eleanor Curtain.

Honig, A. (2002) *Secure Relationships*, Washington, DC: National Association for the Education of Young Children.

Hyson, M. (2002) 'Huh? Eek! Help! Three perspectives on early childhood assessment', *Young Children*, 57(1): 62–4.

Hyson, M. (ed.) (2003) 'NBPTS early childhood/generalist standards, 2nd edn. For teachers of students ages 3–8', in *Preparing Early Childhood Professionals: NAEYC's Standards for Programs*, Washington, DC: National Association for the Education of Young Children. Online. Available http://www.nbpts.org/candidates/guide/whichcert/OIEarlyChild.html (accessed 16 December, 2003).

Jay, J.K. (2003) *Quality Teaching: Reflection as the Heart of Practice*, Lanham, MD: The Scarecrow Press.

Jones, E. and Nimmo, J. (1994) *Emergent Curriculum*, Washington, DC: National Association for the Education of Young Children.

Kagan, S. (2000) 'Making assessment count ... What matters?' *Young Children*, 55(2): 4–5.

Katz, L. (1984) 'The professional early childhood teacher', *Young Children* (July): 3–10.

—— (1988) 'What should young children be doing?' *American Educator*, 12(2): 29–45.

—— (1995a) 'The professional preschool teacher', in L. Katz (ed.) *Talks with Teachers of Young Children: A Collection*, Norwood, NJ: Ablex.

—— (1995b) 'Ethical issues in working with young children', in L. Katz (ed.) *Talks with Teachers of Young Children: A Collection*, Norwood, NJ: Ablex.

—— (1996) 'Children as learners: a developmental approach', *Conference Proceedings, Weaving Webs Conference: Collaborative Teaching and Learning in the Early Years Curriculum*, University of Melbourne (July): 133–46.

—— (1998) 'What can we learn from Reggio Emilia?' in Edwards, C., Gandini, L. and Forman, G. (eds) *The Hundred Languages of Children: The Reggio Emilia Approach – Advanced Reflections*, 2nd edn, Norwood, NJ: Ablex.

Kochan, F.K. (ed.) (2002) *The Organizational and Human Dimensions of Successful Mentoring Programs and Relationships*, Greenwich, CT: Information Age Publishing.

Kostelnik, M.J. (2002) *Children with Special Needs: Lessons for Early Childhood Professionals*, New York: Teachers College Press.

Kostelnik, M.J., Whiren, A., Soderman, A., Stein, L. and Gregory, K. (2001) *Guiding Children's Social Development: Theory to Practice*, 4th edn, Albany, NY: Delmar Publishers, Thomson Learning.

Lambert, E.B. and Clyde, M. (2000) *Re Thinking Early Childhood Theory and Practice*, Katoomba, NSW: Social Science Press.

Landy, S. (2002) *Pathways to Competence: Promoting Healthy Social and Emotional Development in Young Children*, Baltimore, MD: Paul H. Brookes.

Levin, D.E. (2003) *Teaching Young Children in Violent Times. Building a Peaceable Classroom*, 2nd edn, Washington, DC: Educators for Social Responsibility co-published with National Association for the Education of Young Children.

Lubeck, S. (1998a) 'Is developmentally appropriate practice for everyone?', *Childhood Education*, 74: 283–92.

—— (1998b) 'Is developmentally appropriate practice for everyone? A response', *Childhood Education*, 74: 299–301.

Lunt, C. and Williamson, D. (1999) *Children's Experiences Folio: Developmentally Appropriate Experiences for 0–6 Years*, 2nd edn, Melbourne: RMIT Publishing.

MacNaughton, G. (2000) *Rethinking Gender in Early Childhood Education*, St Leonards, NSW: Allen & Unwin.

—— (2003) *Techniques for Teaching Young Children: Choices in Theory and Practice*, Frenchs Forest, NSW: Pearson Education Australia.

Maloney, C. and Barblett, L. (2002) 'Proving quality or improving quality: who's minding the shop?' *Australian Journal of Early Childhood*, 27(1):14–17.

McAfee, O. and Leong, D. (2002) *Assessing and Guiding Young Children's Development and Learning*, 3rd edn, Boston: Allyn & Bacon.

McBurney-Fry, G. (2002) *Improving Your Practicum: A Guide to Better Teaching Practice*, Katoomba, NSW: Social Science Press.

McGrath, H. and Noble, T. (1998) *Different Kids, Same Classroom: Making Mixed Ability Classes Really Work*, Melbourne: Addison Wesley.

Meade-Roberts, J., Jones, E. and Hillard, J. (1993) 'Change making in a primary school: Saedad, California', in E. Jones (ed.) *Growing Teachers: Partnerships in Staff Development*, Washington, DC: National Association for the Education of Young Children.

Meisels, S.J. (2000) 'On the side of the child. Personal reflections on testing, teaching and early childhood education', *Young Children* 55(6): 16–19.

Milne, R. (1997) *Peace Education in Early Childhood*, Richmond: Free Kindergarten Association of Victoria.

National Association for the Education of Young Children (2003) *Early Childhood Curriculum, Assessment and Program Evaluation – Position Statement*. Online Available http://www.naeyc.org (accessed 5 January, 2004).

National Childcare Accreditation Council Inc (NCAC) (2001a) *Quality Improvement and Accreditation Handbook*, 2nd edn, Surry Hills, NSW: NCAC.

—— (2001b) *Quality Improvement and Accreditation Source Book*, Surry Hills, NSW: NCAC.

New, R. (1994) 'Reggio Emilia: its visions and its challenges for educators in the United States', in L. Katz and B. Cesarone (eds) *Reflections on the Reggio Emilia Approach Perspectives from ERIC/EECE: A Monograph Series*, No. 6, Urbana, IL: ERIC Clearinghouse on Elementary and Early Childhood Education.

New Zealand Ministry of Education (1996) *Te Whaariki: Early Childhood Curriculum*, Wellington: Learning Media.

Nisbet, J. and Shucksmith, J. (1986) *Learning Strategies*, London: Routledge and Kegan Paul.

Nixon, D. and Gould, K. (1999) *Emerging: Child Development in the First Three Years*, 2nd edn, Katoomba, NSW: Social Science Press.

Paley, V. (1997) *The Girl with the Brown Crayon*, Cambridge, MA: Harvard University Press.

Penn, H. (2000) 'How do children learn? Early childhood services in a global context', in H. Penn (ed.) *Early Childhood Services: Theory, Policy and Practice*, Buckingham: Open University Press.

Perry, R. (1988) 'An examination of two contrasting approaches to teaching pre-school children and their effects on linguistic and social behaviour', unpublished PhD thesis, Brisbane: University of Queensland.

—— (1989) 'What makes Tim – Tim? Some teachers' thoughts on observation', unpublished report of preschool director's working party, Brisbane: Queensland Department of Education.

—— (1995) *Thinking through Play*, Video and Booklet, Queensland University of Technology.

Perry, R. and Irwin, L. (2000) *Playing with Curriculum*, Brisbane: QUT Publication.

Phillips, C. and Bredekamp, S. (1998) 'Reconsidering early childhood education in the United States: Reflections from our encounters with Reggio Emilia', in C. Edwards, L. Gandini and G. Forman (eds) (1998) *The Hundred Languages of Children: The Reggio Emilia Approach – Advanced Reflections*, 2nd edn, Norwood, NJ: Ablex.

Porter, L. (1999) *Young Children's Behaviour: Practical Approaches for Caregivers and Teachers*, Rosebery, Sydney: MacLennan and Petty.

—— (2003) *Young Children's Behaviour: Practical Approaches for Caregivers and Teachers*, 2nd edn, Eastgardens, NSW: MacLennan and Petty.

Posner, G. (2000) *Field Experience: A Guide to Reflective Teaching*, 5th edn, New York: Longman.

Queensland School Curriculum Council (1998) *Preschool Curriculum Guidelines*, Brisbane: Queensland School Curriculum Council.

Queensland Studies Authority (2002) *Early Years Curriculum Guidelines* (draft) Brisbane: Queensland Studies Authority. Online. Available http://www.qsa. qld.edu.au/preschool/prep/index.html (accessed 18 November 2003).

Rinaldi, C. (1998) 'Projected curriculum constructed through documentation – Progettazione, an interview with Lella Gandini', in C. Edwards, L. Gandini and G. Forman (eds) (1998) *The Hundred Languages of Children: The Reggio Emilia Approach – Advanced Reflections*, 2nd edn, Norwood, NJ: Ablex.

Rogers, B. (1989) *Making a Discipline Plan: Developing Classroom Management Skills*, Melbourne: Thomas Nelson.

Rogoff, B. (1998) 'Cognition as a collaborative process', in W. Damon, (chief ed.) *Handbook of Child Psychology*, 5th edn, Vol. 2 'Cognition, Perception and Language', D. Kuhn and R.S. Siegler (volume eds), New York: John Wiley and Sons, 679–744.

Santrock, J.W. (2001) *Child Development*, 9th edn, Boston, MA: McGraw Hill Higher Education.

Schön, D. (1983) *The Reflective Practitioner*, New York: Basic Books.

—— (1987) *Educating the Reflective Practitioner*, San Francisco, CA: Jossey-Bass.

Shepard, L., Kagan, S. and Wurtz, E. (1998) 'Goal 1 early childhood assessments resource group recommendations', *Young Children*, 53(3): 52–4.

Siraj-Blatchford, I. and Yeok-lin Wong (1999) 'Defining and evaluating "quality" early childhood education in an international context: dilemmas and possibilities', *Early Years*, 20(1): 7–18.

Smith, D.L. and Lovat, T.J. (2003) *Curriculum: Action on Reflection*, 4th edn, Tuggerah, NSW: Social Science Press.

Stacey, M. (1991) *Parents and Teachers Together: Partnership in Primary and Nursery Education*, Buckingham: Open University Press.

Stonehouse, A. (1998) *Our Code of Ethics at Work, AECA Research in Practice Series*, No. 5, revised edn, Canberra: Australian Early Childhood Association.

Stremmel, A. (2002) 'Nurturing professional and personal growth through inquiry', *Young Children*, 57(5): 62–70.

Stringer, E.T. (1999) *Action Research*, 2nd edn, Thousand Oaks, CA: Sage.

Thomas, S. (1991) *The Diary of a Preschool Teacher*, Early Childhood Curriculum Project, Studies Directorate, Brisbane: Queensland Department of Education.

Toffler, A. (1974) *Learning for Tomorrow: The Role of the Future in Education*, New York: Vintage.

Walsh, D.J., Tobin, J.J., and Graue, M.E.(1993) 'The interpretative voice: qualitative research in early childhood education', in B. Spodek (ed.) *Handbook of Research on the Education of Young Children*, New York: Macmillan.

Wellhousen, K. and Wortham, S.C. (2001) *Outdoor Play Every Day: Innovative Play Concepts for Early Childhood*, Albany, NY: Delmar Learning.

Wheatley, K.F. (2003) 'Promoting the use of content standards. Recommendations for teacher educators', *Young Children*, 58(2): 96–102.

Wolfe, P. and Brandt, R. (1998) 'What do we know from brain research?', *Educational Leadership*, 56(3): 8–13.

Woodhead, M. (2000) 'Towards a global paradigm for research into early childhood', in H. Penn (ed.) *Early Childhood Services: Theory, Policy and Practice*, Buckingham: Open University Press.

Woodhead, M., Faulkner, D. and Littleton, K. (1998) *Cultural Worlds of Early Childhood*, London: Routledge.

Woods, P. (1990) *Teacher Skills and Strategies*, Lewes: Falmer Press.

Wortham, S.C., Barbour, A. and Desjean-Perrotta, B. (1998) *Portfolio Assessment: A Handbook for Preschool and Elementary Teachers*, Maryland: ACEI.

Index